SO EMBARRASSING

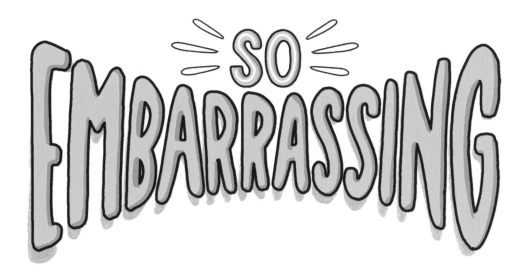

A NOTE FROM THE AUTHOR

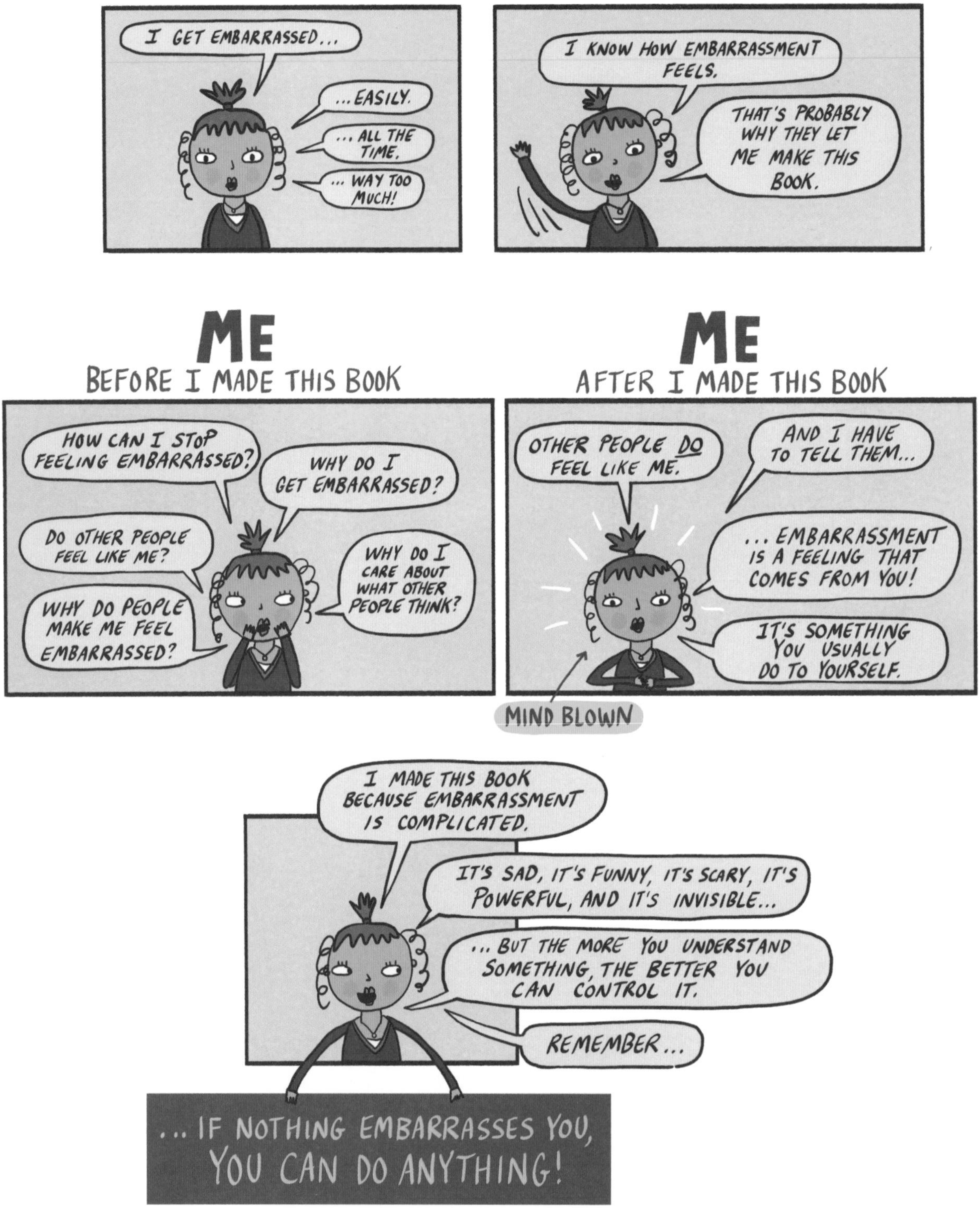
I GET EMBARRASSED...
...EASILY.
...ALL THE TIME.
...WAY TOO MUCH!
I KNOW HOW EMBARRASSMENT FEELS.
THAT'S PROBABLY WHY THEY LET ME MAKE THIS BOOK.
ME
BEFORE I MADE THIS BOOK
HOW CAN I STOP FEELING EMBARRASSED?
WHY DO I GET EMBARRASSED?
DO OTHER PEOPLE FEEL LIKE ME?
WHY DO I CARE ABOUT WHAT OTHER PEOPLE THINK?
WHY DO PEOPLE MAKE ME FEEL EMBARRASSED?
ME
AFTER I MADE THIS BOOK
OTHER PEOPLE DO FEEL LIKE ME.
AND I HAVE TO TELL THEM...
...EMBARRASSMENT IS A FEELING THAT COMES FROM YOU!
IT'S SOMETHING YOU USUALLY DO TO YOURSELF.
MIND BLOWN
I MADE THIS BOOK BECAUSE EMBARRASSMENT IS COMPLICATED.
IT'S SAD, IT'S FUNNY, IT'S SCARY, IT'S POWERFUL, AND IT'S INVISIBLE...
...BUT THE MORE YOU UNDERSTAND SOMETHING, THE BETTER YOU CAN CONTROL IT.
REMEMBER...
...IF NOTHING EMBARRASSES YOU, YOU CAN DO ANYTHING!

SO EMBARRASSING

AWKWARD MOMENTS
AND HOW TO GET THROUGH THEM

CHARISE MERICLE HARPER

WORKMAN PUBLISHING, NEW YORK

UH-OH.

DO YOU WANT A BAG FOR YOUR HEAD?
THIS IS A BOOK ABOUT EMBARRASSMENT.
THINGS COULD GET EMBARRASSING.

DOGS DON'T GET EMBARRASSED!

WATCH!

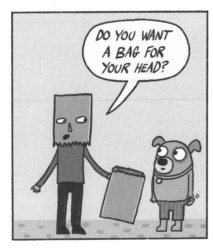

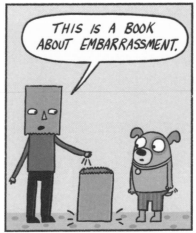

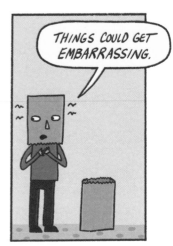

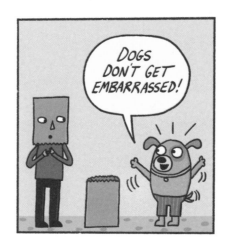

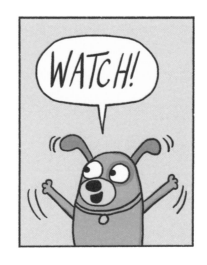

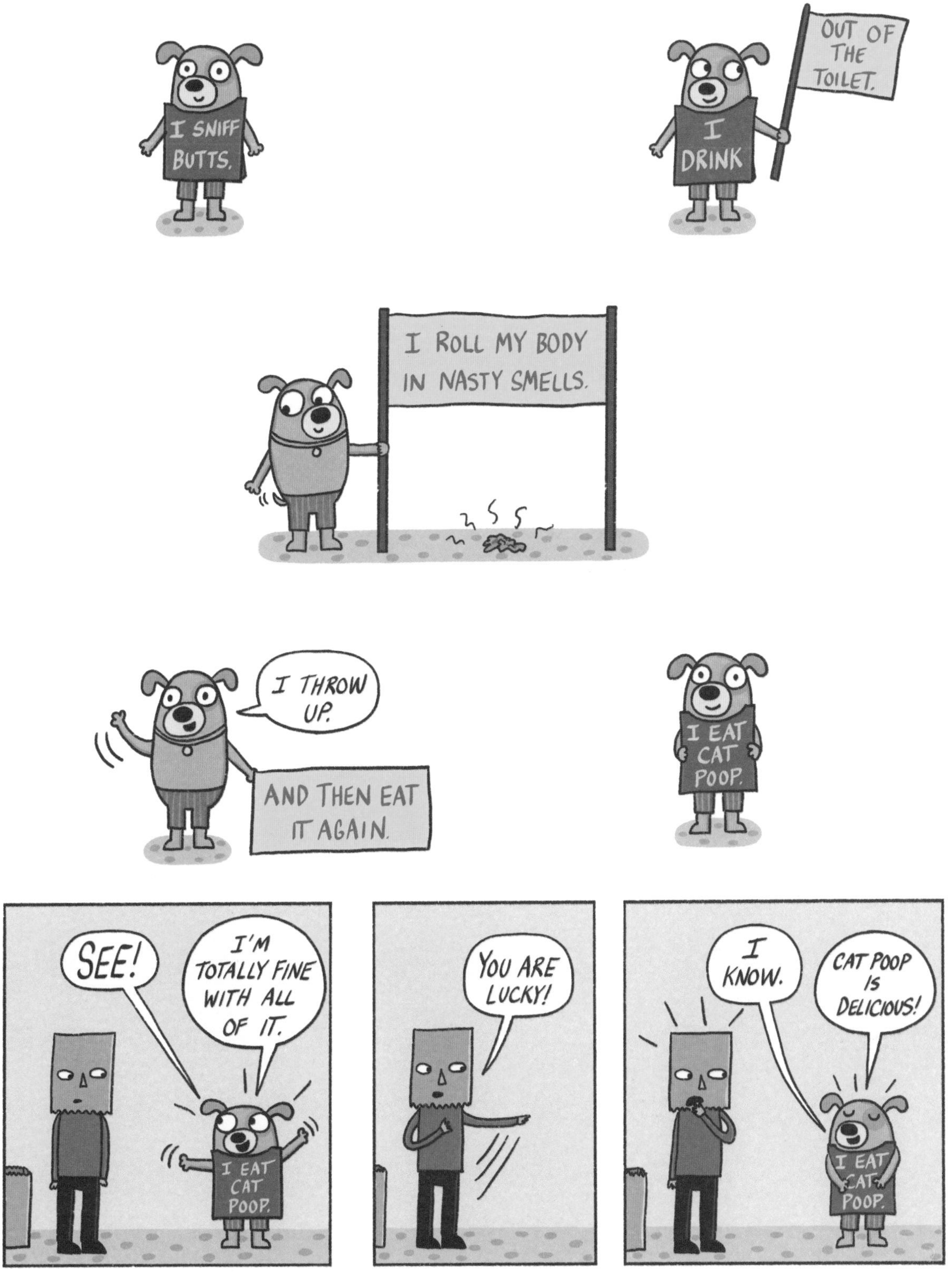

I SNIFF BUTTS.
I DRINK
OUT OF THE TOILET.
I ROLL MY BODY IN NASTY SMELLS.
I THROW UP.
AND THEN EAT IT AGAIN.
I EAT CAT POOP.
SEE!
I'M TOTALLY FINE WITH ALL OF IT.
I EAT CAT POOP.
YOU ARE LUCKY!
I KNOW.
CAT POOP IS DELICIOUS!
I EAT CAT POOP.

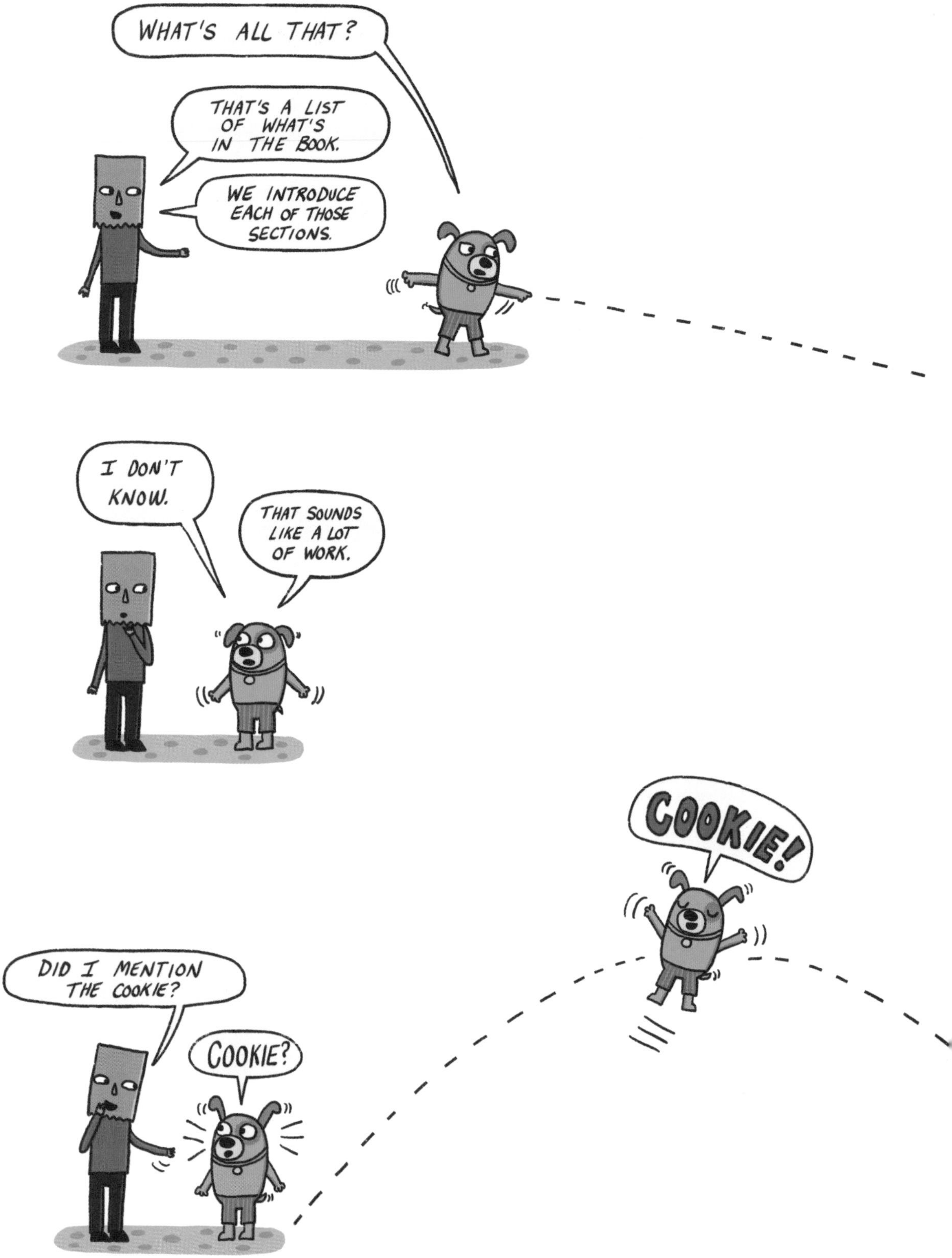
WHAT'S ALL THAT?
THAT'S A LIST OF WHAT'S IN THE BOOK.
WE INTRODUCE EACH OF THOSE SECTIONS.
I DON'T KNOW.
THAT SOUNDS LIKE A LOT OF WORK.
DID I MENTION THE COOKIE?
COOKIE?
COOKIE!

CONTENTS

LOOK FOR BONUS OOPS CLASSICS FUN

I'LL HELP!

LET ME DO IT!

I'LL DO ANYTHING FOR A COOKIE!

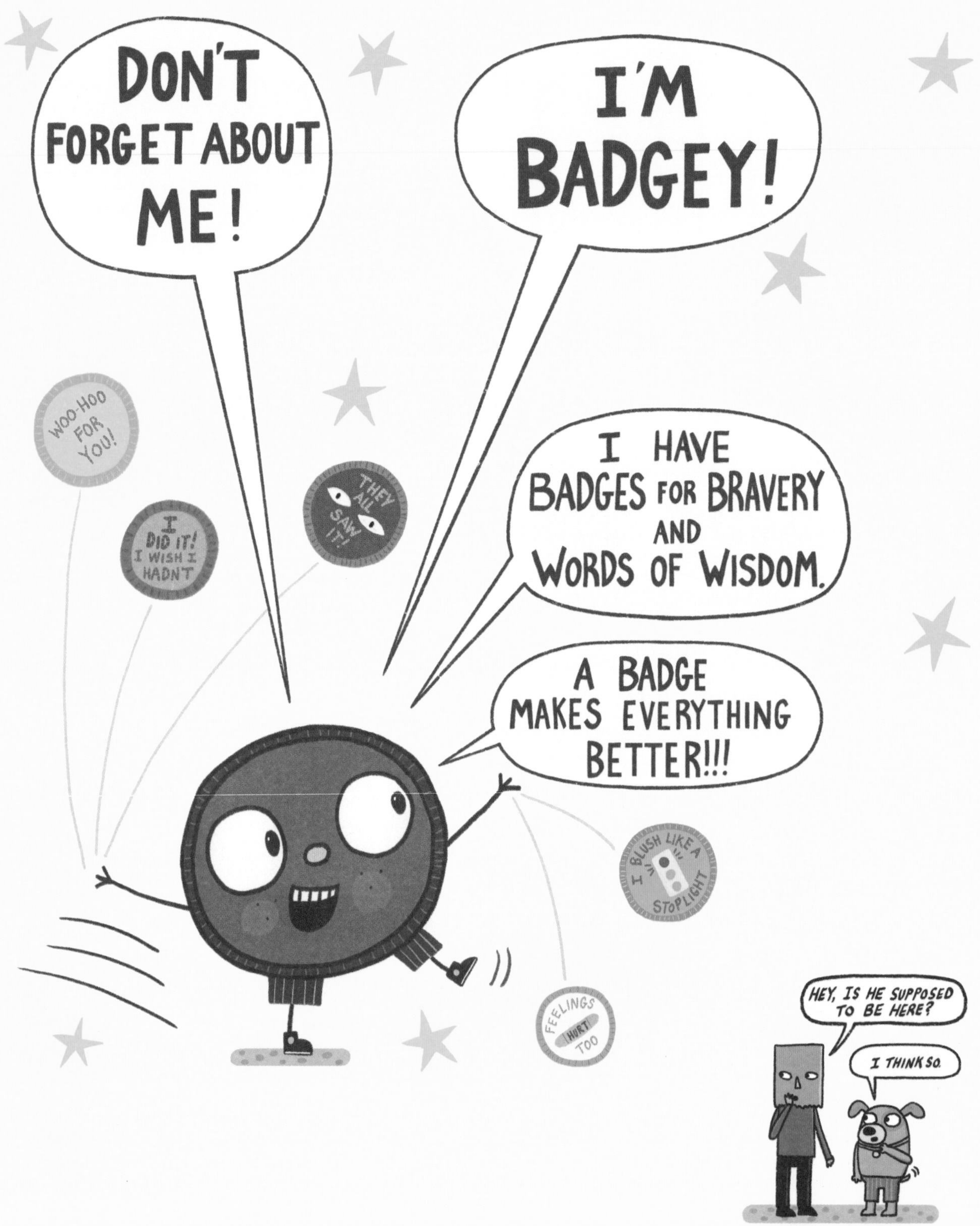
DON'T FORGET ABOUT ME!
I'M BADGEY!
I HAVE BADGES FOR BRAVERY AND WORDS OF WISDOM.
A BADGE MAKES EVERYTHING BETTER!!!
WOO-HOO FOR YOU!
I DID IT! I WISH I HADNT
THEY ALL SAW IT!
I BLUSH LIKE A STOPLIGHT
FEELINGS HURT TOO
HEY, IS HE SUPPOSED TO BE HERE?
I THINK SO.

DISCLAIMER: THERE IS NO GUARANTEE THAT ANY OF THIS WILL HELP, BUT AT LEAST HE IS TRYING.

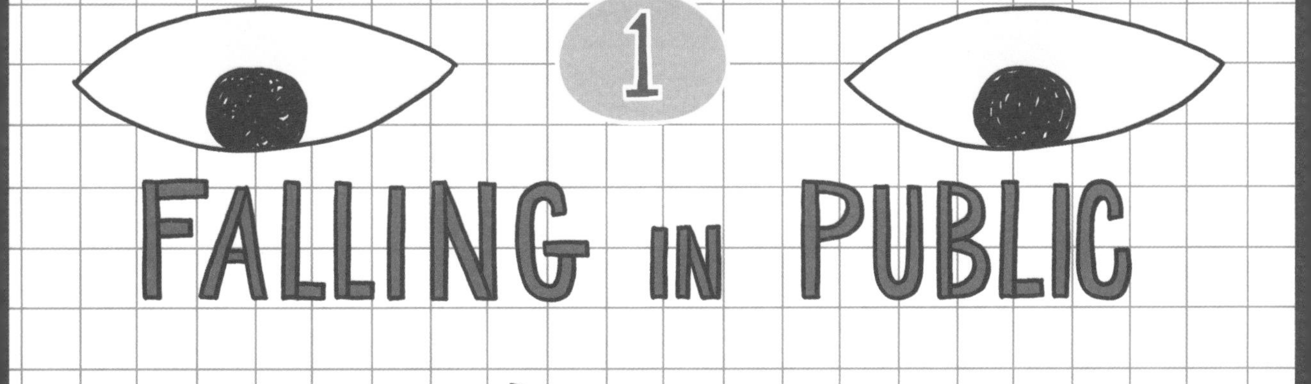

1
FALLING IN PUBLIC

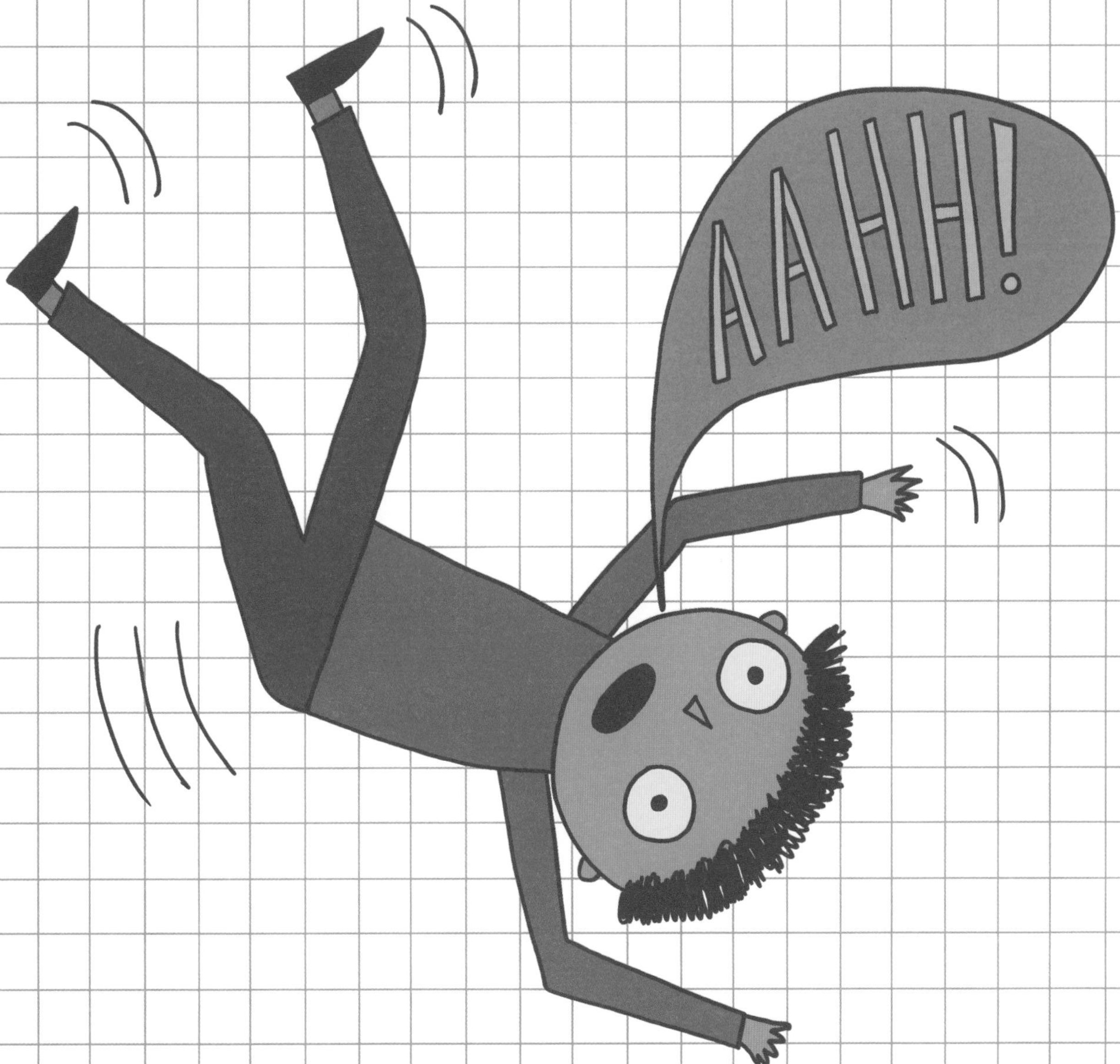
AAHH!

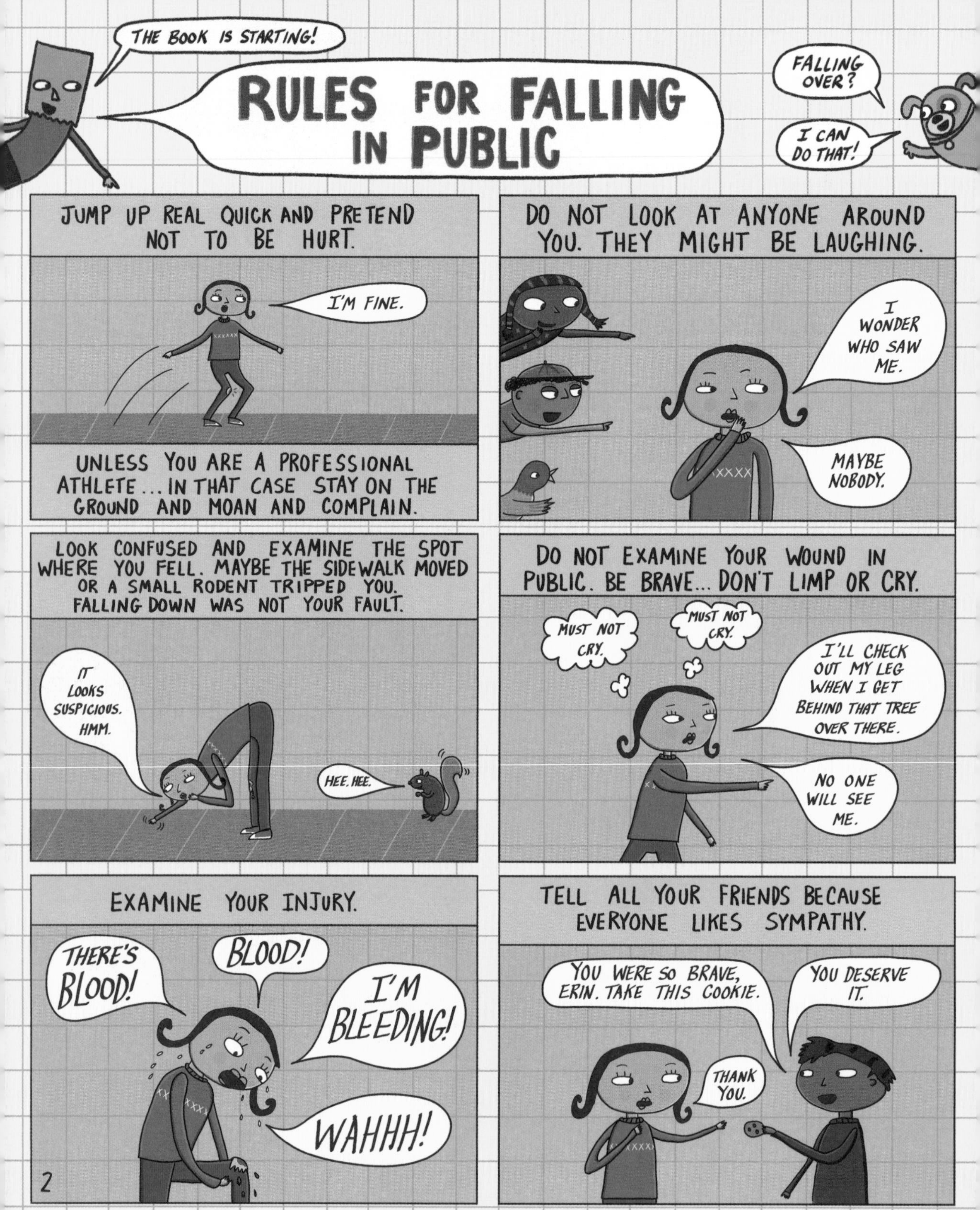
THE BOOK IS STARTING!
RULES FOR FALLING IN PUBLIC
FALLING OVER?
I CAN DO THAT!
JUMP UP REAL QUICK AND PRETEND NOT TO BE HURT.
I'M FINE.
UNLESS YOU ARE A PROFESSIONAL ATHLETE... IN THAT CASE STAY ON THE GROUND AND MOAN AND COMPLAIN.
DO NOT LOOK AT ANYONE AROUND YOU. THEY MIGHT BE LAUGHING.
I WONDER WHO SAW ME.
MAYBE NOBODY.
LOOK CONFUSED AND EXAMINE THE SPOT WHERE YOU FELL. MAYBE THE SIDEWALK MOVED OR A SMALL RODENT TRIPPED YOU. FALLING DOWN WAS NOT YOUR FAULT.
IT LOOKS SUSPICIOUS. HMM.
HEE. HEE.
DO NOT EXAMINE YOUR WOUND IN PUBLIC. BE BRAVE... DON'T LIMP OR CRY.
MUST NOT CRY.
MUST NOT CRY.
I'LL CHECK OUT MY LEG WHEN I GET BEHIND THAT TREE OVER THERE.
NO ONE WILL SEE ME.
EXAMINE YOUR INJURY.
THERE'S BLOOD!
BLOOD!
I'M BLEEDING!
WAHHH!
TELL ALL YOUR FRIENDS BECAUSE EVERYONE LIKES SYMPATHY.
YOU WERE SO BRAVE, ERIN. TAKE THIS COOKIE.
YOU DESERVE IT.
THANK YOU.

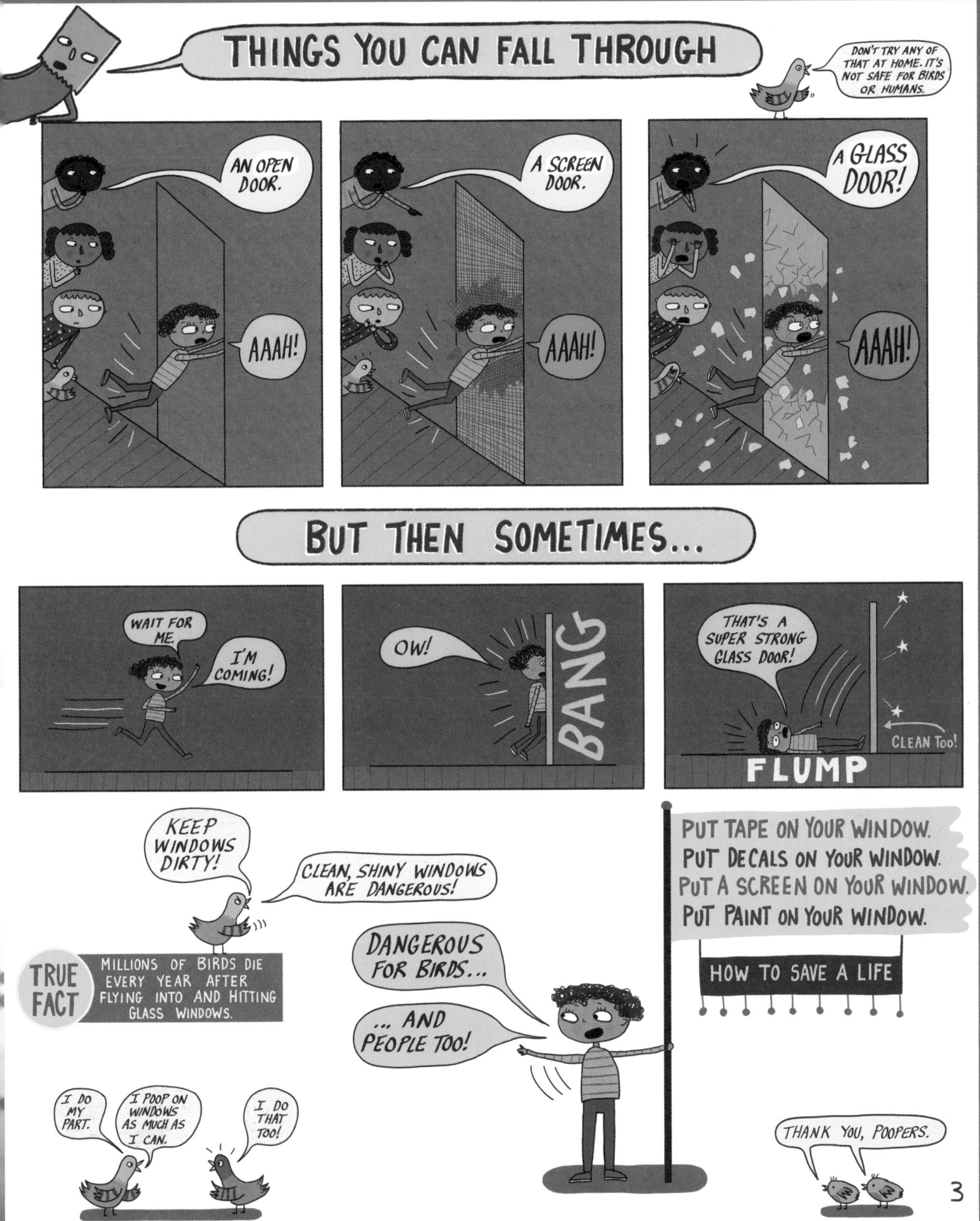
THINGS YOU CAN FALL THROUGH
DON'T TRY ANY OF THAT AT HOME. IT'S NOT SAFE FOR BIRDS OR HUMANS.
AN OPEN DOOR.
AAAH!
A SCREEN DOOR.
AAAH!
A GLASS DOOR!
AAAH!
BUT THEN SOMETIMES...
WAIT FOR ME.
I'M COMING!
OW!
BANG
THAT'S A SUPER STRONG GLASS DOOR!
CLEAN TOO!
FLUMP
KEEP WINDOWS DIRTY!
CLEAN, SHINY WINDOWS ARE DANGEROUS!
TRUE FACT
MILLIONS OF BIRDS DIE EVERY YEAR AFTER FLYING INTO AND HITTING GLASS WINDOWS.
DANGEROUS FOR BIRDS...
... AND PEOPLE TOO!
PUT TAPE ON YOUR WINDOW.
PUT DECALS ON YOUR WINDOW.
PUT A SCREEN ON YOUR WINDOW.
PUT PAINT ON YOUR WINDOW.
HOW TO SAVE A LIFE
I DO MY PART.
I POOP ON WINDOWS AS MUCH AS I CAN.
I DO THAT TOO!
THANK YOU, POOPERS.

HOW TO TELL IF A BODY IS HURT

PAIN!

THERE IS BLOOD!

I HAVE A CUT ON MY HAND!

WHAT DO I DO?

GET AN ADULT TO HELP!

VERBAL FIRST AID FOR A MINI INJURY

YOU ARE SO BRAVE.

YOU'LL BE OKAY.

IT'S JUST A SCRATCH.

LET ME GIVE IT A SLOBBERY, SMOOCHY-SMOOCH, FEEL-BETTER KISS.

IT'S OKAY NOW.

I FEEL BETTER.

WITH WORDS ALONE I HAVE THE POWER TO HEAL.

HA! HA! HA! HA! HA!

SOMETIMES THERE IS LAUGHTER WHEN SOMEONE FALLS DOWN.

BUT FALLING IS ONLY FUNNY IF NO ONE GETS HURT.

AND THAT INCLUDES FEELINGS.

OOPS.

FEELINGS ARE TRICKY.

YOU CAN'T SEE THEM...

...BUT IF THEY GET HURT, YOU CAN REALLY FEEL IT.

FORGIVE ME.

HOW TO TELL IF FEELINGS ARE HURT

FEELINGS HURT TOO

IT'S TRUE!

SAD FACE	WON'T LOOK AT ANYONE	ARMS CROSSED	WON'T TALK TO ANYONE	WANTS TO BE ALONE

FIRST AID FOR HURT FEELINGS SEE PAGE 103

4

EVERYDAY OBJECTS CAN BE HAZARDOUS

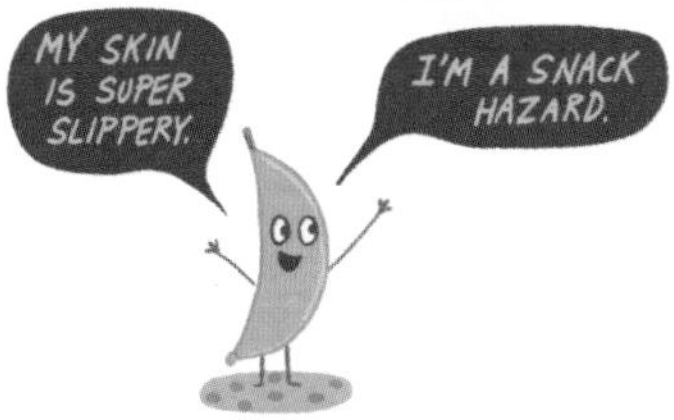

MY SKIN IS SUPER SLIPPERY.
I'M A SNACK HAZARD.

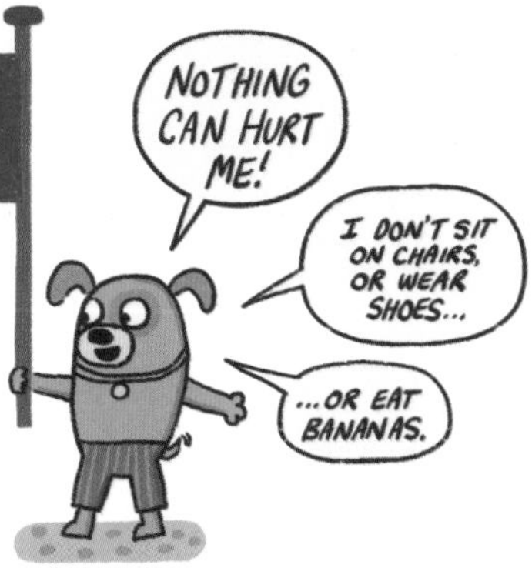

NOTHING CAN HURT ME!
I DON'T SIT ON CHAIRS, OR WEAR SHOES...
...OR EAT BANANAS.

EXAMPLE 1: THE CHAIR

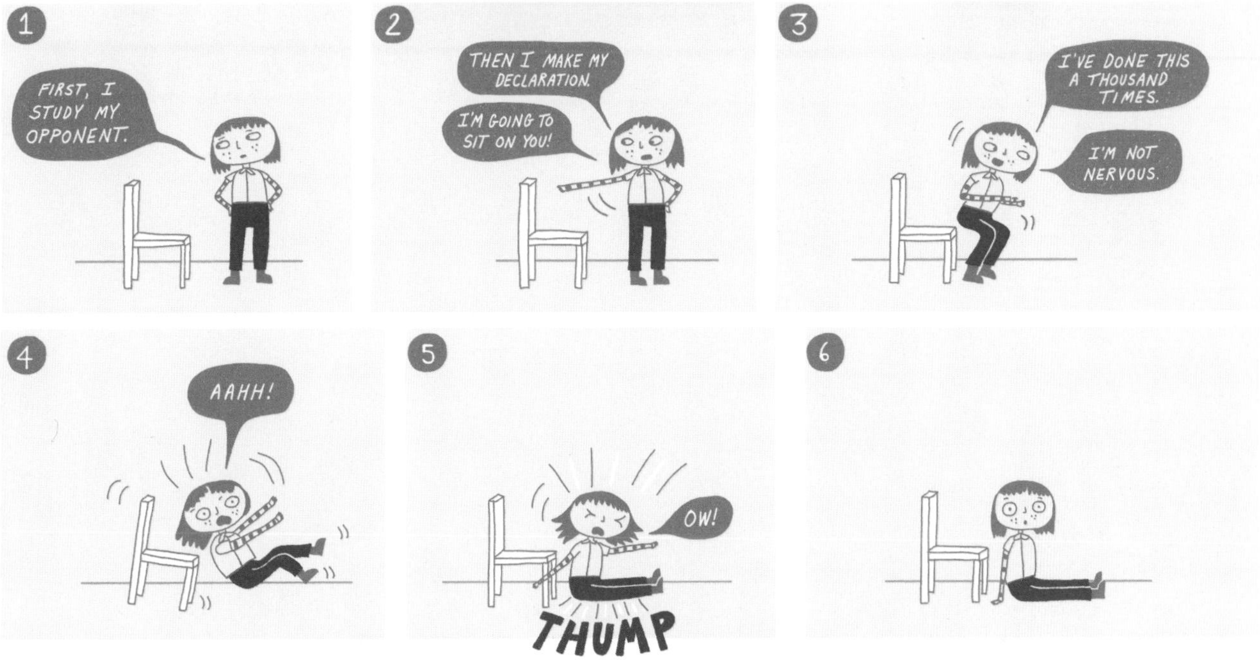

1
FIRST, I STUDY MY OPPONENT.
2
THEN I MAKE MY DECLARATION.
I'M GOING TO SIT ON YOU!
3
I'VE DONE THIS A THOUSAND TIMES.
I'M NOT NERVOUS.
4
AAHH!
5
OW!
THUMP
6

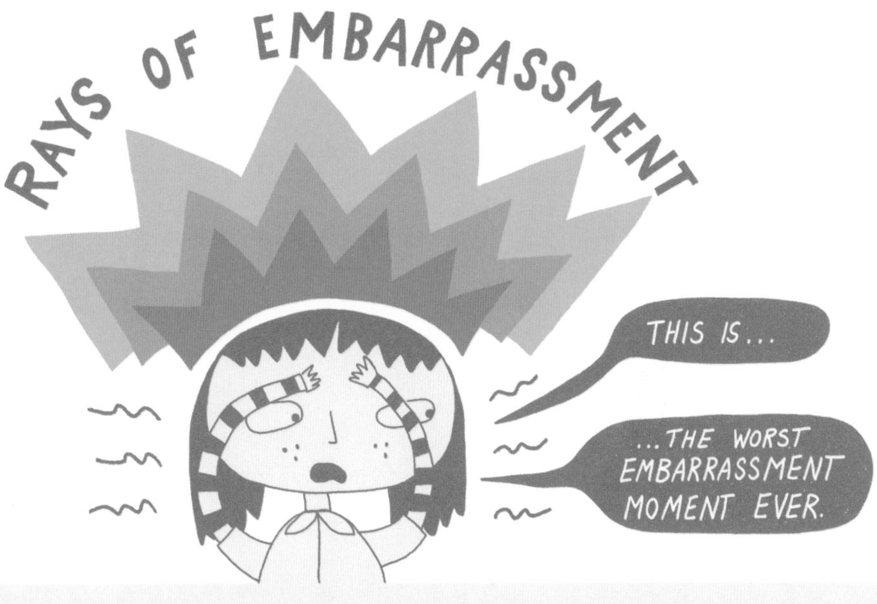

RAYS OF EMBARRASSMENT
THIS IS...
...THE WORST EMBARRASSMENT MOMENT EVER.

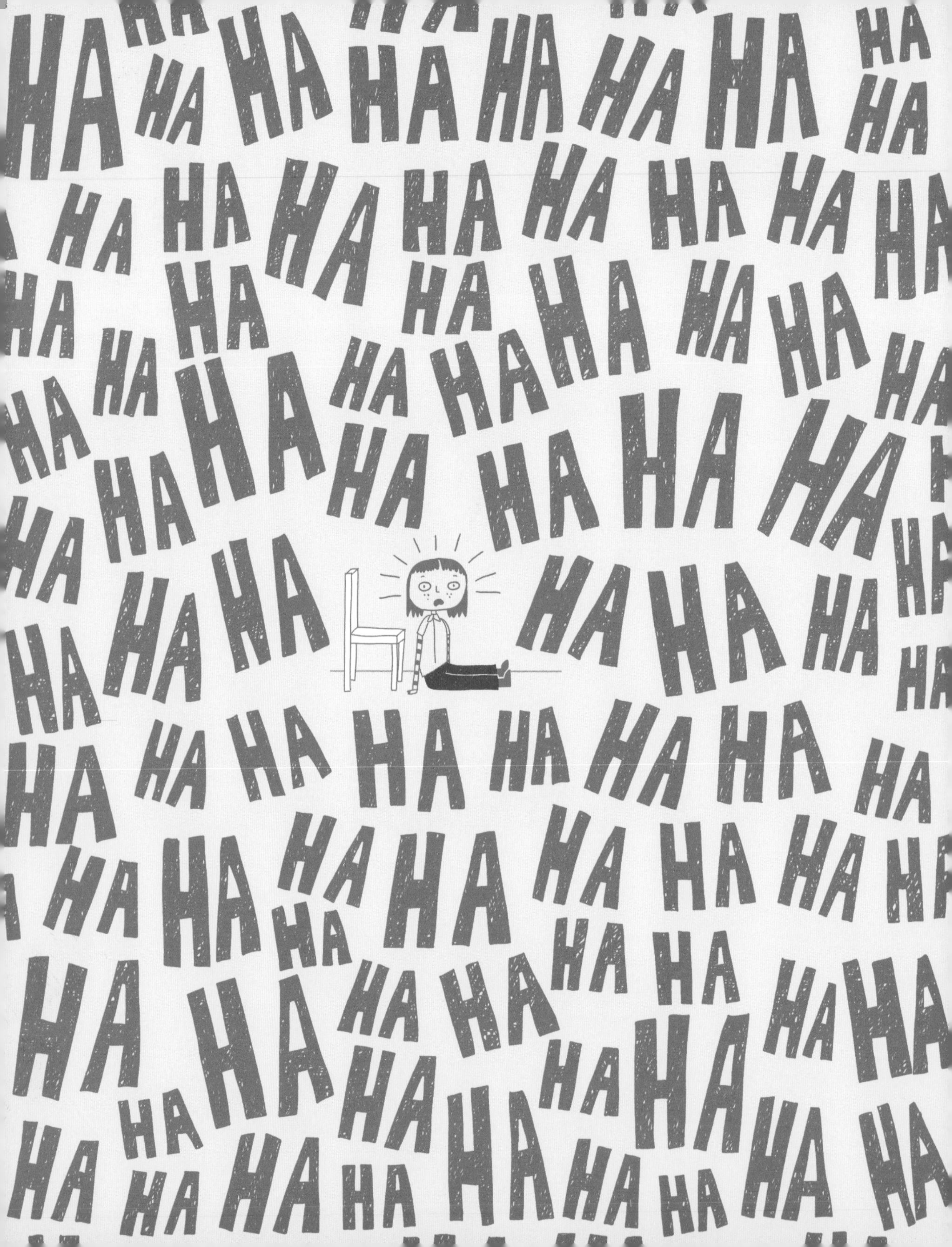
HA HA HA HA HA HA

9
I WAS WRONG.
THIS IS WORSE!
"HA" "HA" THAT WAS AWESOME!
HA HA HA!
"HA" "HA" "HA" "HA"
WHAT A FALL!
"HA" "HA" "HA" "HA" "HA" "HA" "HA" "HA"
DID YOU SEE THAT?
"HA"

10
I WIN.
"HA" "HA" "HA" "HA" "HA"

IT'S NOT A GOOD FEELING TO FIND OUT THAT THE WORLD IS ROOTING FOR THE CHAIR.

DON'T BE SAD, IT CAN HAPPEN TO ANYONE.
I SURVIVED

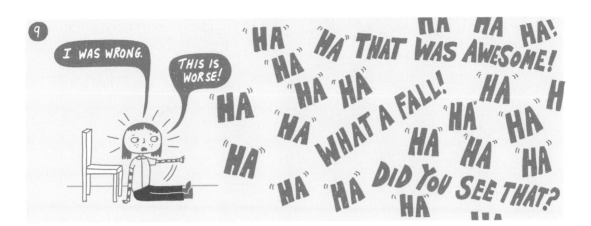

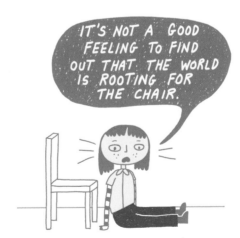

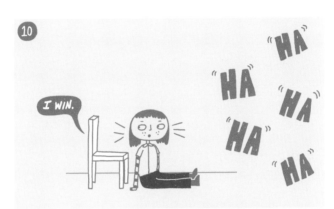

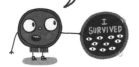

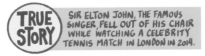

TRUE STORY SIR ELTON JOHN, THE FAMOUS SINGER, FELL OUT OF HIS CHAIR WHILE WATCHING A CELEBRITY TENNIS MATCH IN LONDON IN 2014.

I LIKE THE WORDS OF WISDOM...
... BUT I LOVE THE BADGES!

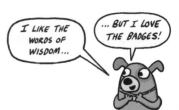

EXAMPLE 2: THE SHOELACE

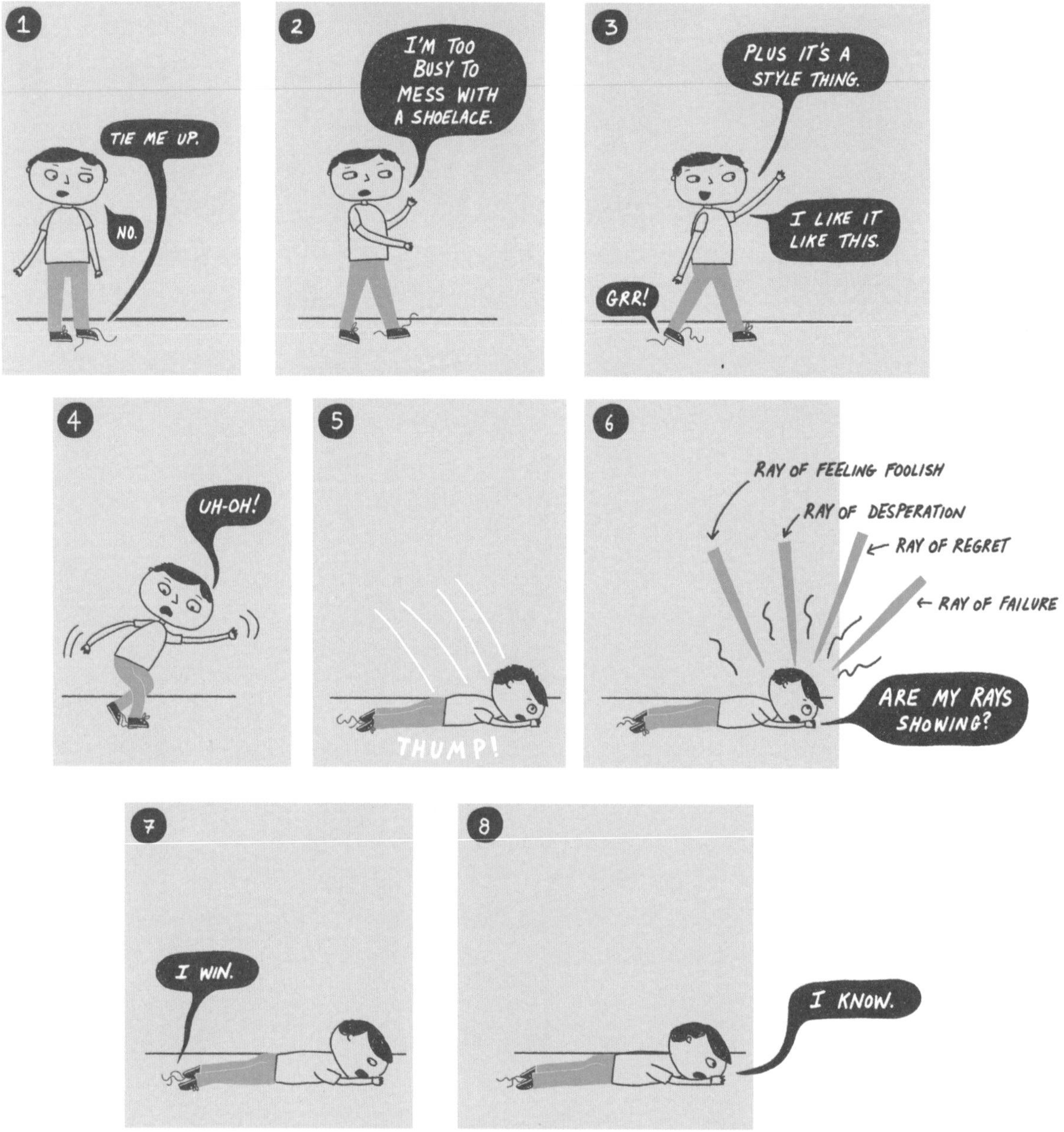
1
TIE ME UP.
NO.
2
I'M TOO BUSY TO MESS WITH A SHOELACE.
3
PLUS IT'S A STYLE THING.
I LIKE IT LIKE THIS.
GRR!
4
UH-OH!
5
THUMP!
6
RAY OF FEELING FOOLISH
RAY OF DESPERATION
RAY OF REGRET
RAY OF FAILURE
ARE MY RAYS SHOWING?
7
I WIN.
8
I KNOW.

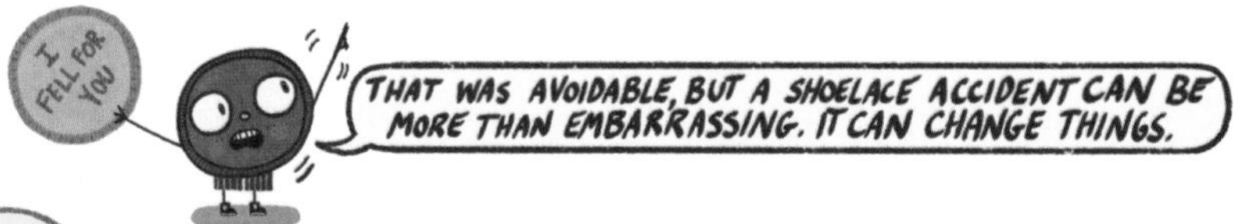
I FELL FOR YOU
THAT WAS AVOIDABLE, BUT A SHOELACE ACCIDENT CAN BE MORE THAN EMBARRASSING. IT CAN CHANGE THINGS.

TRUE STORY PROFESSIONAL BASEBALL PLAYER ALEX RODRIGUEZ (TEXAS RANGERS-SHORTSTOP #3) ONCE TRIPPED AND FELL BECAUSE OF AN UNTIED SHOELACE DURING A GAME AGAINST THE TORONTO BLUE JAYS.

EXAMPLE 3: THE BANANA PEEL

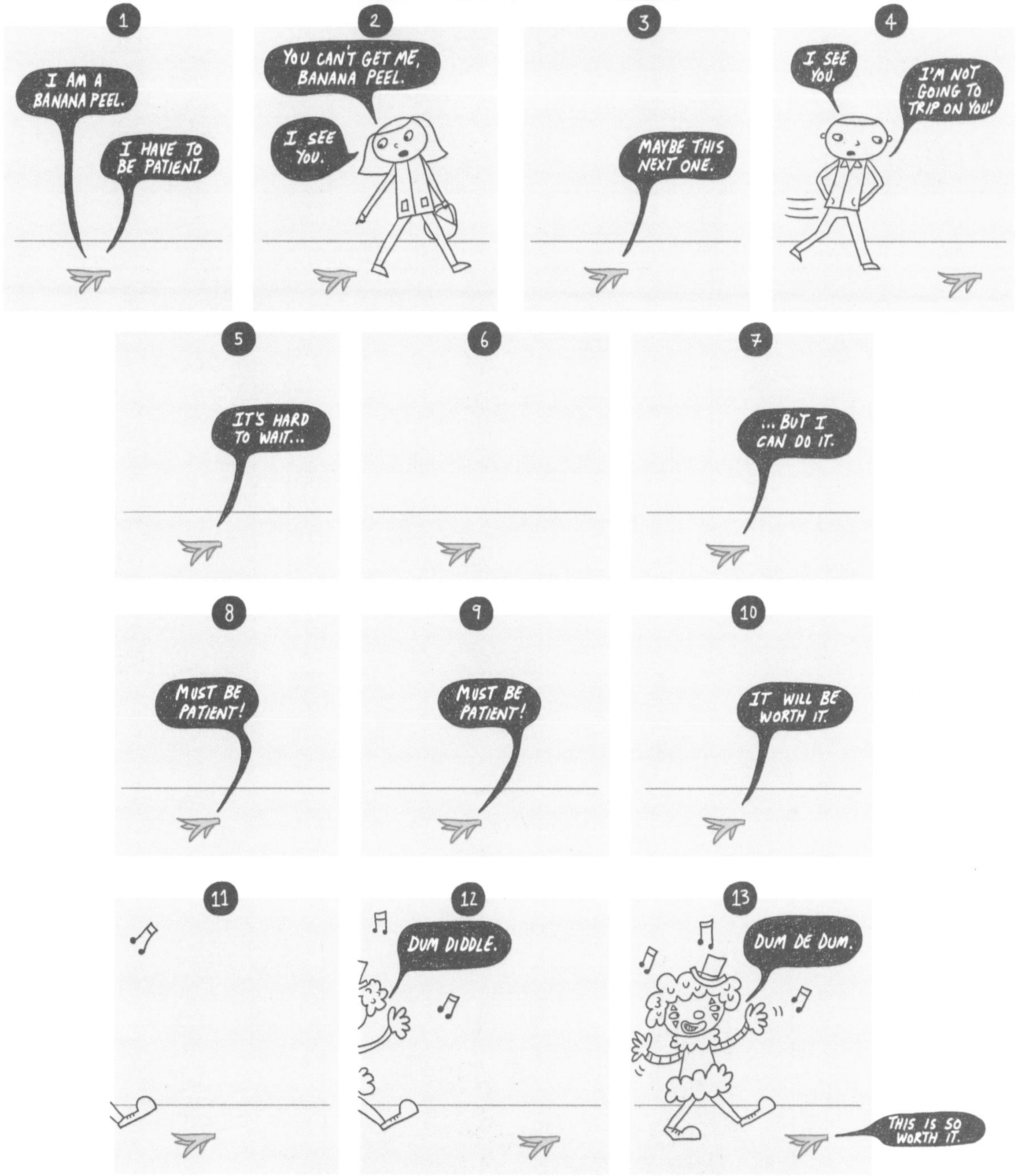
1
I AM A BANANA PEEL.
I HAVE TO BE PATIENT.
2
YOU CAN'T GET ME, BANANA PEEL.
I SEE YOU.
3
MAYBE THIS NEXT ONE.
4
I SEE YOU.
I'M NOT GOING TO TRIP ON YOU!
5
IT'S HARD TO WAIT...
6
7
...BUT I CAN DO IT.
8
MUST BE PATIENT!
9
MUST BE PATIENT!
10
IT WILL BE WORTH IT.
11
12
DUM DIDDLE.
13
DUM DE DUM.
THIS IS SO WORTH IT.

TRUE FACT

IN THE EARLY 1900S PEOPLE COMMONLY THREW THEIR GARBAGE IN THE STREET. A FRESH BANANA PEEL IS MILDLY SLIPPERY, BUT A THREE-DAY-OLD BANANA PEEL IS A SLIPPERY, SLIMY HAZARD. IN 1909 THE CITY OF ST. LOUIS OUTLAWED THE DISPOSAL OF BANANA PEELS ON PUBLIC THOROUGHFARES IN ORDER TO REDUCE BANANA-RELATED INJURIES.

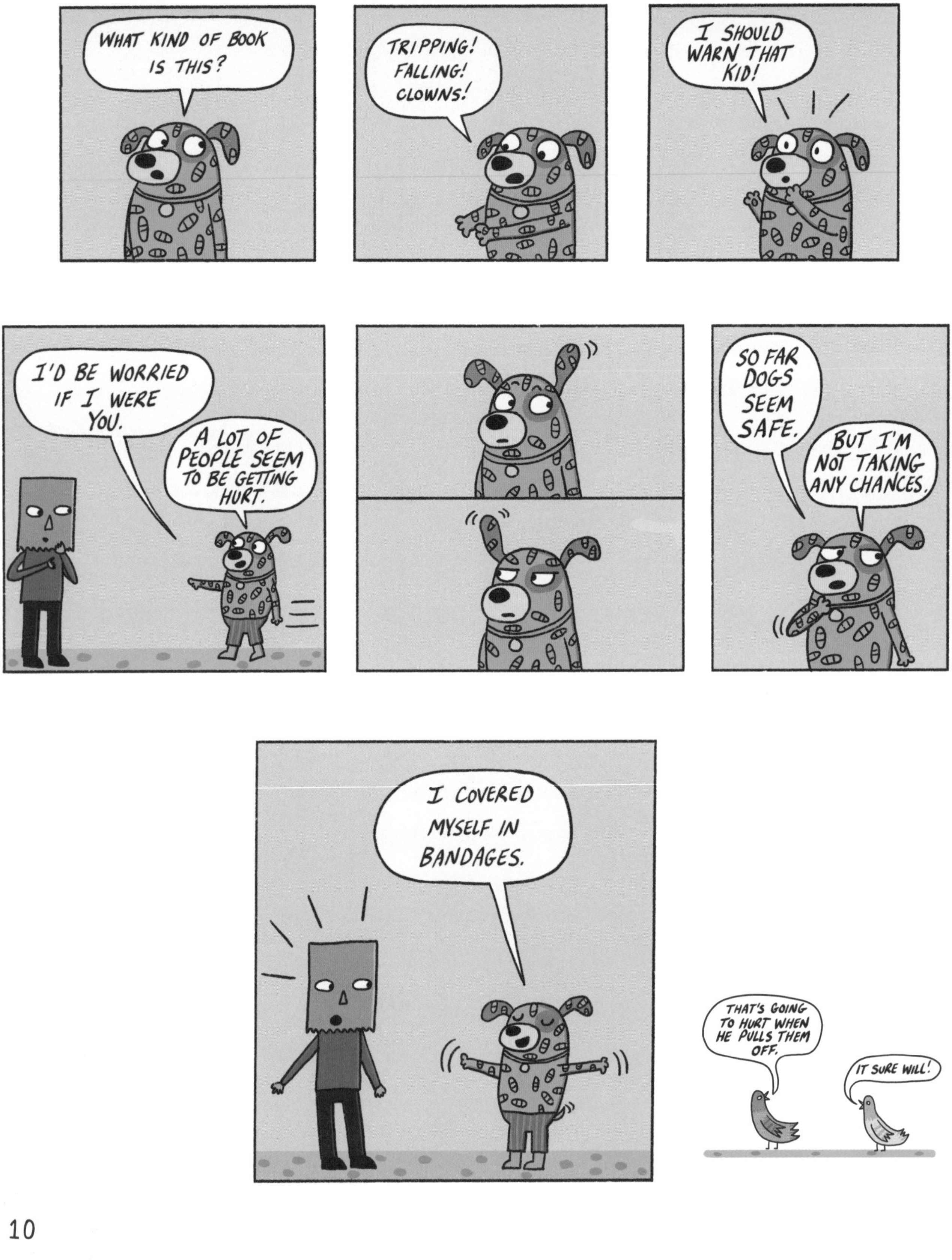
WHAT KIND OF BOOK IS THIS?
TRIPPING! FALLING! CLOWNS!
I SHOULD WARN THAT KID!
I'D BE WORRIED IF I WERE YOU.
A LOT OF PEOPLE SEEM TO BE GETTING HURT.
SO FAR DOGS SEEM SAFE.
BUT I'M NOT TAKING ANY CHANCES.
I COVERED MYSELF IN BANDAGES.
THAT'S GOING TO HURT WHEN HE PULLS THEM OFF.
IT SURE WILL!

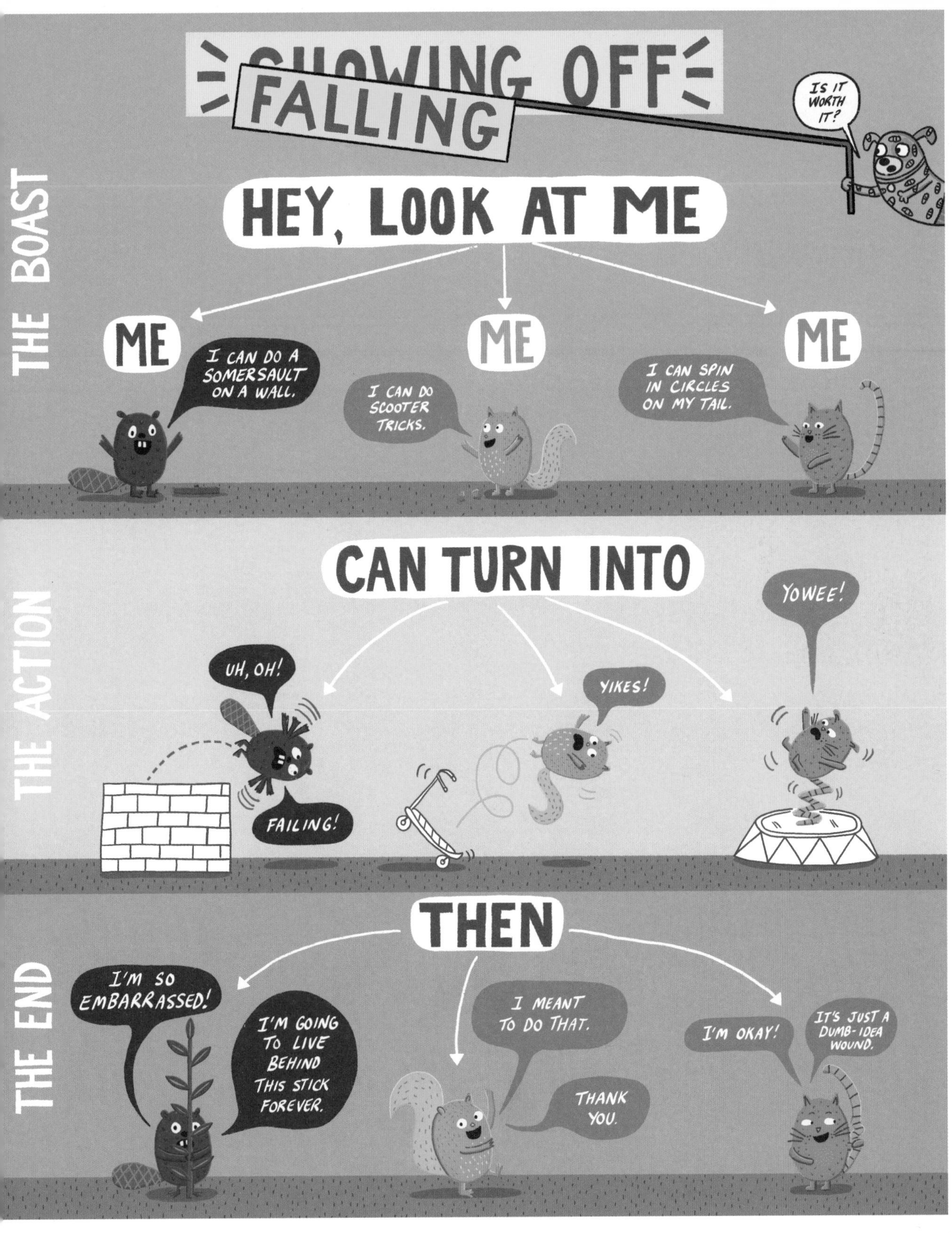
SHOWING OFF
FALLING
IS IT WORTH IT?
THE BOAST
HEY, LOOK AT ME
ME
I CAN DO A SOMERSAULT ON A WALL.
ME
I CAN DO SCOOTER TRICKS.
ME
I CAN SPIN IN CIRCLES ON MY TAIL.
THE ACTION
CAN TURN INTO
UH, OH!
FAILING!
YIKES!
YOWEE!
THE END
THEN
I'M SO EMBARRASSED!
I'M GOING TO LIVE BEHIND THIS STICK FOREVER.
I MEANT TO DO THAT.
THANK YOU.
I'M OKAY!
IT'S JUST A DUMB-IDEA WOUND.

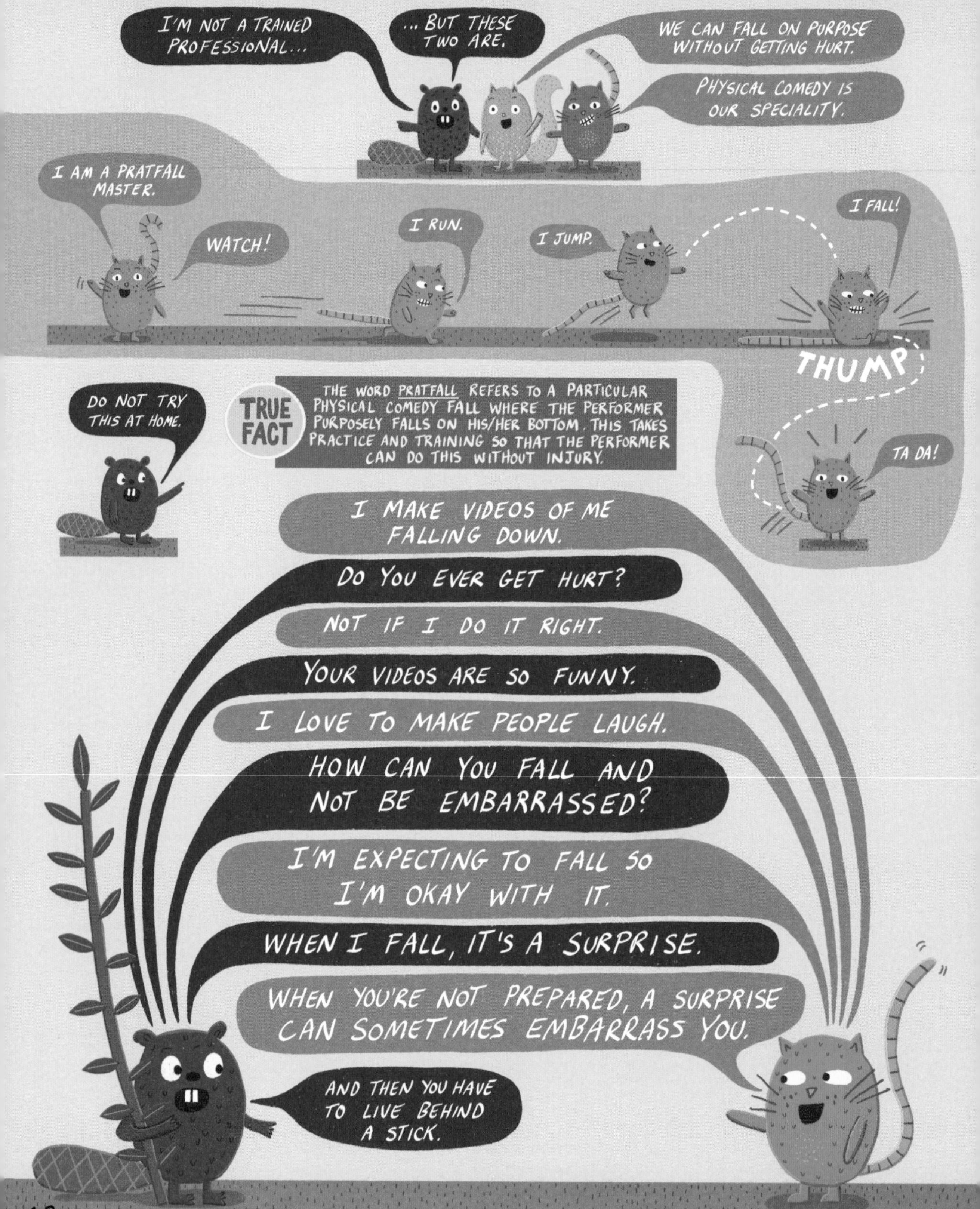
I'M NOT A TRAINED PROFESSIONAL...
... BUT THESE TWO ARE.
WE CAN FALL ON PURPOSE WITHOUT GETTING HURT.
PHYSICAL COMEDY IS OUR SPECIALITY.
I AM A PRATFALL MASTER.
WATCH!
I RUN.
I JUMP.
I FALL!
THUMP
TA DA!
DO NOT TRY THIS AT HOME.
TRUE FACT
THE WORD PRATFALL REFERS TO A PARTICULAR PHYSICAL COMEDY FALL WHERE THE PERFORMER PURPOSELY FALLS ON HIS/HER BOTTOM. THIS TAKES PRACTICE AND TRAINING SO THAT THE PERFORMER CAN DO THIS WITHOUT INJURY.
I MAKE VIDEOS OF ME FALLING DOWN.
DO YOU EVER GET HURT?
NOT IF I DO IT RIGHT.
YOUR VIDEOS ARE SO FUNNY.
I LOVE TO MAKE PEOPLE LAUGH.
HOW CAN YOU FALL AND NOT BE EMBARRASSED?
I'M EXPECTING TO FALL SO I'M OKAY WITH IT.
WHEN I FALL, IT'S A SURPRISE.
WHEN YOU'RE NOT PREPARED, A SURPRISE CAN SOMETIMES EMBARRASS YOU.
AND THEN YOU HAVE TO LIVE BEHIND A STICK.

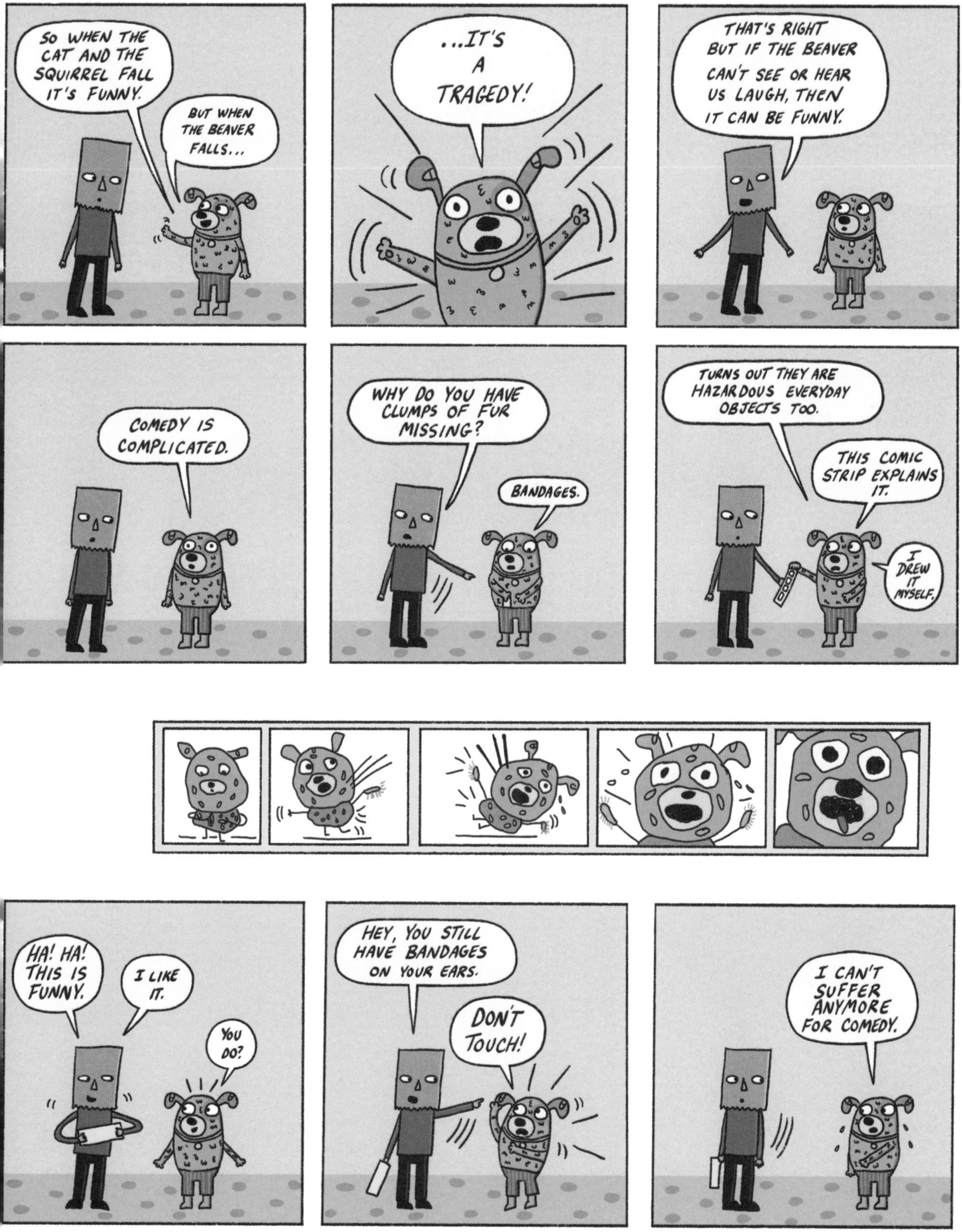

SO WHEN THE CAT AND THE SQUIRREL FALL IT'S FUNNY.
BUT WHEN THE BEAVER FALLS...
...IT'S A TRAGEDY!
THAT'S RIGHT BUT IF THE BEAVER CAN'T SEE OR HEAR US LAUGH, THEN IT CAN BE FUNNY.
COMEDY IS COMPLICATED.
WHY DO YOU HAVE CLUMPS OF FUR MISSING?
BANDAGES.
TURNS OUT THEY ARE HAZARDOUS EVERYDAY OBJECTS TOO.
THIS COMIC STRIP EXPLAINS IT.
I DREW IT MYSELF.
HA! HA! THIS IS FUNNY.
I LIKE IT.
YOU DO?
HEY, YOU STILL HAVE BANDAGES ON YOUR EARS.
DON'T TOUCH!
I CAN'T SUFFER ANYMORE FOR COMEDY.

 # FALLING IN PUBLIC IS AN

"I DID SOMETHING WRONG AND EVERYONE SAW IT"

PEOPLE OF DIFFERENT CULTURES FIND FALLING FUNNY.

KIND OF MISTAKE.

SCIENTISTS DON'T KNOW WHY PEOPLE LAUGH AT FALLING.

IT MAKES PEOPLE LAUGH.

PEOPLE AREN'T USUALLY LAUGHING TO BE MEAN. THEY CAN'T HELP IT.

IT CAN BE

THE URGE TO LAUGH MIGHT BE HARDWIRED INTO OUR BRAINS.

EMBARRASSING!

SO, WHAT DO YOU DO IF IT HAPPENS TO YOU?

I SURVIVED A FALL

ACCEPT YOUR MISTAKE AND SHRUG IT OFF?

ACCEPT YOUR EMBARRASSMENT? EVERYONE MAKES MISTAKES.

MAKE A JOKE OF IT?

PRETEND YOU DID IT ON PURPOSE?

RUN AWAY AND HIDE?

THERE IS NO WRONG ANSWER.

YOU DESERVE A BADGE. WEAR IT PROUDLY.

THAT IS PRETTY GOOD ADVICE.

BADGEY IS A BONUS!

2

LOOK! A SOCIAL OOPS

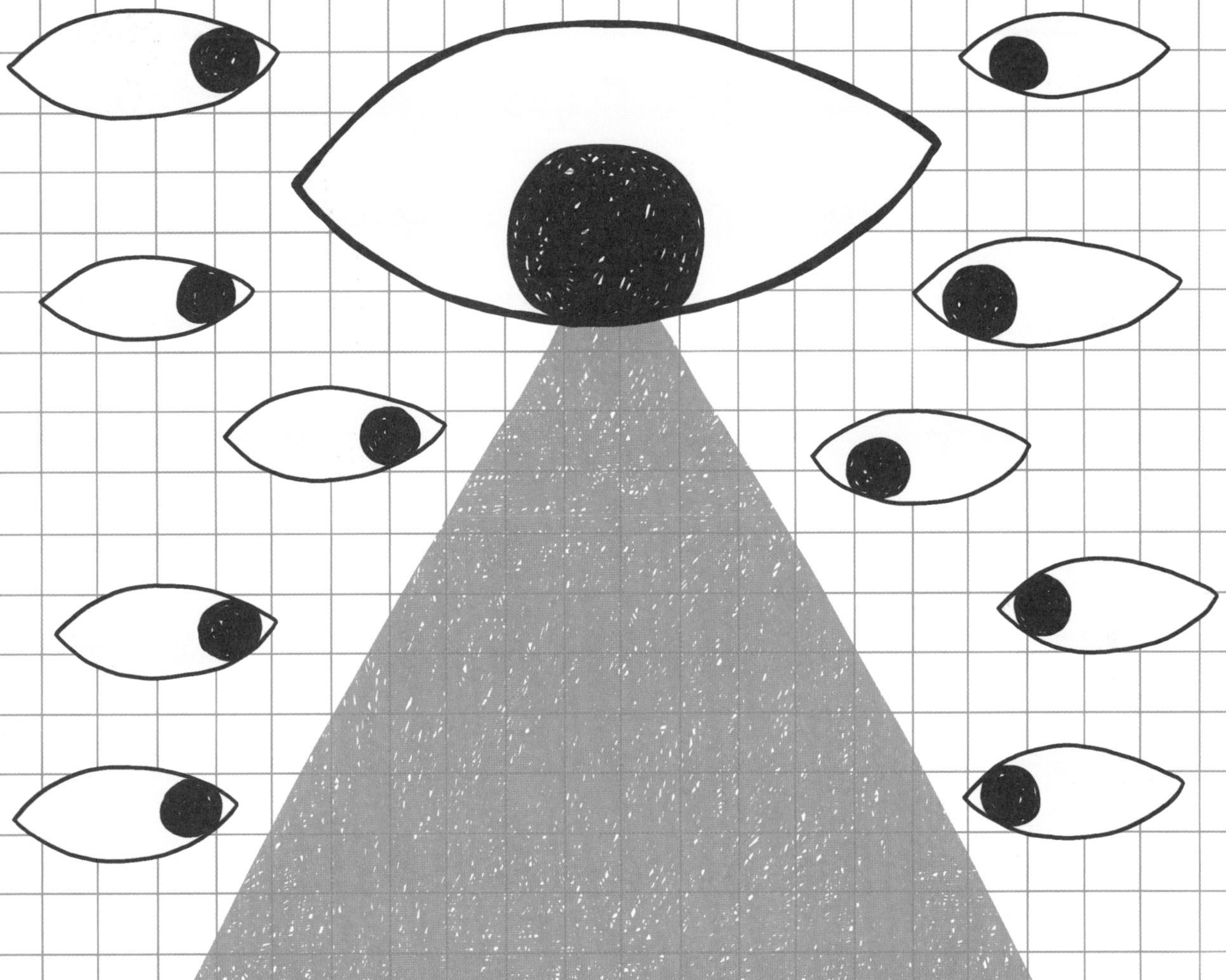
IMAGINE YOURSELF HERE

THE TROUBLE WITH HANDS

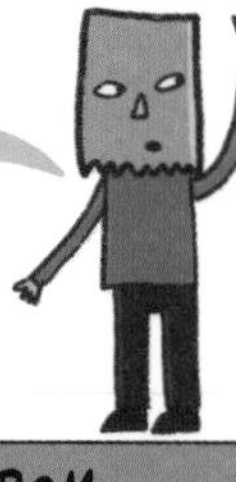

EVERYBODY LIKES A GOOD WAVE. THERE ARE MANY VARIETIES TO CHOOSE FROM.

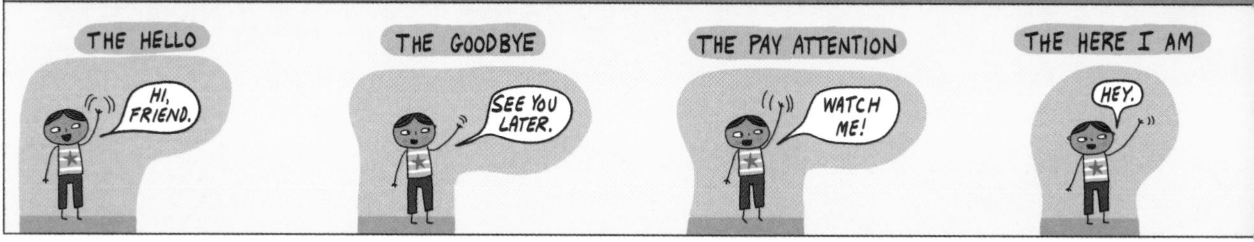
THE HELLO
HI, FRIEND.
THE GOODBYE
SEE YOU LATER.
THE PAY ATTENTION
WATCH ME!
THE HERE I AM
HEY.

A BIG FAVORITE IS THE TRANSPORTATION WAVE. THIS WAVE OFTEN HAPPENS BETWEEN COMPLETE STRANGERS—USUALLY WHEN ONE STRANGER IS MOVING AND THE OTHER STRANGER IS STANDING STILL.

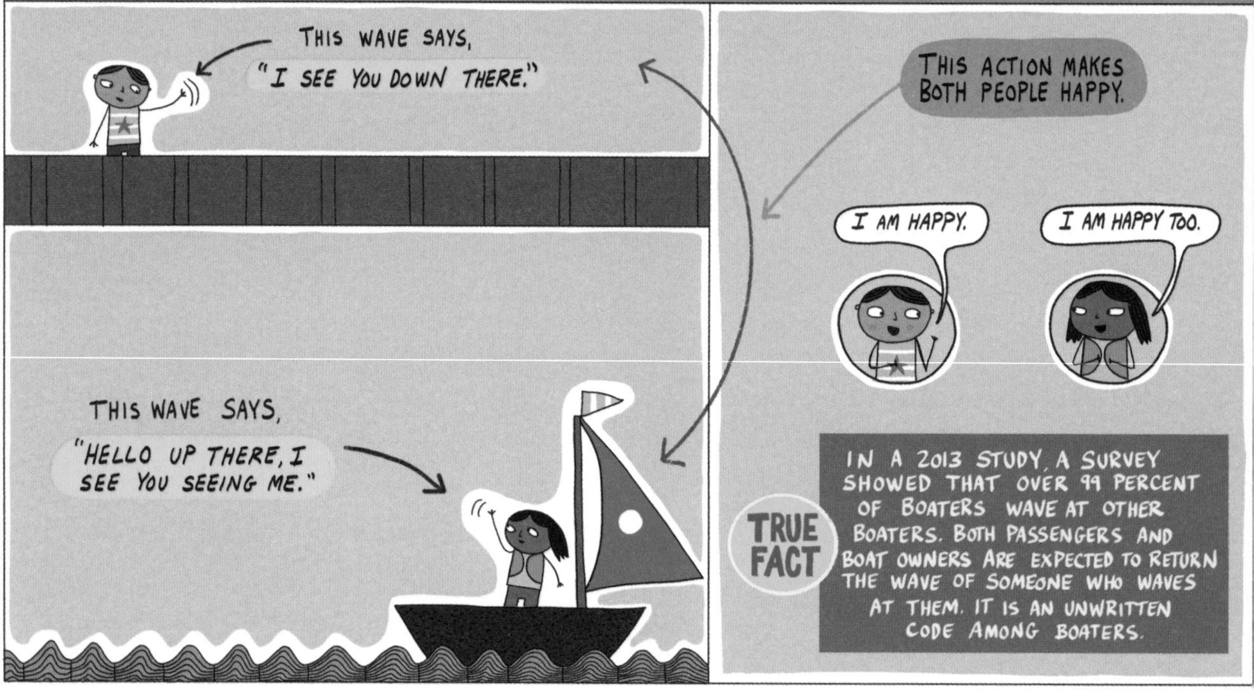
THIS WAVE SAYS,
"I SEE YOU DOWN THERE."
THIS WAVE SAYS,
"HELLO UP THERE, I SEE YOU SEEING ME."
THIS ACTION MAKES BOTH PEOPLE HAPPY.
I AM HAPPY.
I AM HAPPY TOO.
TRUE FACT
IN A 2013 STUDY, A SURVEY SHOWED THAT OVER 99 PERCENT OF BOATERS WAVE AT OTHER BOATERS. BOTH PASSENGERS AND BOAT OWNERS ARE EXPECTED TO RETURN THE WAVE OF SOMEONE WHO WAVES AT THEM. IT IS AN UNWRITTEN CODE AMONG BOATERS.

PEOPLE ALSO LIKE TO DO THE TRANSPORTATION WAVE FROM THESE.

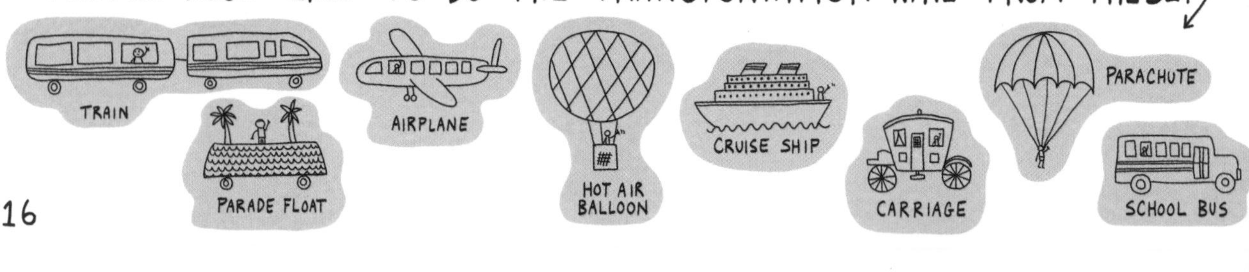
TRAIN
PARADE FLOAT
AIRPLANE
HOT AIR BALLOON
CRUISE SHIP
CARRIAGE
PARACHUTE
SCHOOL BUS

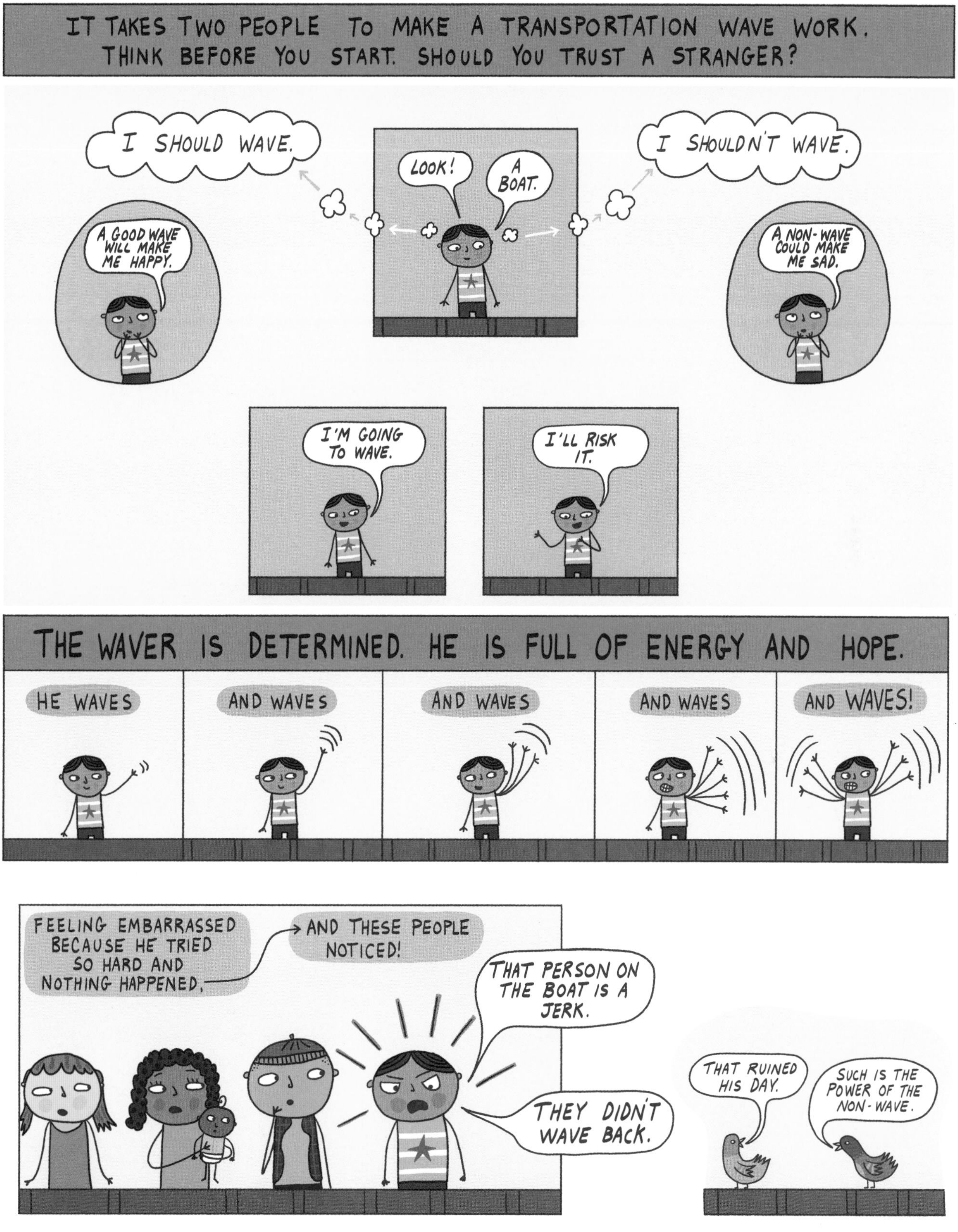
IT TAKES TWO PEOPLE TO MAKE A TRANSPORTATION WAVE WORK. THINK BEFORE YOU START. SHOULD YOU TRUST A STRANGER?
I SHOULD WAVE.
A GOOD WAVE WILL MAKE ME HAPPY.
LOOK!
A BOAT.
I SHOULDN'T WAVE.
A NON-WAVE COULD MAKE ME SAD.
I'M GOING TO WAVE.
I'LL RISK IT.
THE WAVER IS DETERMINED. HE IS FULL OF ENERGY AND HOPE.
HE WAVES
AND WAVES
AND WAVES
AND WAVES
AND WAVES!
FEELING EMBARRASSED BECAUSE HE TRIED SO HARD AND NOTHING HAPPENED,
AND THESE PEOPLE NOTICED!
THAT PERSON ON THE BOAT IS A JERK.
THEY DIDN'T WAVE BACK.
THAT RUINED HIS DAY.
SUCH IS THE POWER OF THE NON-WAVE.

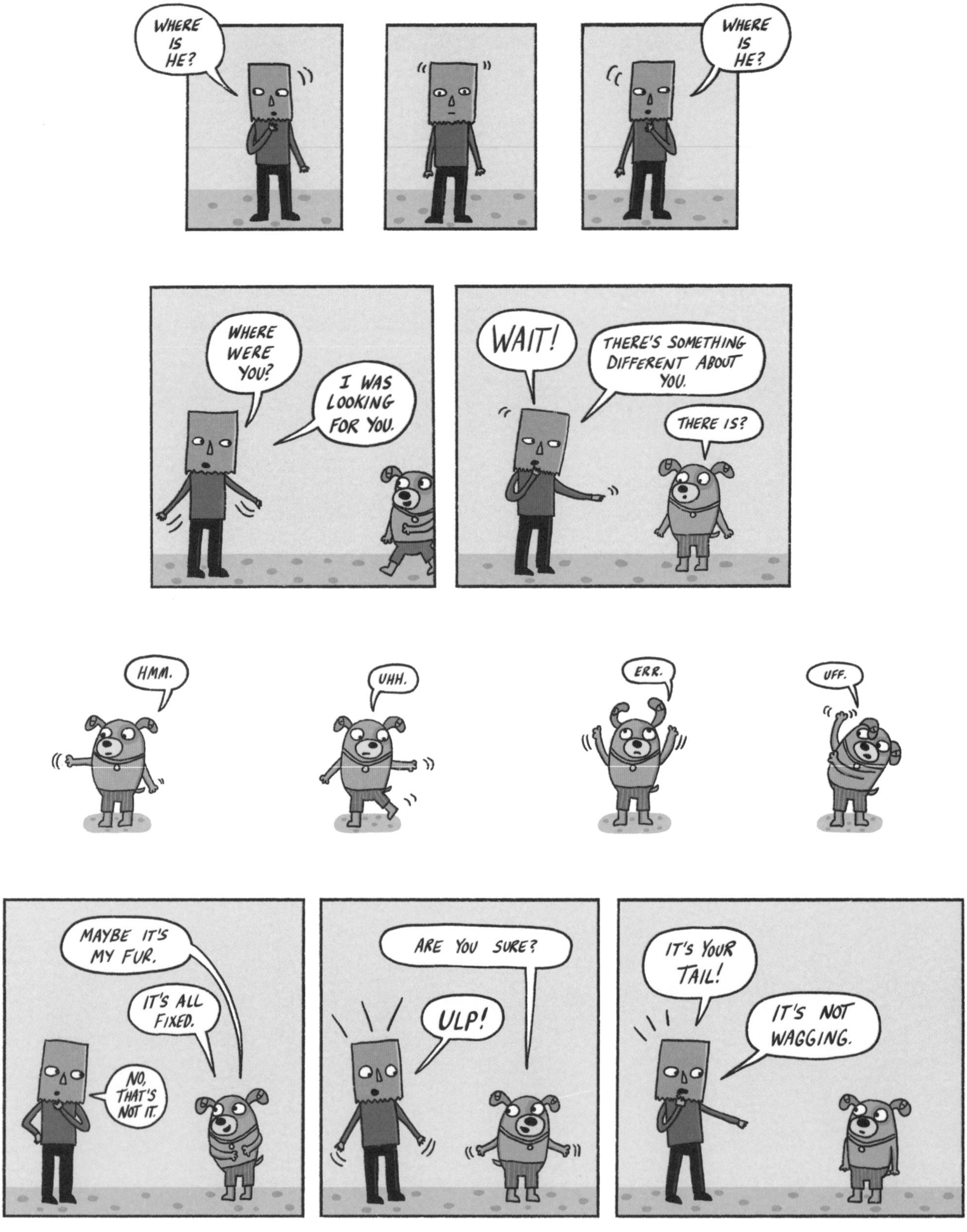
WHERE IS HE?
WHERE IS HE?
WHERE WERE YOU?
I WAS LOOKING FOR YOU.
WAIT!
THERE'S SOMETHING DIFFERENT ABOUT YOU.
THERE IS?
HMM.
UHH.
ERR.
UFF.
MAYBE IT'S MY FUR.
IT'S ALL FIXED.
NO, THAT'S NOT IT.
ARE YOU SURE?
ULP!
IT'S YOUR TAIL!
IT'S NOT WAGGING.

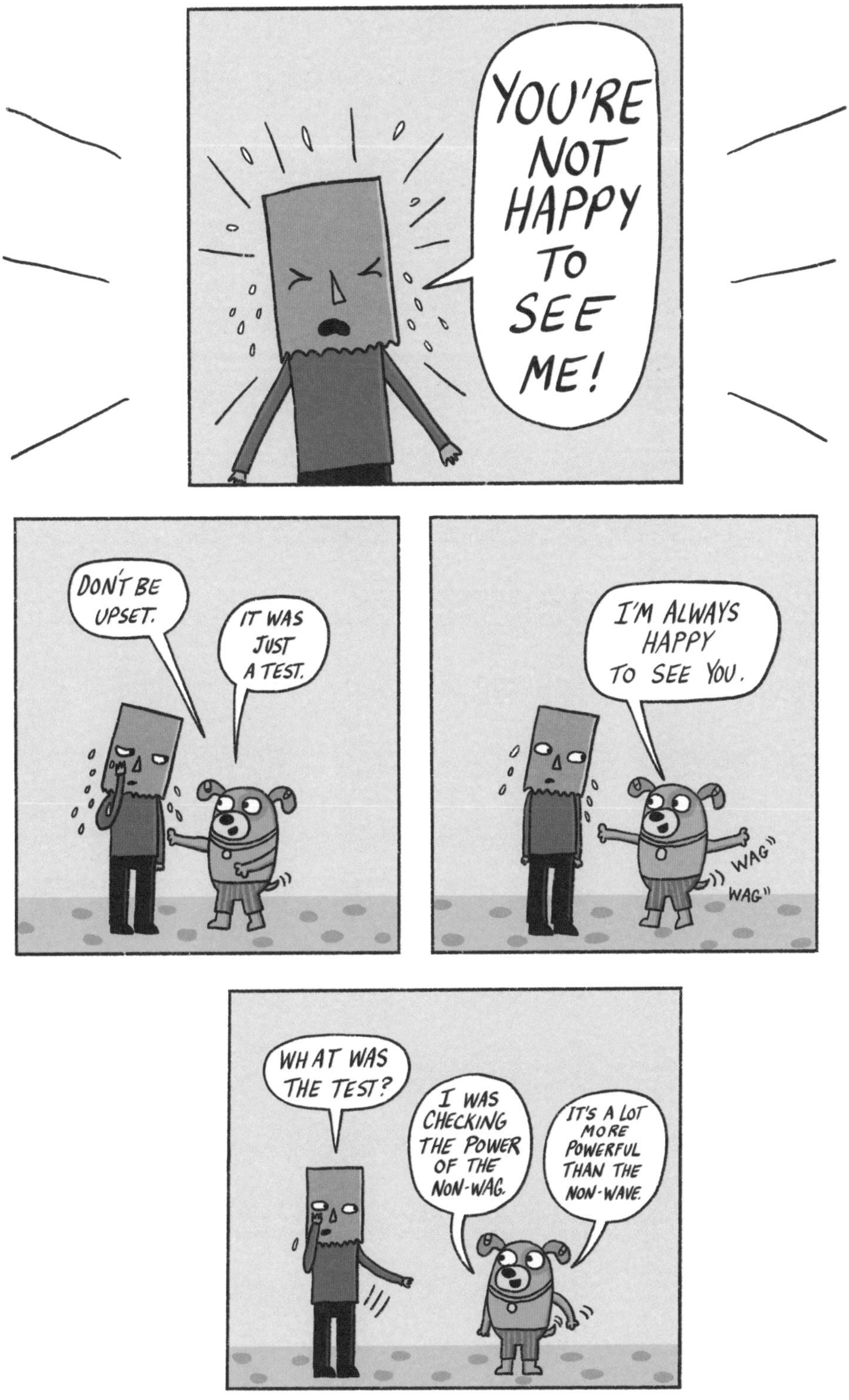
YOU'RE NOT HAPPY TO SEE ME!
DON'T BE UPSET.
IT WAS JUST A TEST.
I'M ALWAYS HAPPY TO SEE YOU.
WAG
WAG
WHAT WAS THE TEST?
I WAS CHECKING THE POWER OF THE NON-WAG.
IT'S A LOT MORE POWERFUL THAN THE NON-WAVE.

IS IT TIME FOR A COOKIE?

NOT EVEN CLOSE!

WE'RE NOT EVEN CLOSE TO BEING DONE.

I THINK SOMEONE IS EMBARRASSED ABOUT CRYING.

THERE WERE REAL TEARS,

I DIDN'T KNOW THAT WOULD HAPPEN.

TALKING ABOUT IT IN FRONT OF EVERYBODY <u>DOES NOT</u> MAKE ME FEEL LESS EMBARRASSED!

NOW EVERYONE KNOWS ABOUT IT!

THAT IS TRUE!

I'M SORRY.

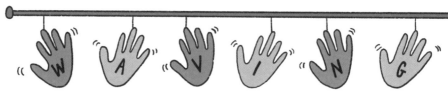

W A V I N G

THERE ARE LOTS OF WAYS FOR A WAVE TO GO WRONG.   EXAMPLE 1   NOT FOR YOU.

WHO IS THAT WAVING OVER THERE?

IT LOOKS LIKE JERRI.

WHY IS SHE WAVING AT ME?

I HARDLY KNOW HER.

WOW, SHE REALLY IS WAVING.

I GUESS SHE WANTS MY ATTENTION.

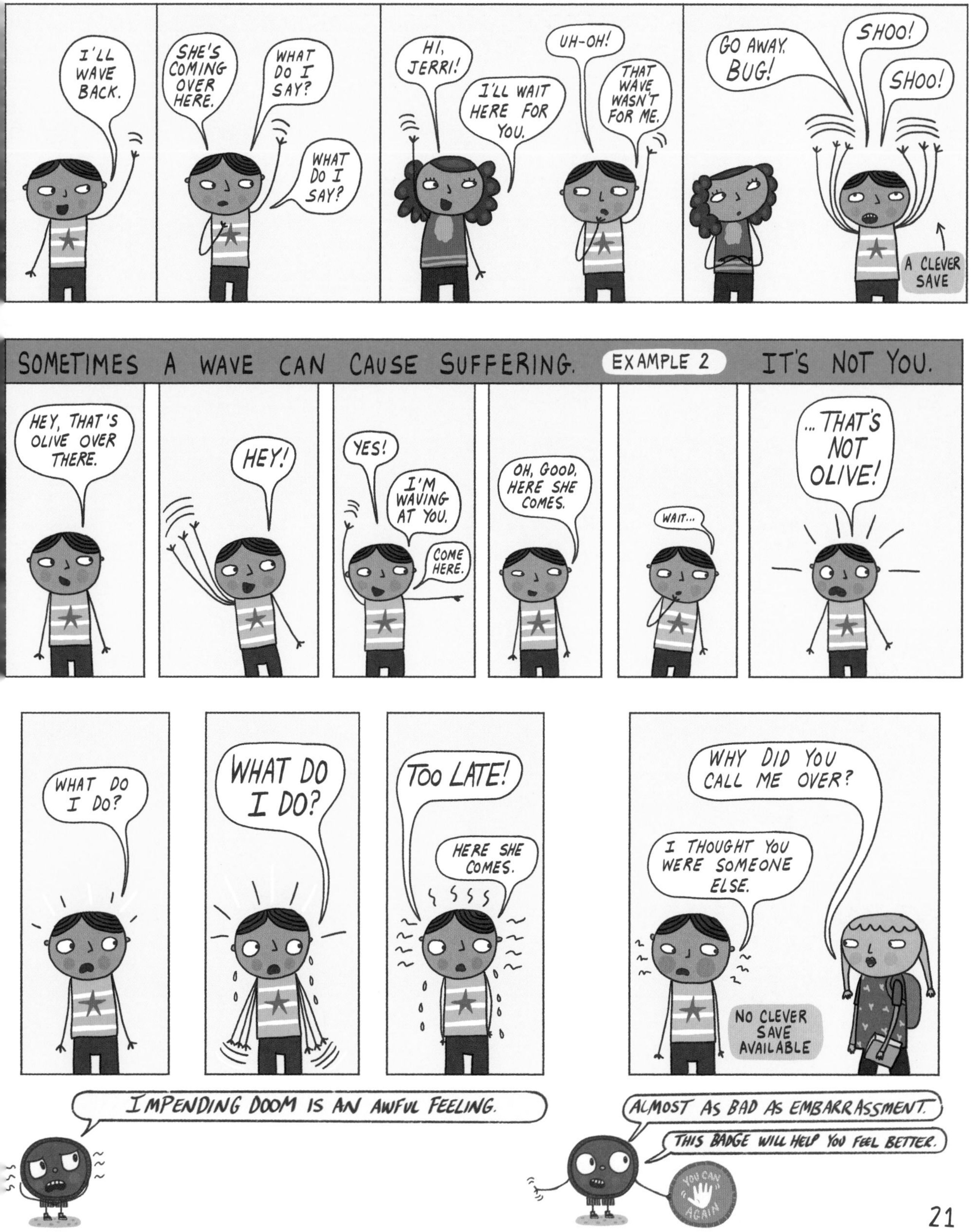
I'LL WAVE BACK.
SHE'S COMING OVER HERE.
WHAT DO I SAY?
WHAT DO I SAY?
HI, JERRI!
I'LL WAIT HERE FOR YOU.
UH-OH!
THAT WAVE WASN'T FOR ME.
GO AWAY. BUG!
SHOO!
SHOO!
A CLEVER SAVE
SOMETIMES A WAVE CAN CAUSE SUFFERING.
EXAMPLE 2
IT'S NOT YOU.
HEY, THAT'S OLIVE OVER THERE.
HEY!
YES!
I'M WAVING AT YOU.
COME HERE.
OH, GOOD. HERE SHE COMES.
WAIT...
...THAT'S NOT OLIVE!
WHAT DO I DO?
WHAT DO I DO?
TOO LATE!
HERE SHE COMES.
WHY DID YOU CALL ME OVER?
I THOUGHT YOU WERE SOMEONE ELSE.
NO CLEVER SAVE AVAILABLE
IMPENDING DOOM IS AN AWFUL FEELING.
ALMOST AS BAD AS EMBARRASSMENT.
THIS BADGE WILL HELP YOU FEEL BETTER.
YOU CAN "" AGAIN

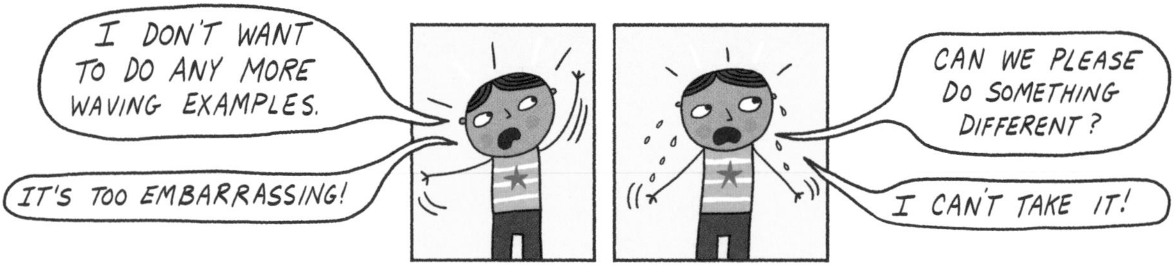
I DON'T WANT TO DO ANY MORE WAVING EXAMPLES.
IT'S TOO EMBARRASSING!
CAN WE PLEASE DO SOMETHING DIFFERENT?
I CAN'T TAKE IT!

WHY IS A WAVE MISTAKE SO EMBARRASSING?

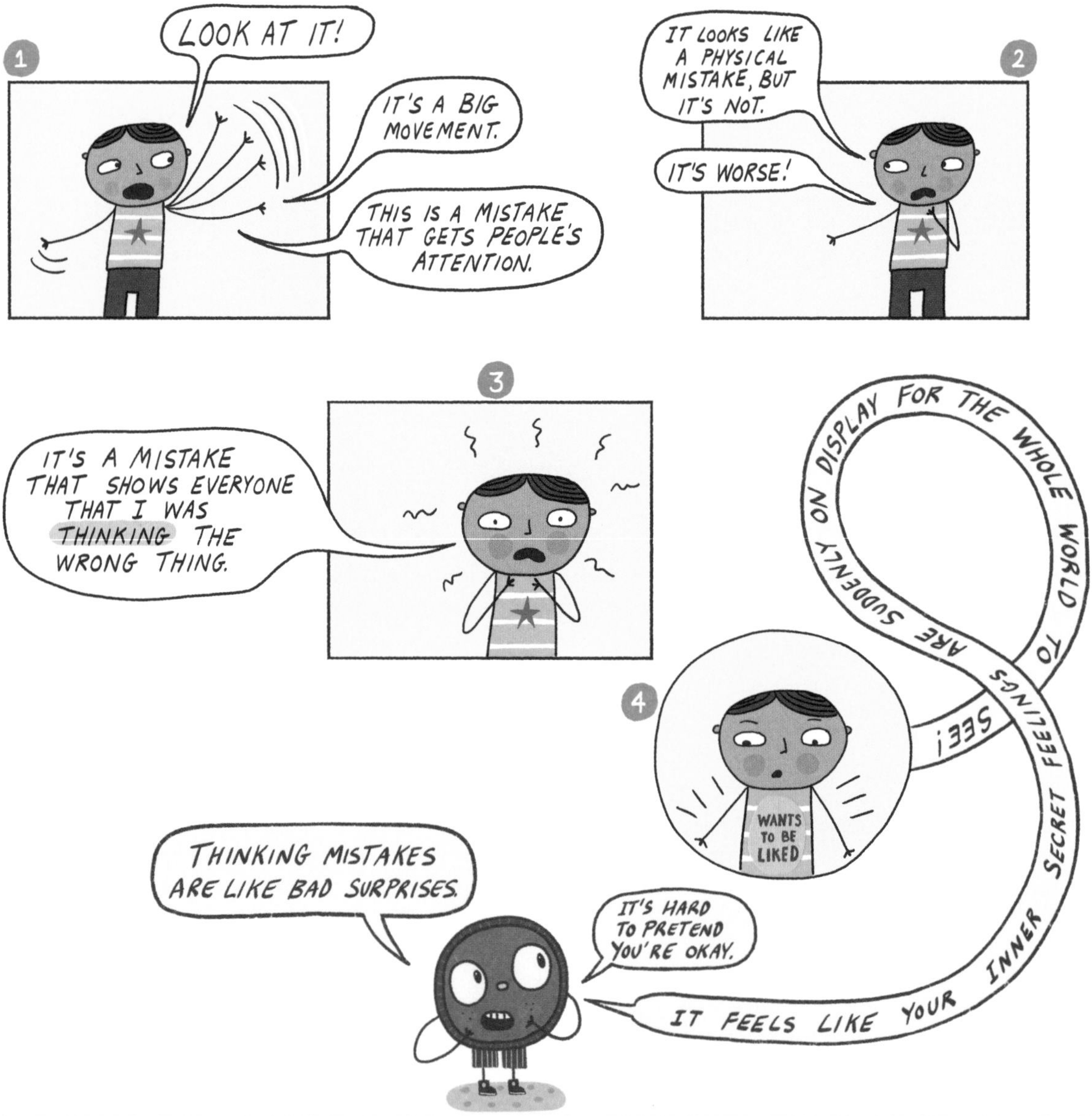
1
LOOK AT IT!
IT'S A BIG MOVEMENT.
THIS IS A MISTAKE THAT GETS PEOPLE'S ATTENTION.
2
IT LOOKS LIKE A PHYSICAL MISTAKE, BUT IT'S NOT.
IT'S WORSE!
3
IT'S A MISTAKE THAT SHOWS EVERYONE THAT I WAS THINKING THE WRONG THING.
4
WANTS TO BE LIKED
THINKING MISTAKES ARE LIKE BAD SURPRISES.
IT'S HARD TO PRETEND YOU'RE OKAY.
IT FEELS LIKE YOUR INNER SECRET FEELINGS ARE SUDDENLY ON DISPLAY FOR THE WHOLE WORLD TO SEE!

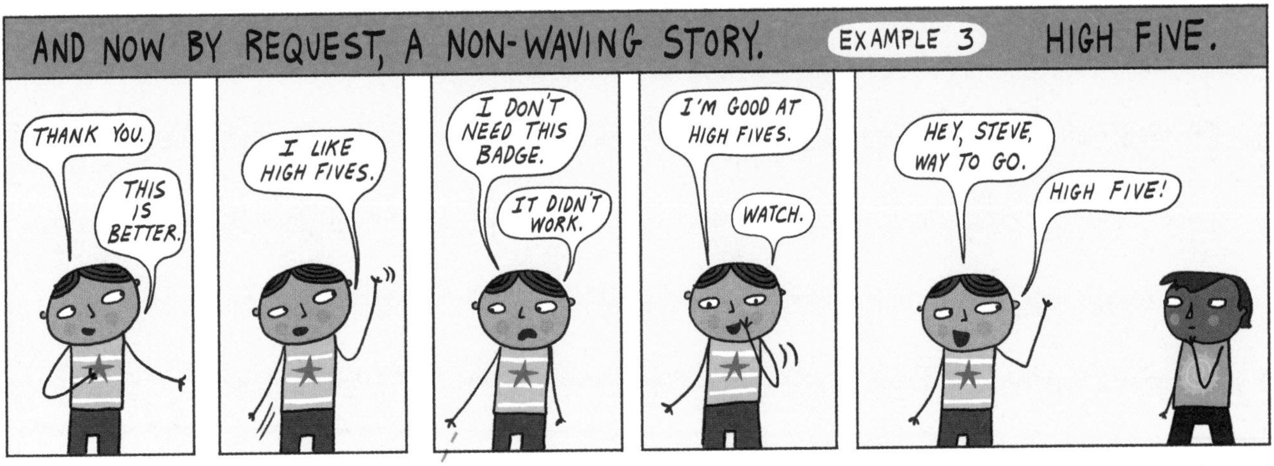
AND NOW BY REQUEST, A NON-WAVING STORY.
EXAMPLE 3
HIGH FIVE.
THANK YOU.
THIS IS BETTER.
I LIKE HIGH FIVES.
I DON'T NEED THIS BADGE.
IT DIDN'T WORK.
I'M GOOD AT HIGH FIVES.
WATCH.
HEY, STEVE, WAY TO GO.
HIGH FIVE!

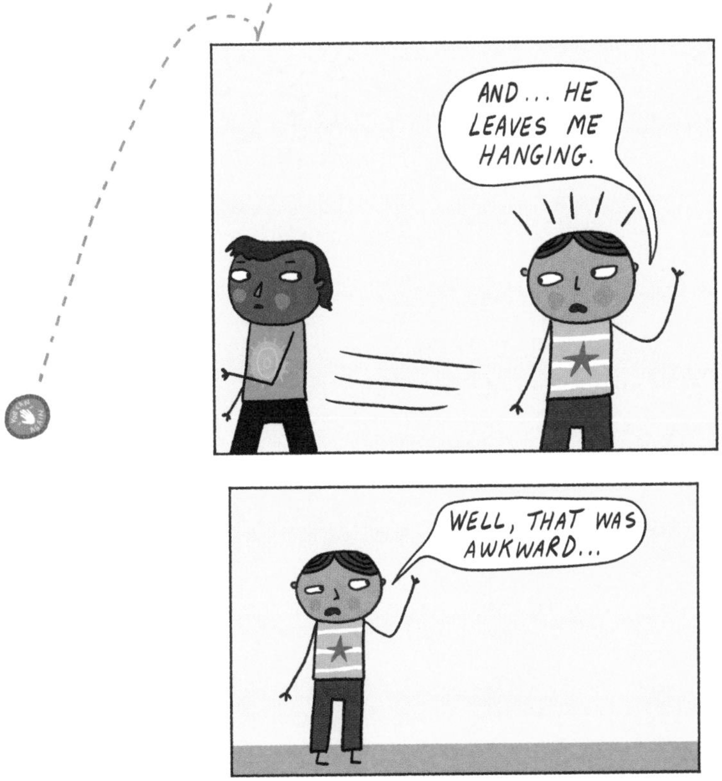
AND... HE LEAVES ME HANGING.
WELL, THAT WAS AWKWARD...

TRUE FACT

THE THIRD THURSDAY OF APRIL IS NATIONAL HIGH FIVE DAY. IT WAS STARTED BY A GROUP OF UNIVERSITY OF VIRGINIA STUDENTS IN 2002. VARIATIONS OF THE HIGH FIVE INCLUDE:

THE AIR FIVE
HIGH FIVE GESTURE BETWEEN TWO PEOPLE BUT NO PHYSICAL CONTACT.

THE DOUBLE HIGH FIVE
USING BOTH HANDS TO HIGH-FIVE AT THE SAME TIME.

THE SELF HIGH FIVE
A PERSON GIVES THEMSELVES A HIGH FIVE IN CELEBRATION.

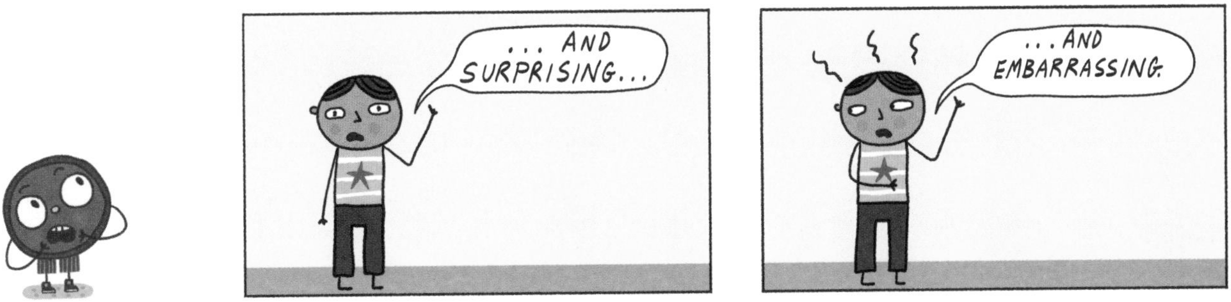
... AND SURPRISING...
... AND EMBARRASSING.

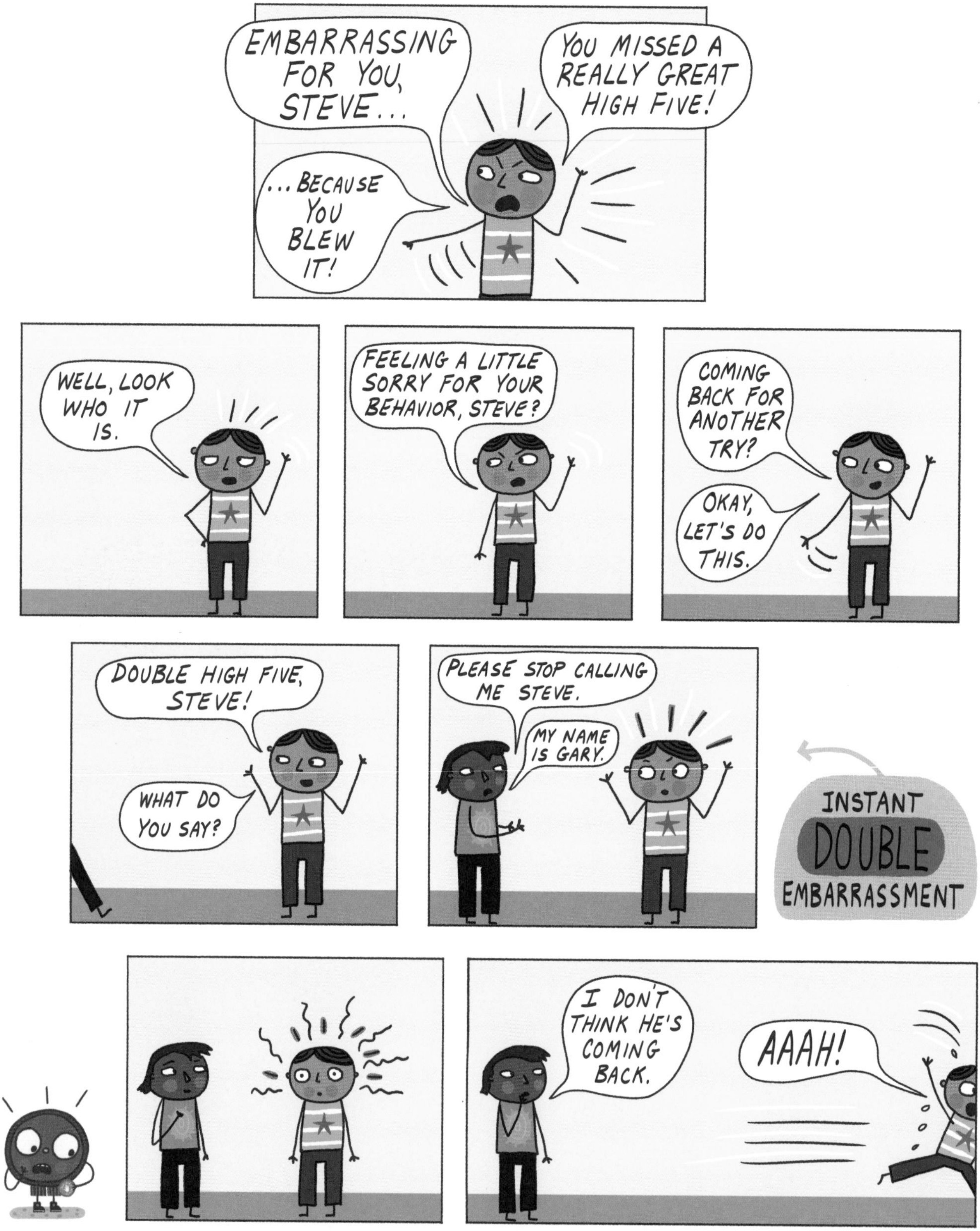
EMBARRASSING FOR YOU, STEVE...
YOU MISSED A REALLY GREAT HIGH FIVE!
...BECAUSE YOU BLEW IT!
WELL, LOOK WHO IT IS.
FEELING A LITTLE SORRY FOR YOUR BEHAVIOR, STEVE?
COMING BACK FOR ANOTHER TRY?
OKAY, LET'S DO THIS.
DOUBLE HIGH FIVE, STEVE!
WHAT DO YOU SAY?
PLEASE STOP CALLING ME STEVE.
MY NAME IS GARY.
INSTANT DOUBLE EMBARRASSMENT
I DON'T THINK HE'S COMING BACK.
AAAH!

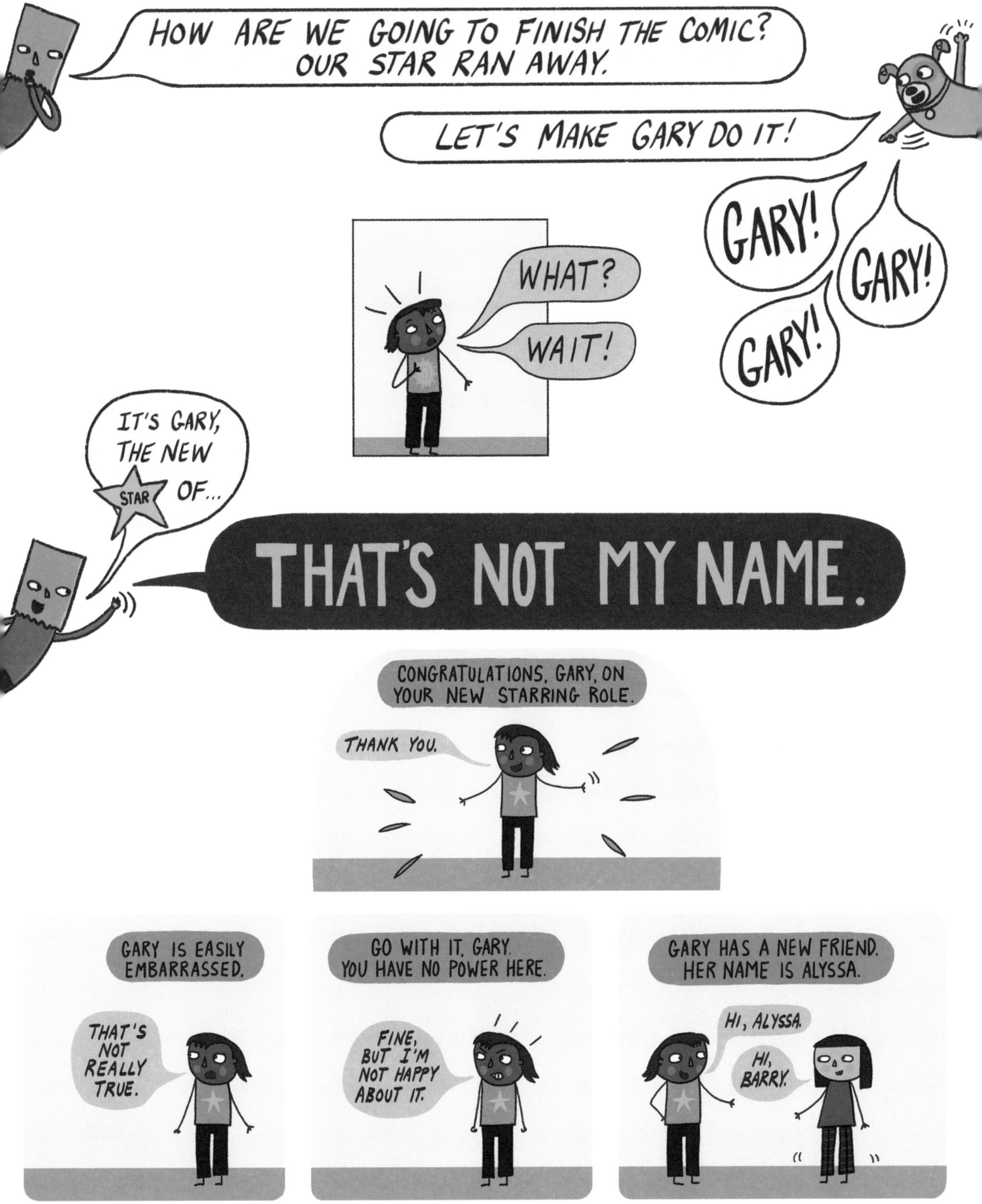
HOW ARE WE GOING TO FINISH THE COMIC? OUR STAR RAN AWAY.
LET'S MAKE GARY DO IT!
GARY!
GARY!
GARY!
WHAT?
WAIT!
IT'S GARY, THE NEW STAR OF...
THAT'S NOT MY NAME.
CONGRATULATIONS, GARY, ON YOUR NEW STARRING ROLE.
THANK YOU.
GARY IS EASILY EMBARRASSED.
THAT'S NOT REALLY TRUE.
GO WITH IT, GARY. YOU HAVE NO POWER HERE.
FINE, BUT I'M NOT HAPPY ABOUT IT.
GARY HAS A NEW FRIEND. HER NAME IS ALYSSA.
HI, ALYSSA.
HI, BARRY.

UH-OH, ALYSSA GOT GARY'S NAME WRONG. WHAT WILL EASILY EMBARRASSED GARY DO?

LET ME GUESS.

I DO NOTHING?

THAT'S RIGHT, GARY, YOU DO NOT CORRECT HER. BECAUSE YOU ARE TOO EMBARRASSED TO SAY ANYTHING.

THIS BARRY THING IS PAINFUL.

BARRY, DO YOU WANT TO GET SOME ICE CREAM?

SURE.

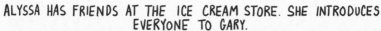

ALYSSA HAS FRIENDS AT THE ICE CREAM STORE. SHE INTRODUCES EVERYONE TO GARY.

UH-OH!

HEY, EVERYONE, THIS IS BARRY!

SUPER SCOOP

SUNDAE

$1 25

THIS IS NOT GOOD!

HI, BARRY!

SUPER SCOOP

SUNDAE

$1 25

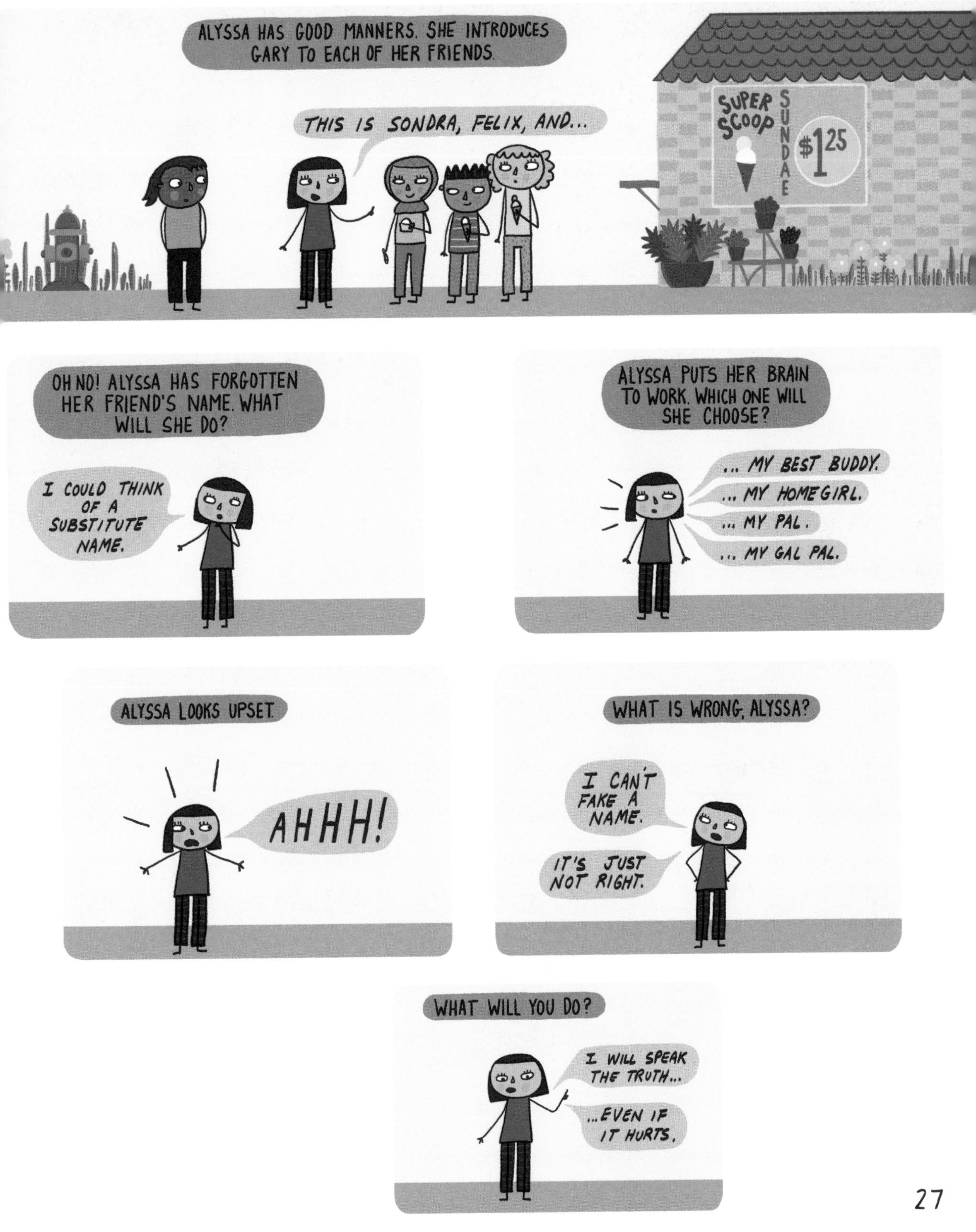
ALYSSA HAS GOOD MANNERS. SHE INTRODUCES GARY TO EACH OF HER FRIENDS.
THIS IS SONDRA, FELIX, AND...
SUPER SCOOP SUNDAE $1.25
OH NO! ALYSSA HAS FORGOTTEN HER FRIEND'S NAME. WHAT WILL SHE DO?
I COULD THINK OF A SUBSTITUTE NAME.
ALYSSA PUTS HER BRAIN TO WORK. WHICH ONE WILL SHE CHOOSE?
... MY BEST BUDDY.
... MY HOMEGIRL.
... MY PAL.
... MY GAL PAL.
ALYSSA LOOKS UPSET.
AHHH!
WHAT IS WRONG, ALYSSA?
I CAN'T FAKE A NAME.
IT'S JUST NOT RIGHT.
WHAT WILL YOU DO?
I WILL SPEAK THE TRUTH...
...EVEN IF IT HURTS.

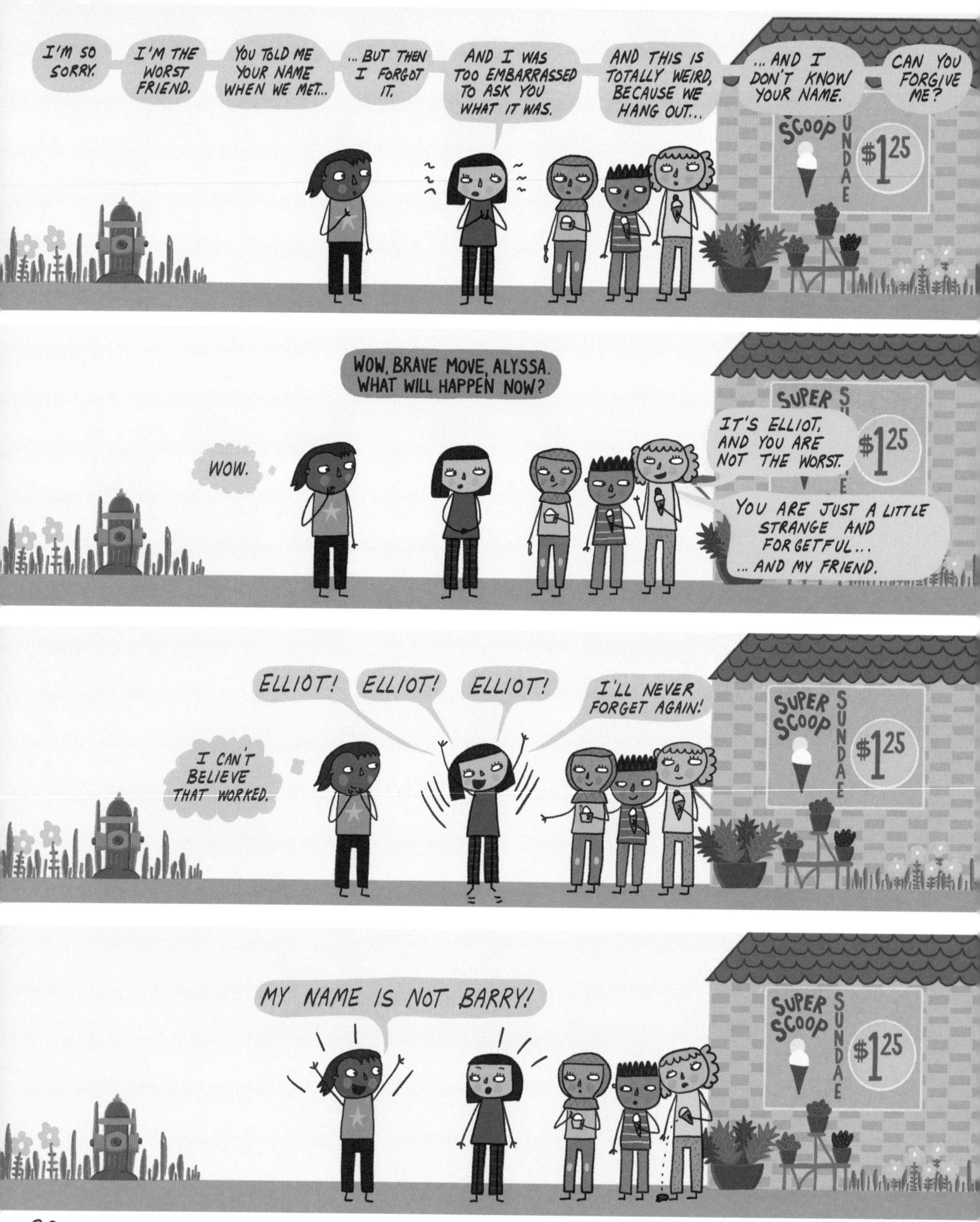
I'M SO SORRY.
I'M THE WORST FRIEND.
YOU TOLD ME YOUR NAME WHEN WE MET...
... BUT THEN I FORGOT IT.
AND I WAS TOO EMBARRASSED TO ASK YOU WHAT IT WAS.
AND THIS IS TOTALLY WEIRD, BECAUSE WE HANG OUT...
... AND I DON'T KNOW YOUR NAME.
CAN YOU FORGIVE ME?
SCOOP
$1.25
WOW, BRAVE MOVE, ALYSSA. WHAT WILL HAPPEN NOW?
WOW.
IT'S ELLIOT, AND YOU ARE NOT THE WORST.
YOU ARE JUST A LITTLE STRANGE AND FORGETFUL...
... AND MY FRIEND.
ELLIOT!
ELLIOT!
ELLIOT!
I'LL NEVER FORGET AGAIN!
I CAN'T BELIEVE THAT WORKED.
SUPER SCOOP SUNDAE
$1.25
MY NAME IS NOT BARRY!
SUPER SCOOP SUNDAE
$1.25

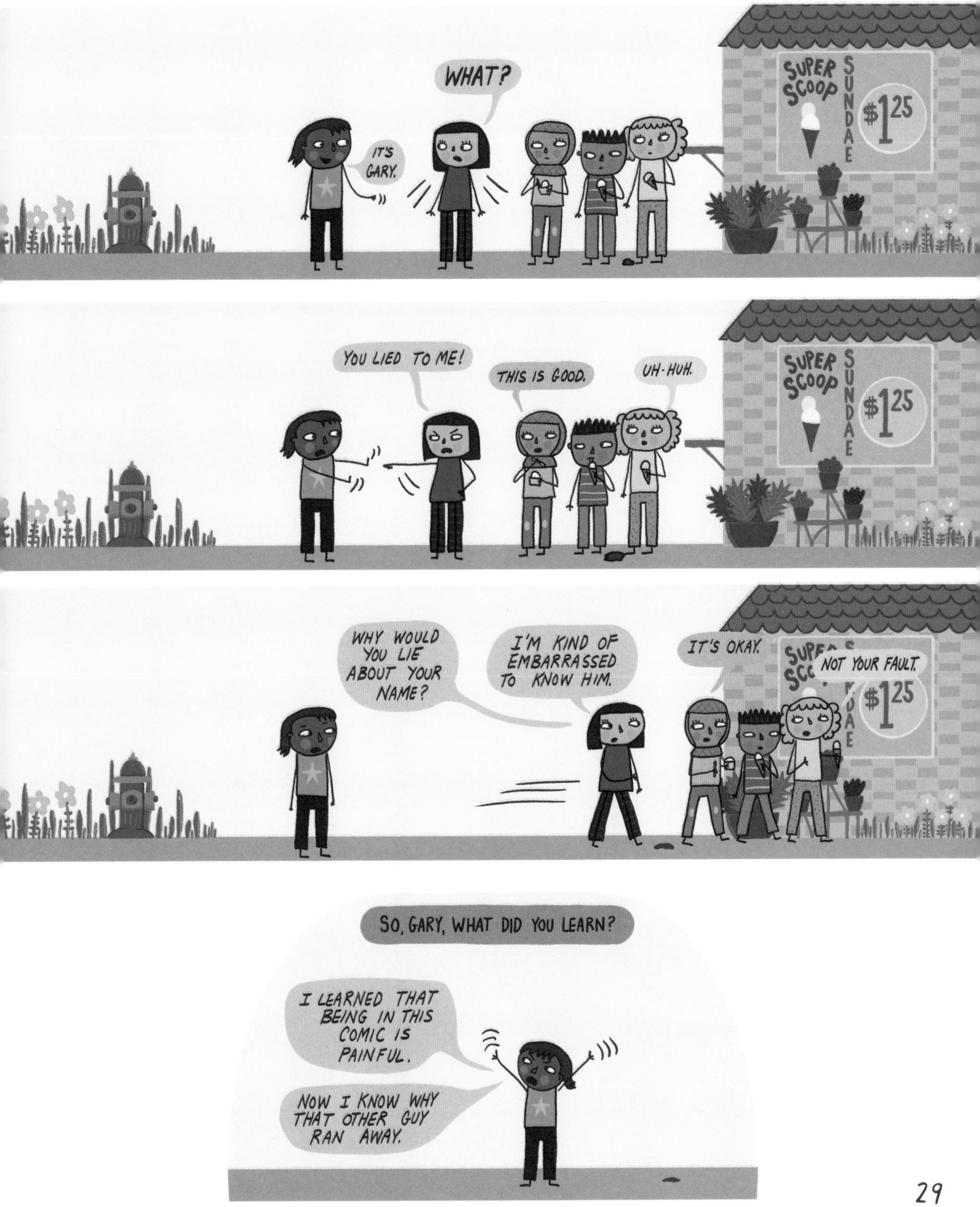
WHAT?
IT'S GARY.
SUPER SCOOP SUNDAE $1.25
YOU LIED TO ME!
THIS IS GOOD.
UH-HUH.
WHY WOULD YOU LIE ABOUT YOUR NAME?
I'M KIND OF EMBARRASSED TO KNOW HIM.
IT'S OKAY.
NOT YOUR FAULT.
SO, GARY, WHAT DID YOU LEARN?
I LEARNED THAT BEING IN THIS COMIC IS PAINFUL.
NOW I KNOW WHY THAT OTHER GUY RAN AWAY.

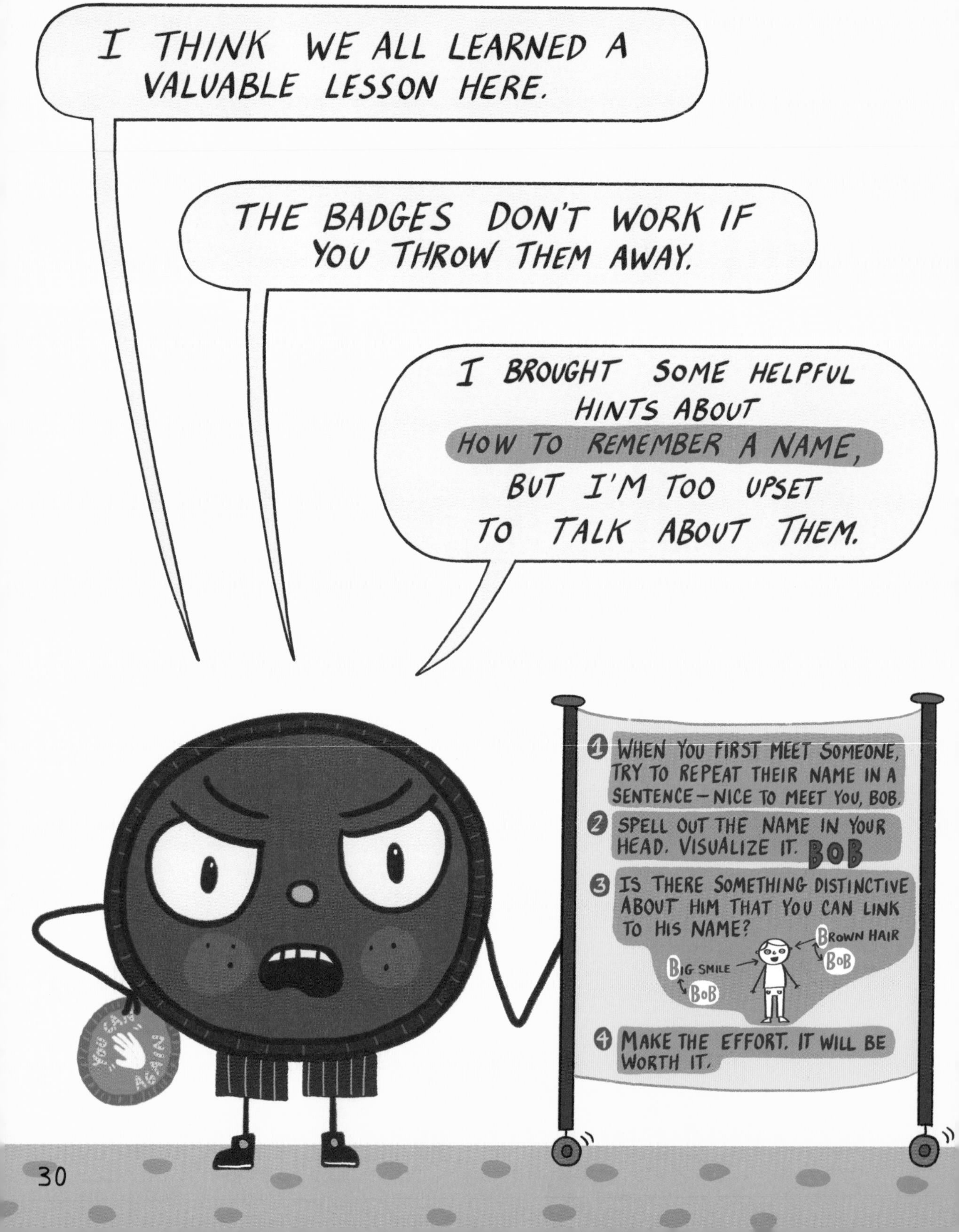
I THINK WE ALL LEARNED A VALUABLE LESSON HERE.
THE BADGES DON'T WORK IF YOU THROW THEM AWAY.
I BROUGHT SOME HELPFUL HINTS ABOUT HOW TO REMEMBER A NAME, BUT I'M TOO UPSET TO TALK ABOUT THEM.
1 WHEN YOU FIRST MEET SOMEONE, TRY TO REPEAT THEIR NAME IN A SENTENCE—NICE TO MEET YOU, BOB.
2 SPELL OUT THE NAME IN YOUR HEAD. VISUALIZE IT. BOB
3 IS THERE SOMETHING DISTINCTIVE ABOUT HIM THAT YOU CAN LINK TO HIS NAME?
BROWN HAIR
BOB
BIG SMILE
BOB
4 MAKE THE EFFORT. IT WILL BE WORTH IT.

3

IT'S ON YOU AND IT SHOULDN'T BE

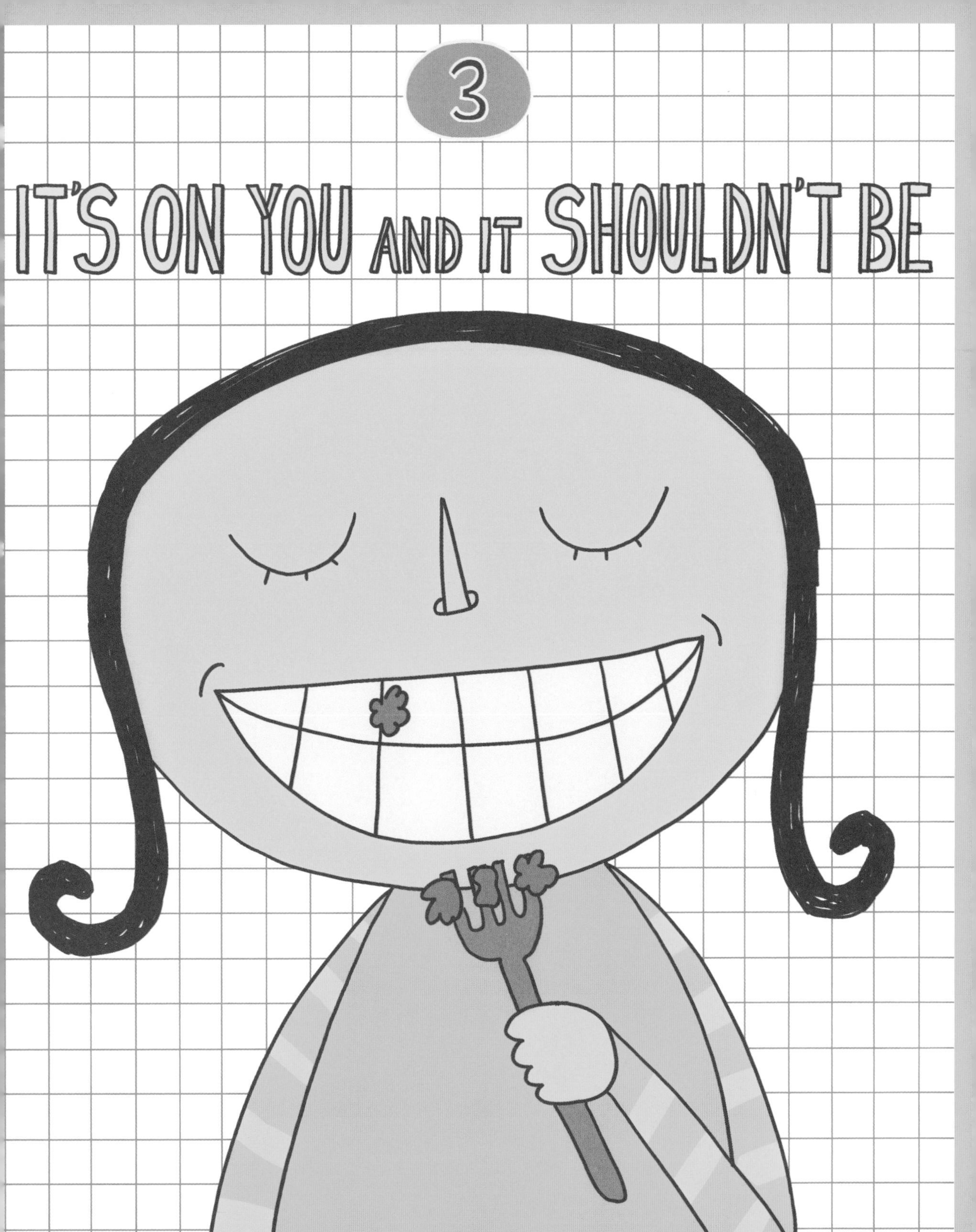

STUFF IN THEIR TEETH

STARRING REBECCA

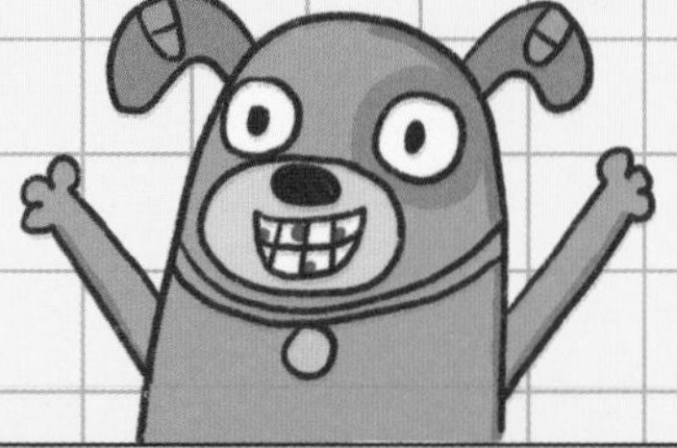

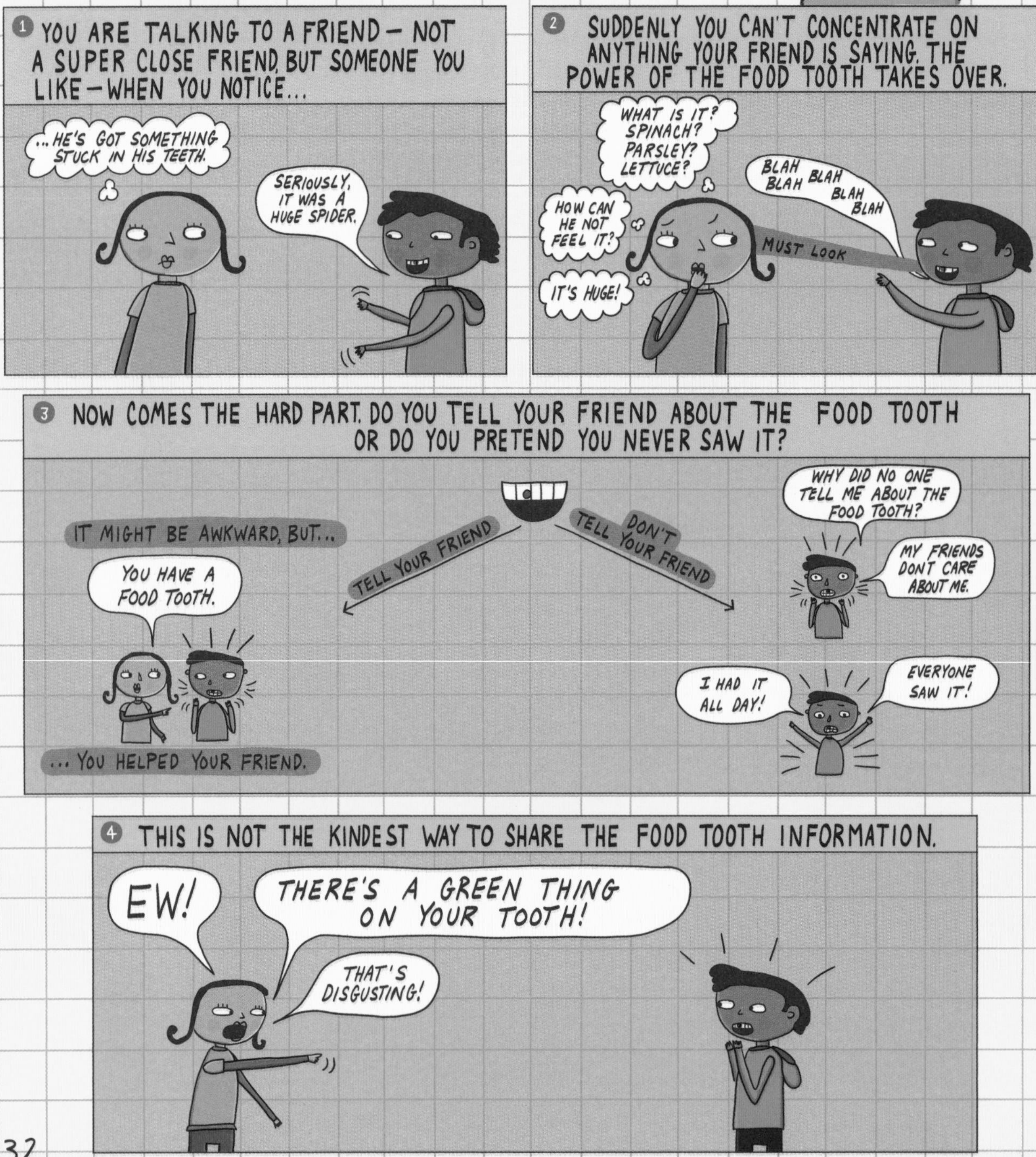

1 YOU ARE TALKING TO A FRIEND — NOT A SUPER CLOSE FRIEND, BUT SOMEONE YOU LIKE — WHEN YOU NOTICE...
...HE'S GOT SOMETHING STUCK IN HIS TEETH.
SERIOUSLY, IT WAS A HUGE SPIDER.
2 SUDDENLY YOU CAN'T CONCENTRATE ON ANYTHING YOUR FRIEND IS SAYING. THE POWER OF THE FOOD TOOTH TAKES OVER.
WHAT IS IT? SPINACH? PARSLEY? LETTUCE?
HOW CAN HE NOT FEEL IT?
IT'S HUGE!
BLAH BLAH BLAH BLAH BLAH
MUST LOOK
3 NOW COMES THE HARD PART. DO YOU TELL YOUR FRIEND ABOUT THE FOOD TOOTH OR DO YOU PRETEND YOU NEVER SAW IT?
TELL YOUR FRIEND
DON'T TELL YOUR FRIEND
IT MIGHT BE AWKWARD, BUT...
YOU HAVE A FOOD TOOTH.
... YOU HELPED YOUR FRIEND.
WHY DID NO ONE TELL ME ABOUT THE FOOD TOOTH?
MY FRIENDS DONT CARE ABOUT ME.
I HAD IT ALL DAY!
EVERYONE SAW IT!
4 THIS IS NOT THE KINDEST WAY TO SHARE THE FOOD TOOTH INFORMATION.
EW!
THERE'S A GREEN THING ON YOUR TOOTH!
THAT'S DISGUSTING!

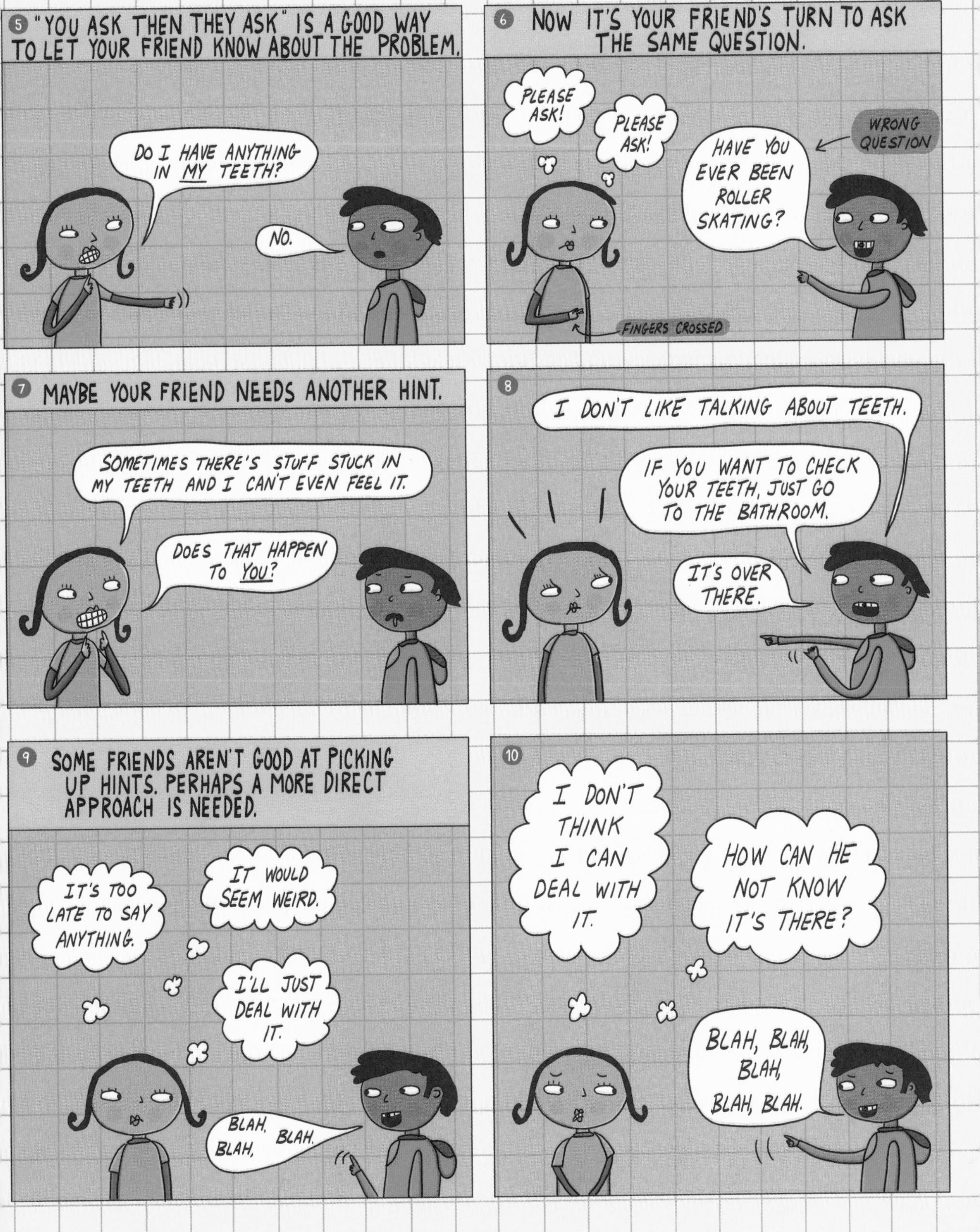
5 "YOU ASK THEN THEY ASK" IS A GOOD WAY TO LET YOUR FRIEND KNOW ABOUT THE PROBLEM.
DO I HAVE ANYTHING IN MY TEETH?
NO.
6 NOW IT'S YOUR FRIEND'S TURN TO ASK THE SAME QUESTION.
PLEASE ASK!
PLEASE ASK!
HAVE YOU EVER BEEN ROLLER SKATING?
WRONG QUESTION
FINGERS CROSSED
7 MAYBE YOUR FRIEND NEEDS ANOTHER HINT.
SOMETIMES THERE'S STUFF STUCK IN MY TEETH AND I CAN'T EVEN FEEL IT.
DOES THAT HAPPEN TO YOU?
8
I DON'T LIKE TALKING ABOUT TEETH.
IF YOU WANT TO CHECK YOUR TEETH, JUST GO TO THE BATHROOM.
IT'S OVER THERE.
9 SOME FRIENDS AREN'T GOOD AT PICKING UP HINTS. PERHAPS A MORE DIRECT APPROACH IS NEEDED.
IT'S TOO LATE TO SAY ANYTHING.
IT WOULD SEEM WEIRD.
I'LL JUST DEAL WITH IT.
BLAH, BLAH, BLAH.
10
I DON'T THINK I CAN DEAL WITH IT.
HOW CAN HE NOT KNOW IT'S THERE?
BLAH, BLAH, BLAH, BLAH, BLAH.

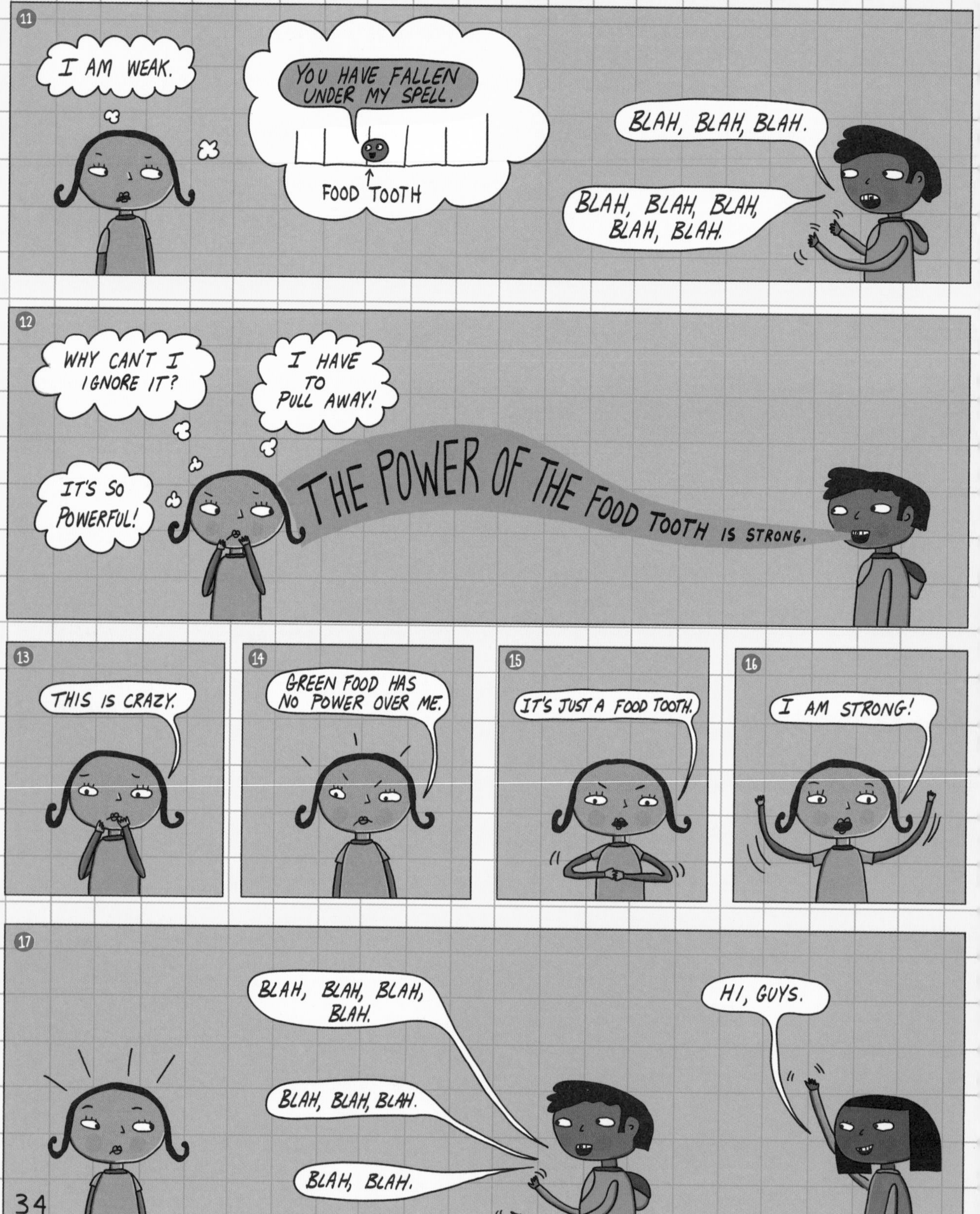
I AM WEAK.
YOU HAVE FALLEN UNDER MY SPELL.
FOOD TOOTH
BLAH, BLAH, BLAH.
BLAH, BLAH, BLAH, BLAH, BLAH.
WHY CAN'T I IGNORE IT?
I HAVE TO PULL AWAY!
IT'S SO POWERFUL!
THE POWER OF THE FOOD TOOTH IS STRONG.
THIS IS CRAZY.
GREEN FOOD HAS NO POWER OVER ME.
IT'S JUST A FOOD TOOTH.
I AM STRONG!
BLAH, BLAH, BLAH, BLAH.
BLAH, BLAH, BLAH.
BLAH, BLAH.
HI, GUYS.

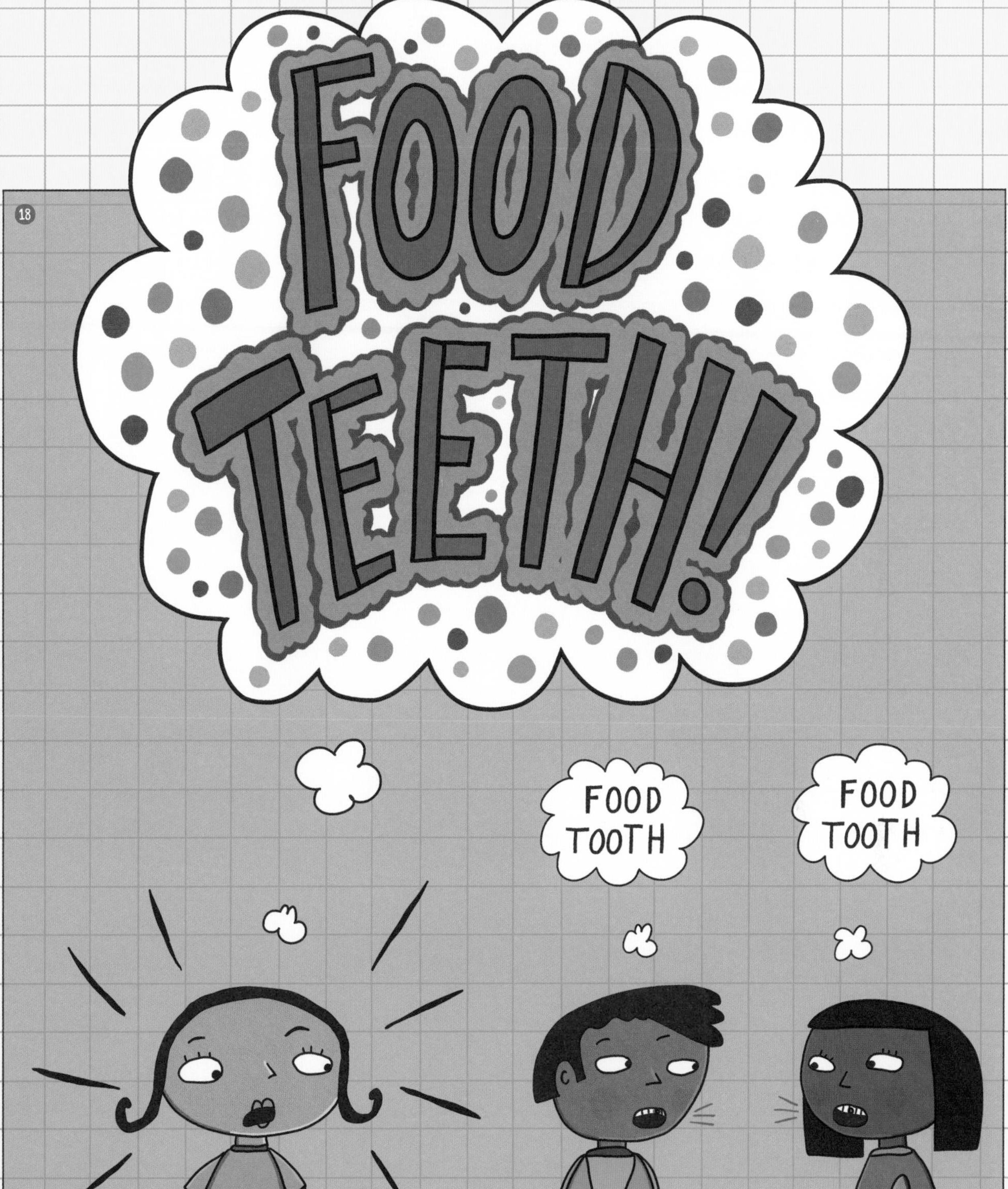
18
FOOD TEETH!!
FOOD TOOTH
FOOD TOOTH

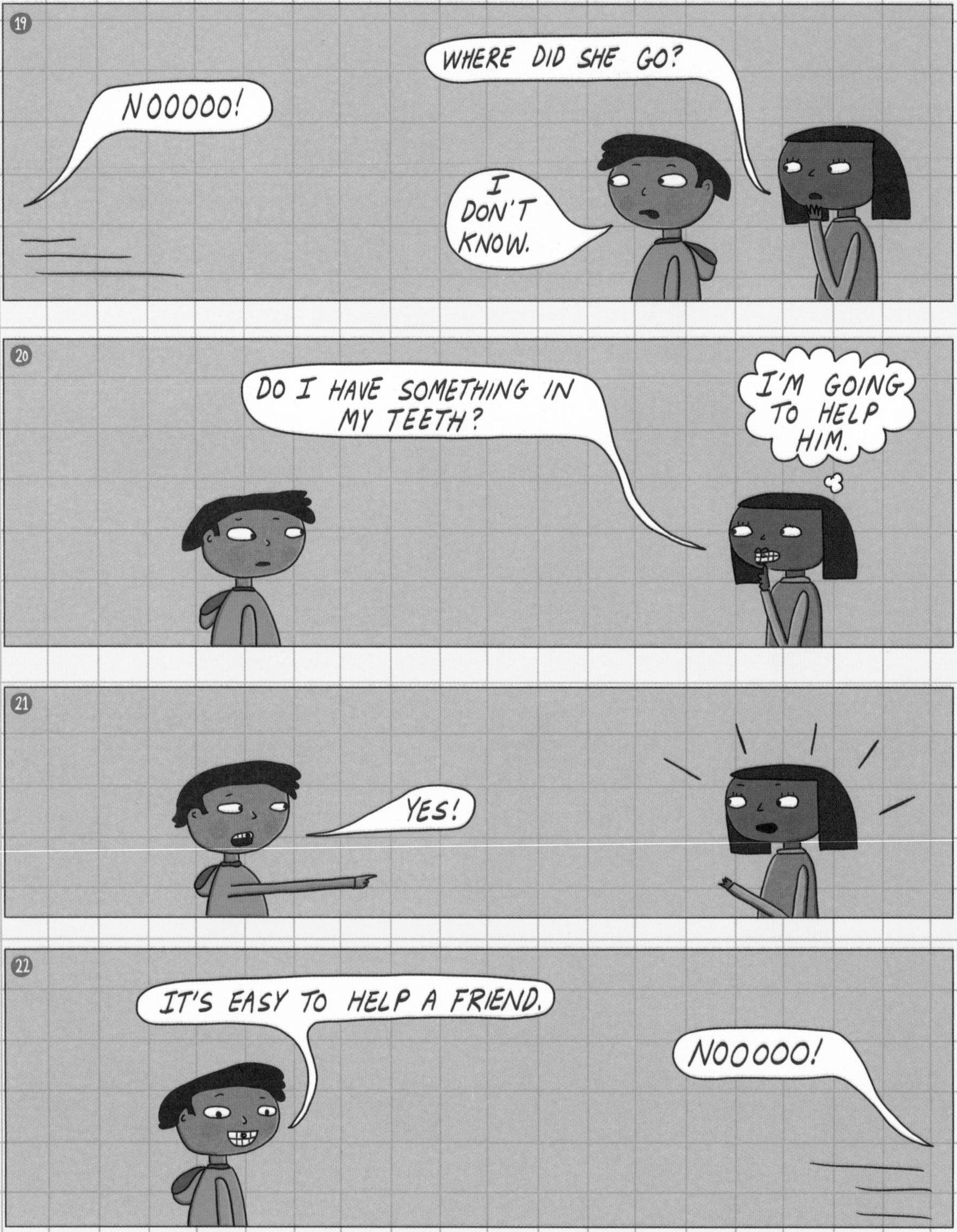
19
WHERE DID SHE GO?
NOOOOO!
I DON'T KNOW.
20
DO I HAVE SOMETHING IN MY TEETH?
I'M GOING TO HELP HIM.
21
YES!
22
IT'S EASY TO HELP A FRIEND.
NOOOOO!

TRUE FACT THERE IS EVIDENCE THAT PEOPLE FLOSSED THEIR TEETH IN PREHISTORIC TIMES. THEY MOST LIKELY USED SMALL SHARP STICKS OR REEDS. MODERN DENTAL FLOSS WAS INVENTED IN 1815 BY LEVI SPEAR PARMLY, A DENTIST IN NEW ORLEANS.

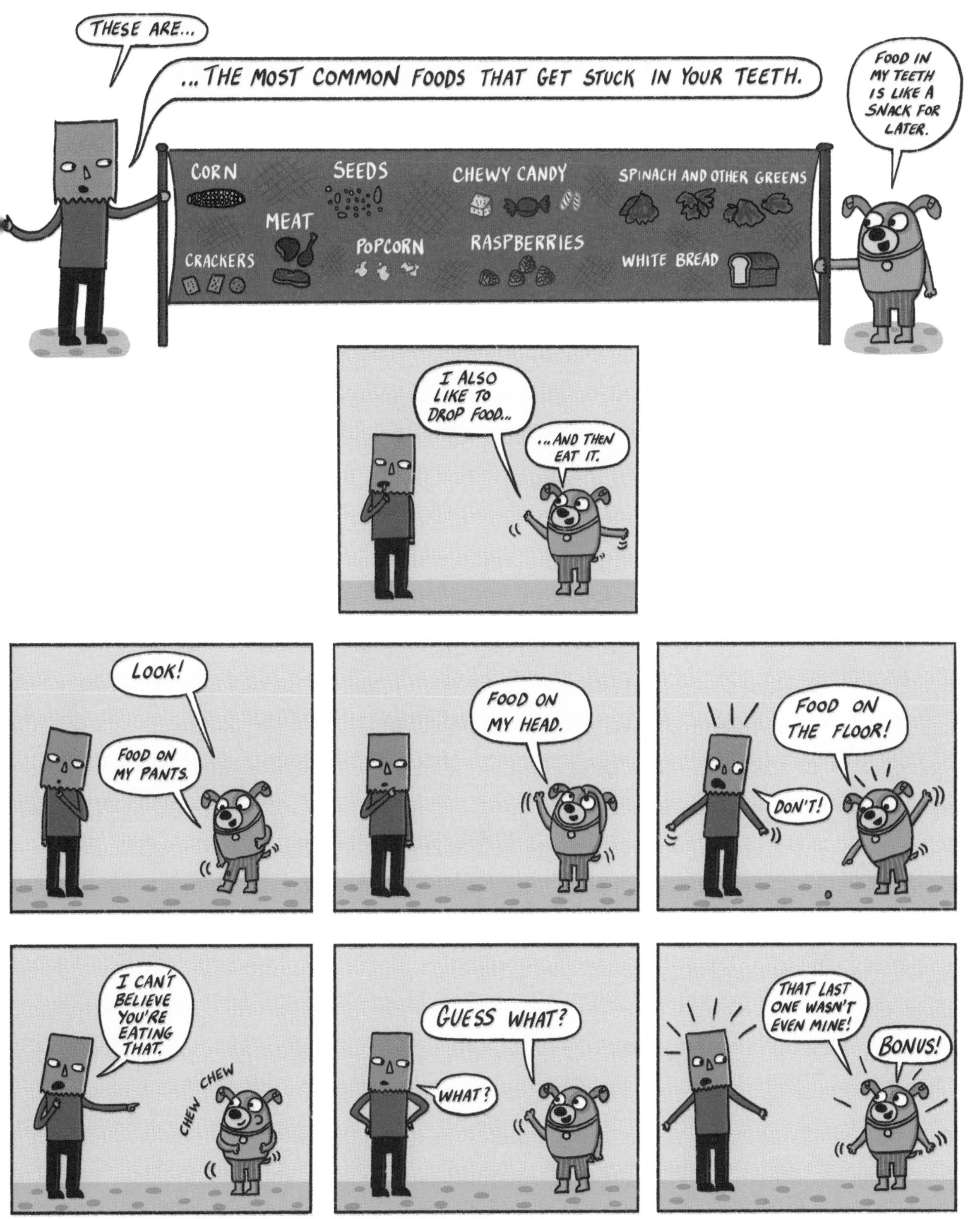
THESE ARE...
...THE MOST COMMON FOODS THAT GET STUCK IN YOUR TEETH.
FOOD IN MY TEETH IS LIKE A SNACK FOR LATER.
CORN
SEEDS
CHEWY CANDY
SPINACH AND OTHER GREENS
MEAT
CRACKERS
POPCORN
RASPBERRIES
WHITE BREAD
I ALSO LIKE TO DROP FOOD...
...AND THEN EAT IT.
LOOK!
FOOD ON MY PANTS.
FOOD ON MY HEAD.
FOOD ON THE FLOOR!
DON'T!
I CAN'T BELIEVE YOU'RE EATING THAT.
CHEW CHEW
GUESS WHAT?
WHAT?
THAT LAST ONE WASN'T EVEN MINE!
BONUS!

BONUS OOPS CLASSICS

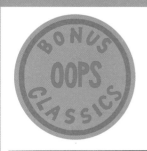

YOU PEED YOUR PANTS...
...OR DID YOU?

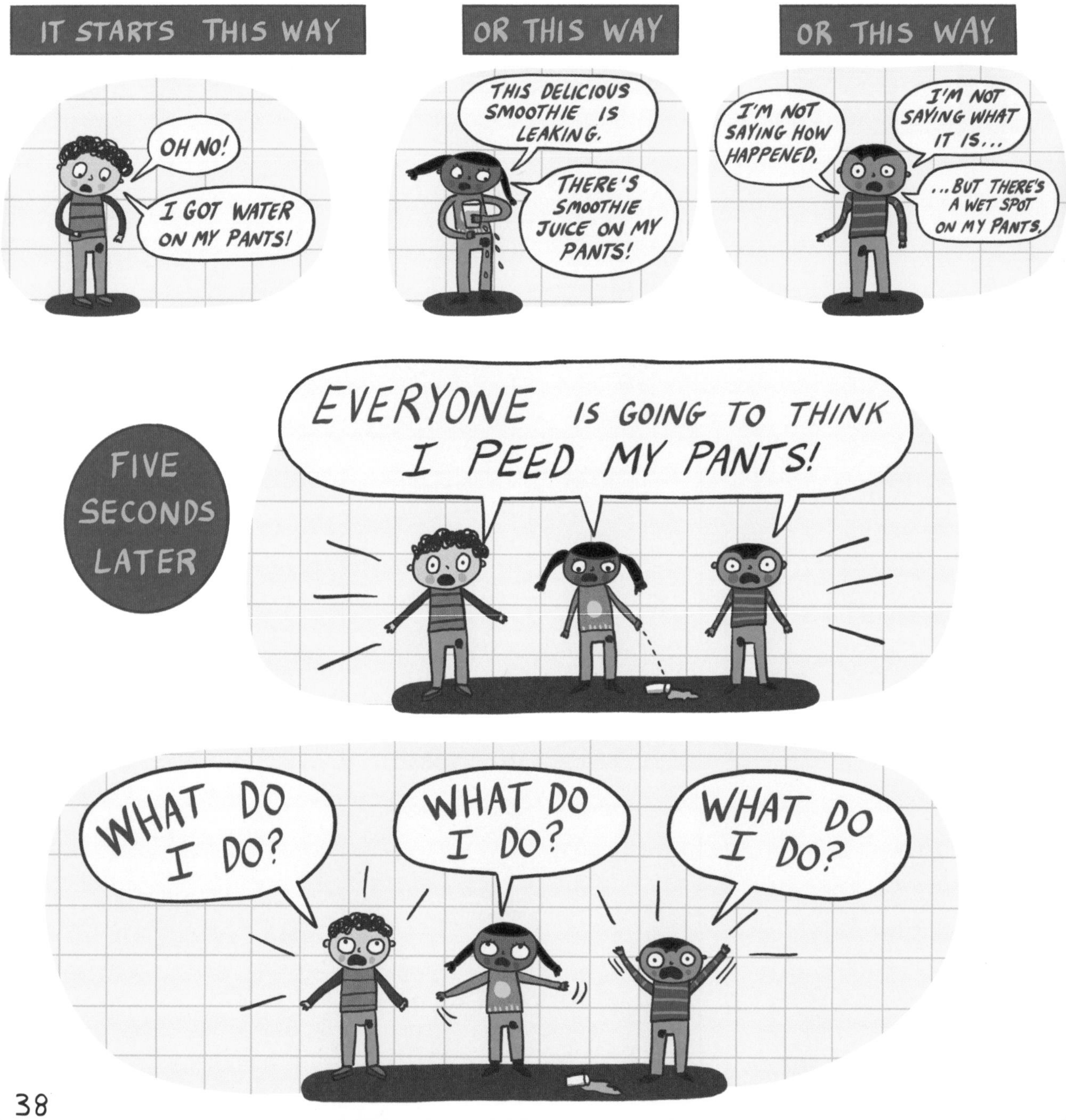

IT STARTS THIS WAY
OH NO!
I GOT WATER ON MY PANTS!
OR THIS WAY
THIS DELICIOUS SMOOTHIE IS LEAKING.
THERE'S SMOOTHIE JUICE ON MY PANTS!
OR THIS WAY.
I'M NOT SAYING HOW HAPPENED.
I'M NOT SAYING WHAT IT IS...
...BUT THERE'S A WET SPOT ON MY PANTS.
FIVE SECONDS LATER
EVERYONE IS GOING TO THINK I PEED MY PANTS!
WHAT DO I DO?
WHAT DO I DO?
WHAT DO I DO?

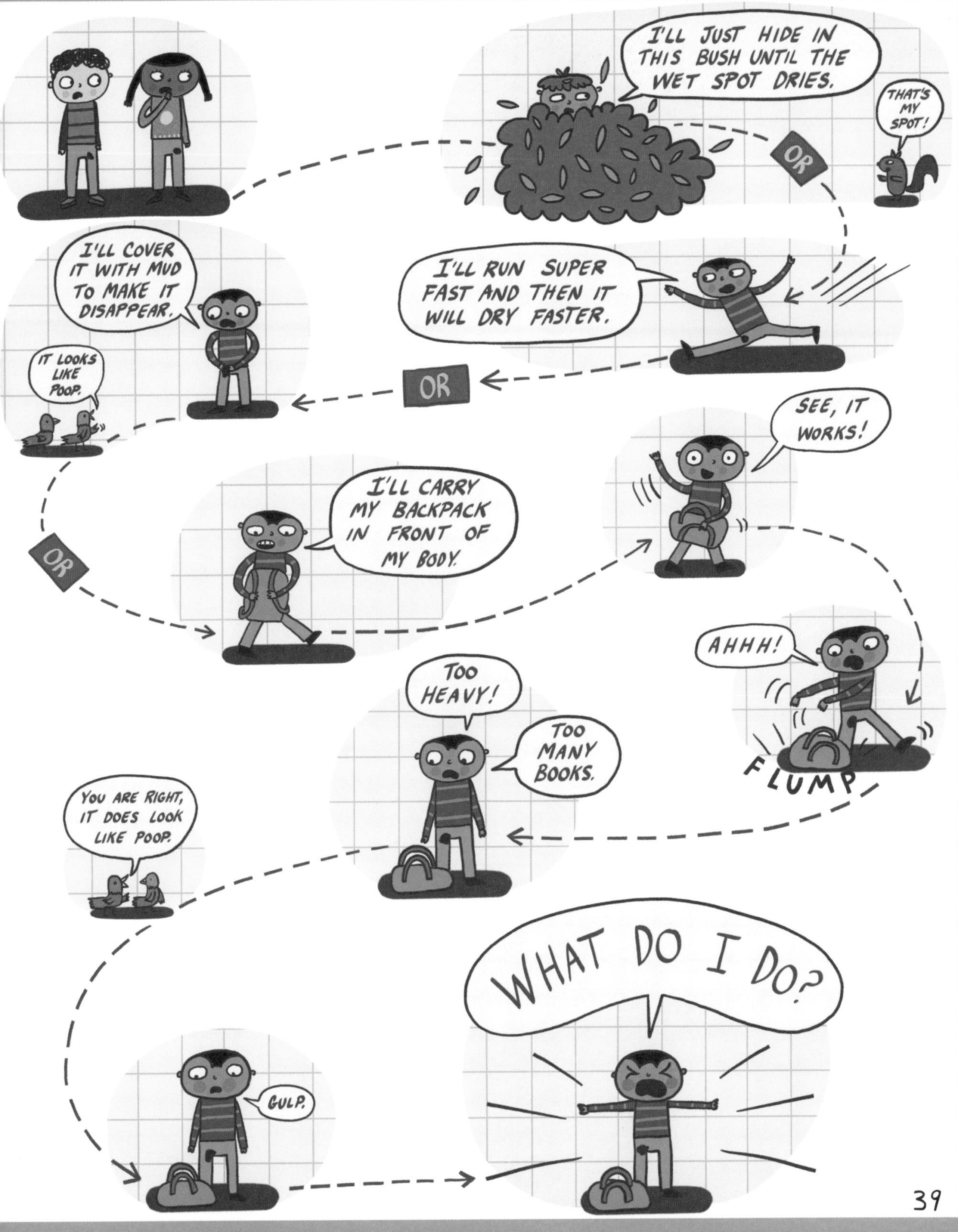

I'LL JUST HIDE IN THIS BUSH UNTIL THE WET SPOT DRIES.
THAT'S MY SPOT!
OR
I'LL RUN SUPER FAST AND THEN IT WILL DRY FASTER.
OR
I'LL COVER IT WITH MUD TO MAKE IT DISAPPEAR.
IT LOOKS LIKE POOP.
OR
I'LL CARRY MY BACKPACK IN FRONT OF MY BODY.
SEE, IT WORKS!
AHHH!
FLUMP
TOO HEAVY!
TOO MANY BOOKS.
YOU ARE RIGHT, IT DOES LOOK LIKE POOP.
GULP.
WHAT DO I DO?

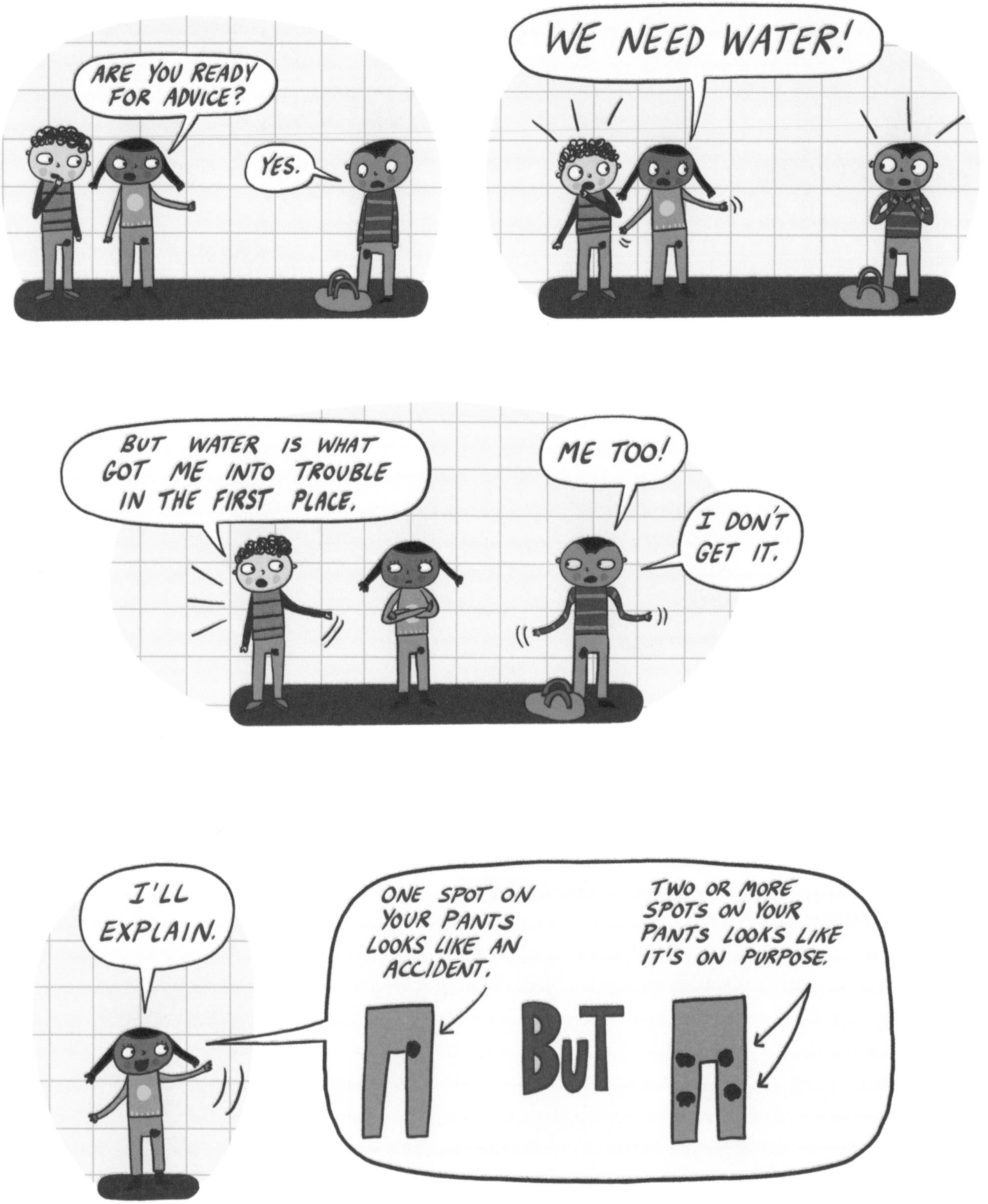
ARE YOU READY FOR ADVICE?
YES.
WE NEED WATER!
BUT WATER IS WHAT GOT ME INTO TROUBLE IN THE FIRST PLACE.
ME TOO!
I DON'T GET IT.
I'LL EXPLAIN.
ONE SPOT ON YOUR PANTS LOOKS LIKE AN ACCIDENT.
BUT
TWO OR MORE SPOTS ON YOUR PANTS LOOKS LIKE IT'S ON PURPOSE.

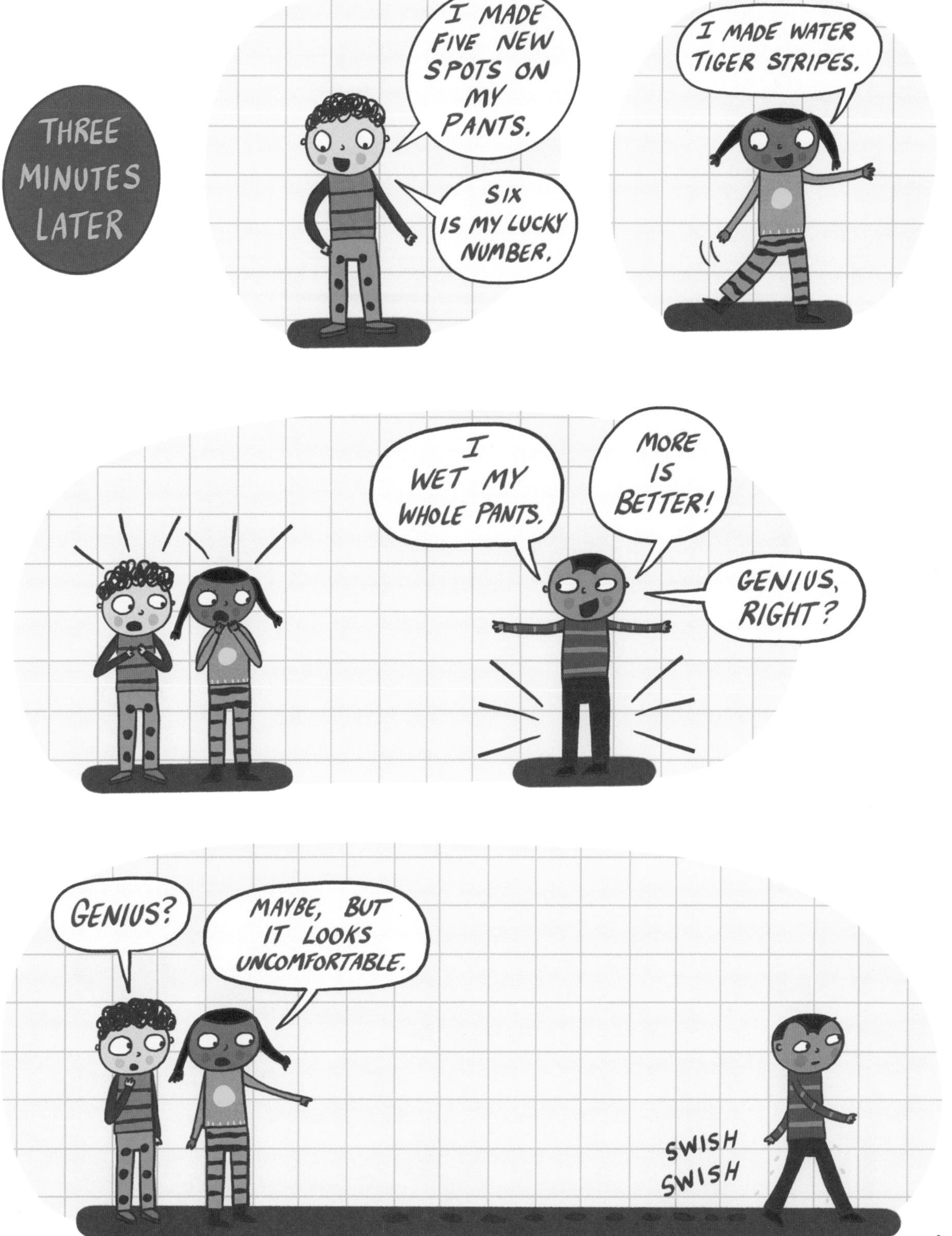
THREE MINUTES LATER
I MADE FIVE NEW SPOTS ON MY PANTS.
SIX IS MY LUCKY NUMBER.
I MADE WATER TIGER STRIPES.
I WET MY WHOLE PANTS.
MORE IS BETTER!
GENIUS, RIGHT?
GENIUS?
MAYBE, BUT IT LOOKS UNCOMFORTABLE.
SWISH SWISH

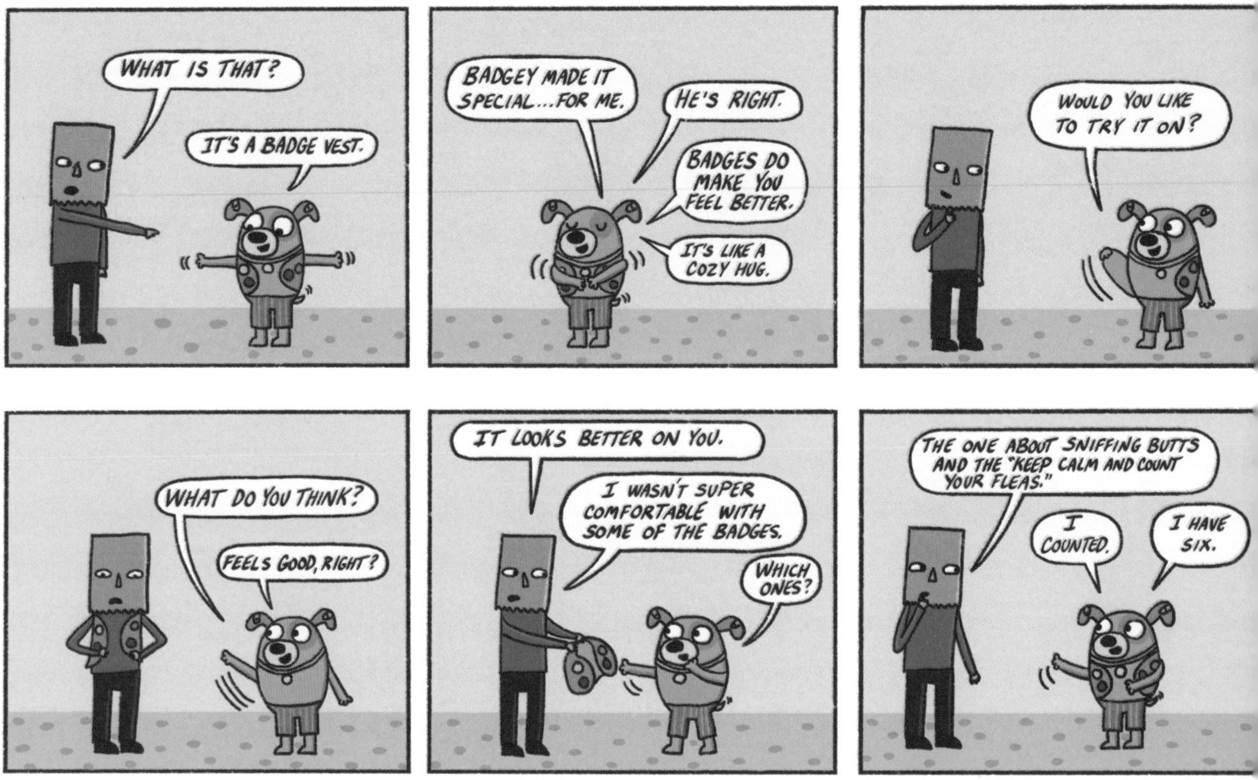
WHAT IS THAT?
IT'S A BADGE VEST.
BADGEY MADE IT SPECIAL...FOR ME.
HE'S RIGHT.
BADGES DO MAKE YOU FEEL BETTER.
IT'S LIKE A COZY HUG.
WOULD YOU LIKE TO TRY IT ON?
WHAT DO YOU THINK?
FEELS GOOD, RIGHT?
IT LOOKS BETTER ON YOU.
I WASN'T SUPER COMFORTABLE WITH SOME OF THE BADGES.
WHICH ONES?
THE ONE ABOUT SNIFFING BUTTS AND THE "KEEP CALM AND COUNT YOUR FLEAS."
I COUNTED.
I HAVE SIX.

THE TAGS A TRUE STORY

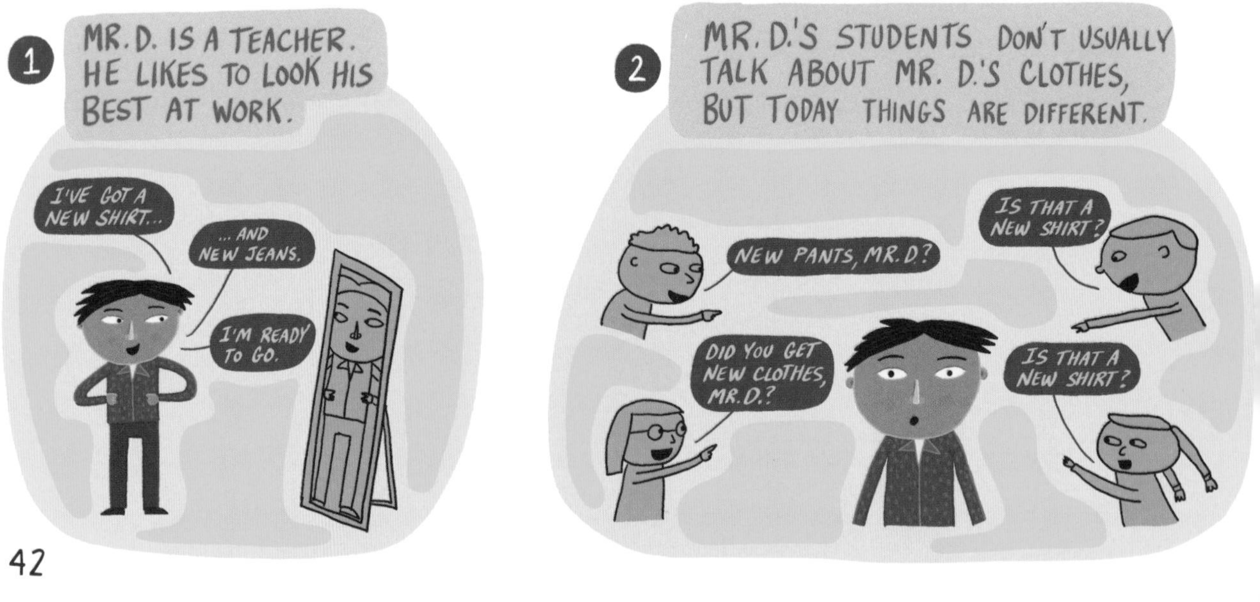
1
MR. D. IS A TEACHER. HE LIKES TO LOOK HIS BEST AT WORK.
I'VE GOT A NEW SHIRT...
... AND NEW JEANS.
I'M READY TO GO.
2
MR. D.'S STUDENTS DON'T USUALLY TALK ABOUT MR. D.'S CLOTHES, BUT TODAY THINGS ARE DIFFERENT.
NEW PANTS, MR. D?
IS THAT A NEW SHIRT?
DID YOU GET NEW CLOTHES, MR. D.?
IS THAT A NEW SHIRT?

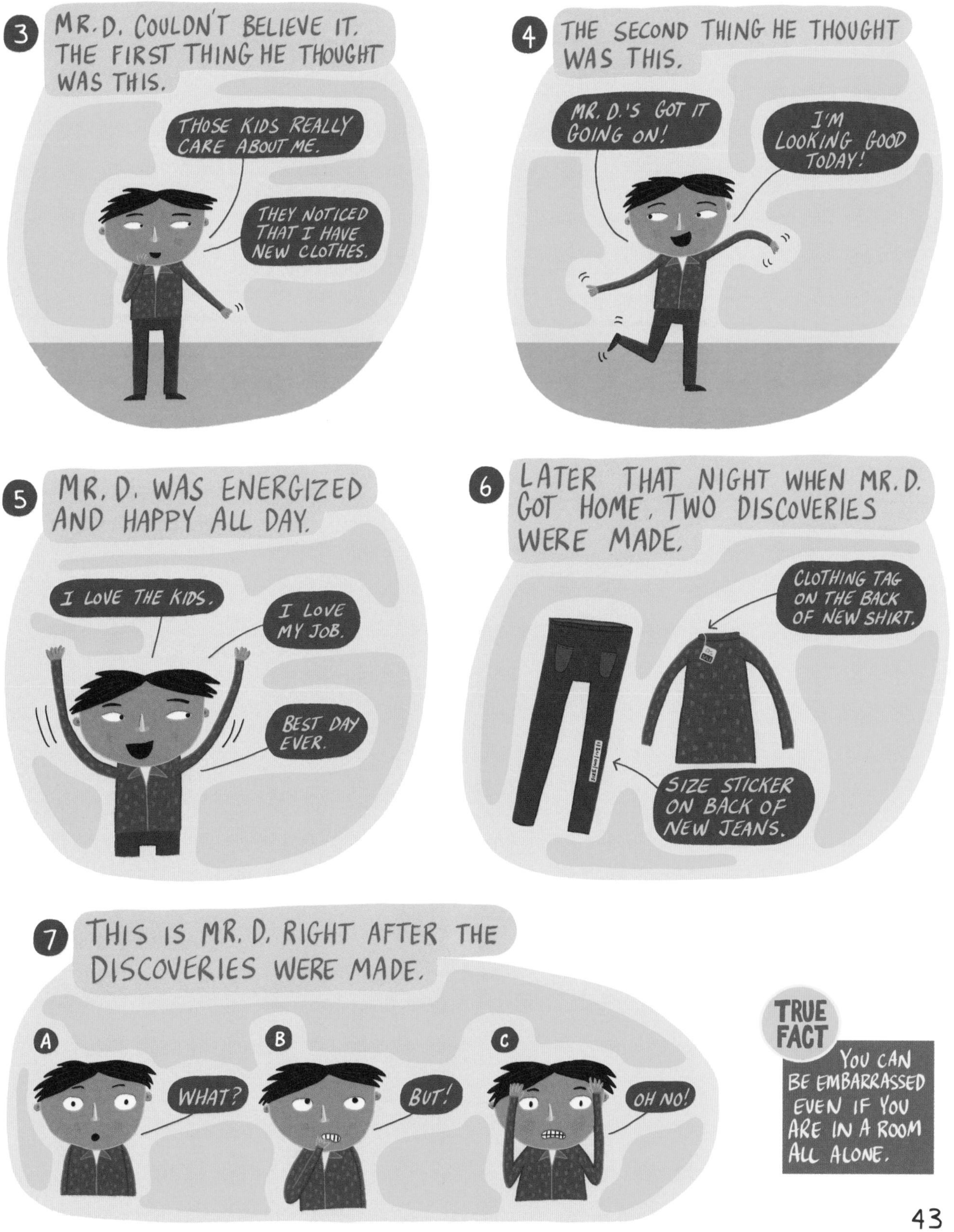
3
MR. D. COULDN'T BELIEVE IT. THE FIRST THING HE THOUGHT WAS THIS.
THOSE KIDS REALLY CARE ABOUT ME.
THEY NOTICED THAT I HAVE NEW CLOTHES.
4
THE SECOND THING HE THOUGHT WAS THIS.
MR. D.'S GOT IT GOING ON!
I'M LOOKING GOOD TODAY!
5
MR. D. WAS ENERGIZED AND HAPPY ALL DAY.
I LOVE THE KIDS.
I LOVE MY JOB.
BEST DAY EVER.
6
LATER THAT NIGHT WHEN MR. D. GOT HOME, TWO DISCOVERIES WERE MADE.
CLOTHING TAG ON THE BACK OF NEW SHIRT.
SIZE STICKER ON BACK OF NEW JEANS.
7
THIS IS MR. D. RIGHT AFTER THE DISCOVERIES WERE MADE.
A
WHAT?
B
BUT!
C
OH NO!
TRUE FACT
YOU CAN BE EMBARRASSED EVEN IF YOU ARE IN A ROOM ALL ALONE.

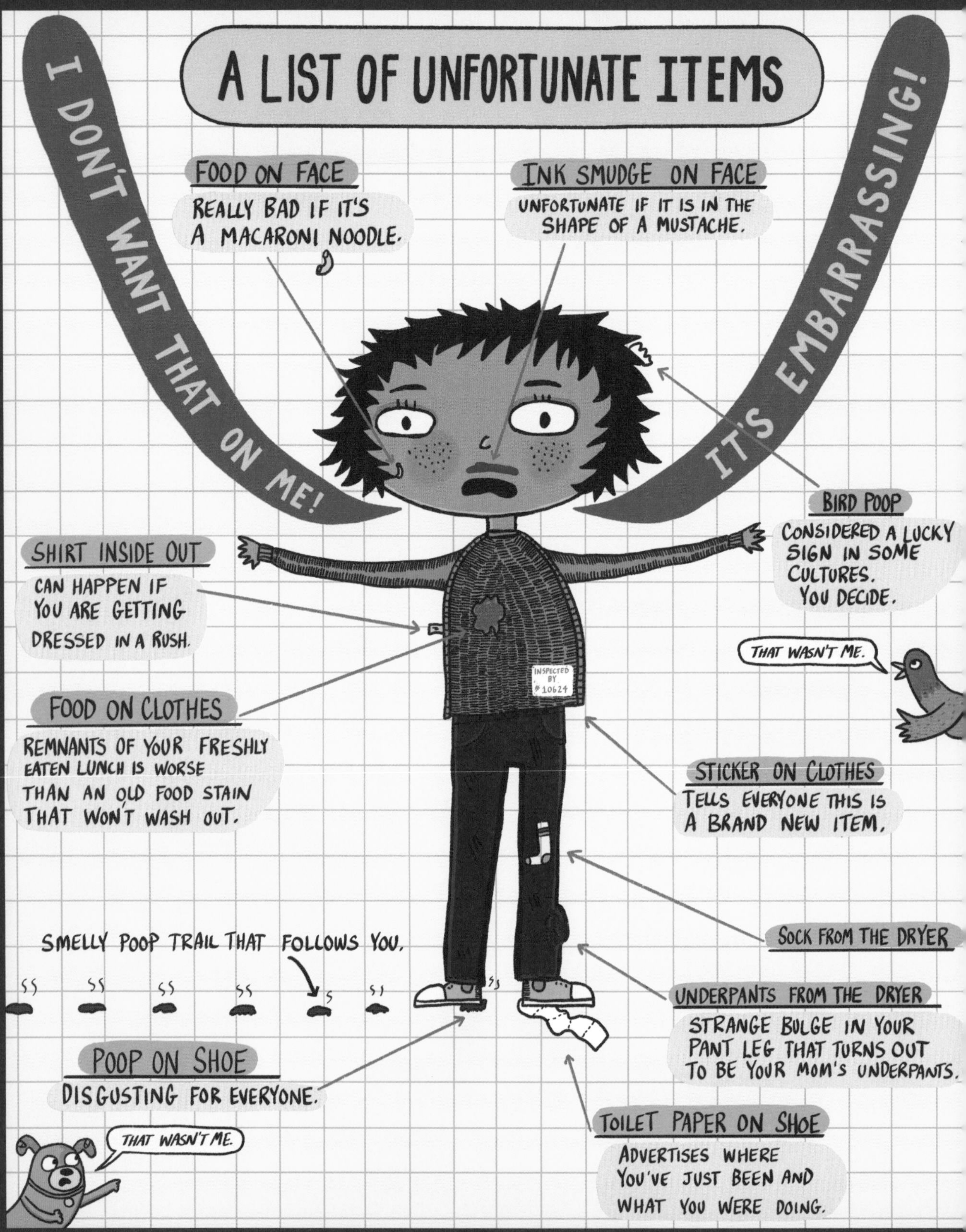

A LIST OF UNFORTUNATE ITEMS
I DON'T WANT THAT ON ME!
IT'S EMBARRASSING!
FOOD ON FACE
REALLY BAD IF IT'S A MACARONI NOODLE.
INK SMUDGE ON FACE
UNFORTUNATE IF IT IS IN THE SHAPE OF A MUSTACHE.
BIRD POOP
CONSIDERED A LUCKY SIGN IN SOME CULTURES. YOU DECIDE.
SHIRT INSIDE OUT
CAN HAPPEN IF YOU ARE GETTING DRESSED IN A RUSH.
THAT WASN'T ME.
INSPECTED BY #10624
FOOD ON CLOTHES
REMNANTS OF YOUR FRESHLY EATEN LUNCH IS WORSE THAN AN OLD FOOD STAIN THAT WON'T WASH OUT.
STICKER ON CLOTHES
TELLS EVERYONE THIS IS A BRAND NEW ITEM.
SOCK FROM THE DRYER
SMELLY POOP TRAIL THAT FOLLOWS YOU.
UNDERPANTS FROM THE DRYER
STRANGE BULGE IN YOUR PANT LEG THAT TURNS OUT TO BE YOUR MOM'S UNDERPANTS.
POOP ON SHOE
DISGUSTING FOR EVERYONE.
THAT WASN'T ME.
TOILET PAPER ON SHOE
ADVERTISES WHERE YOU'VE JUST BEEN AND WHAT YOU WERE DOING.

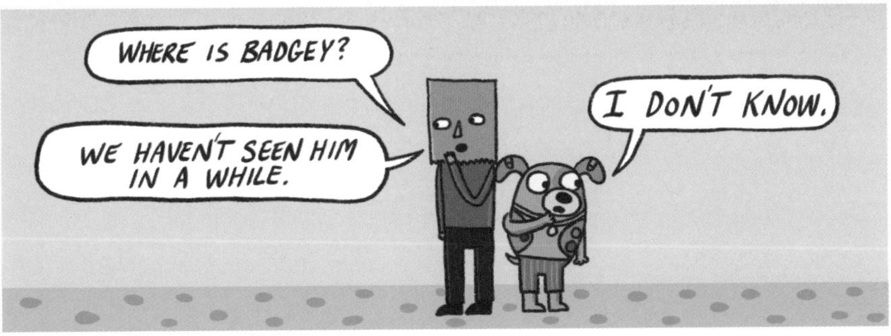
WHERE IS BADGEY?
WE HAVEN'T SEEN HIM IN A WHILE.
I DON'T KNOW.

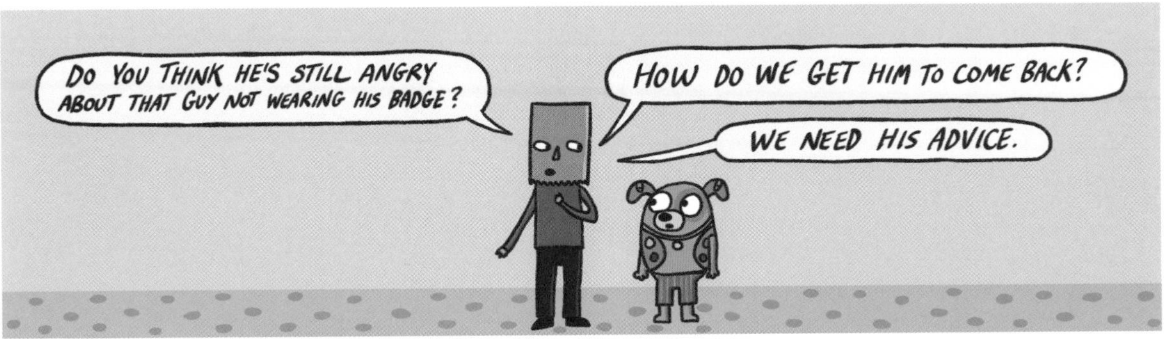
DO YOU THINK HE'S STILL ANGRY ABOUT THAT GUY NOT WEARING HIS BADGE?
HOW DO WE GET HIM TO COME BACK?
WE NEED HIS ADVICE.

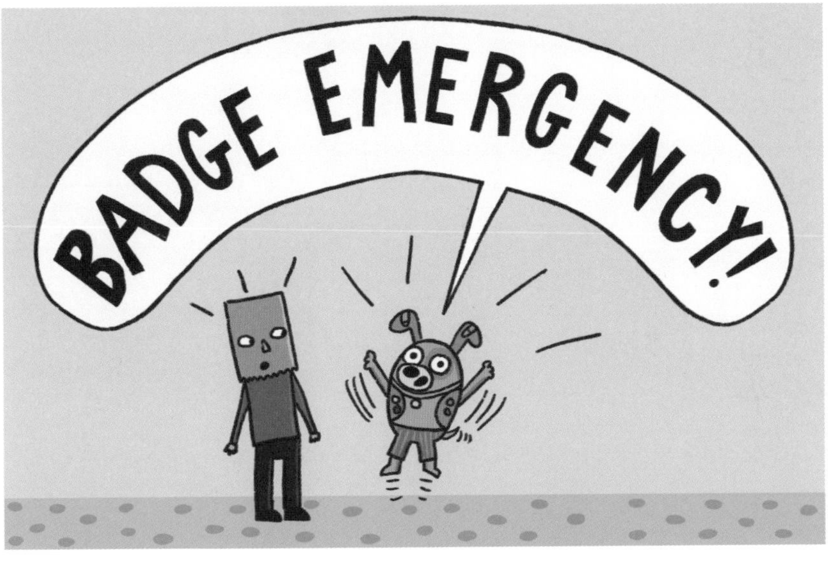
BADGE EMERGENCY!

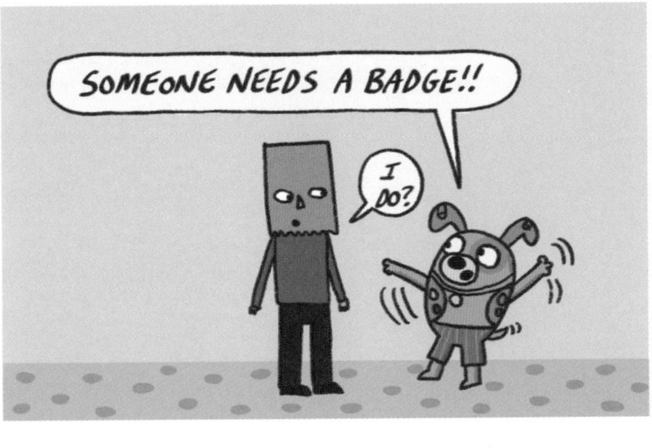
SOMEONE NEEDS A BADGE!!
I DO?

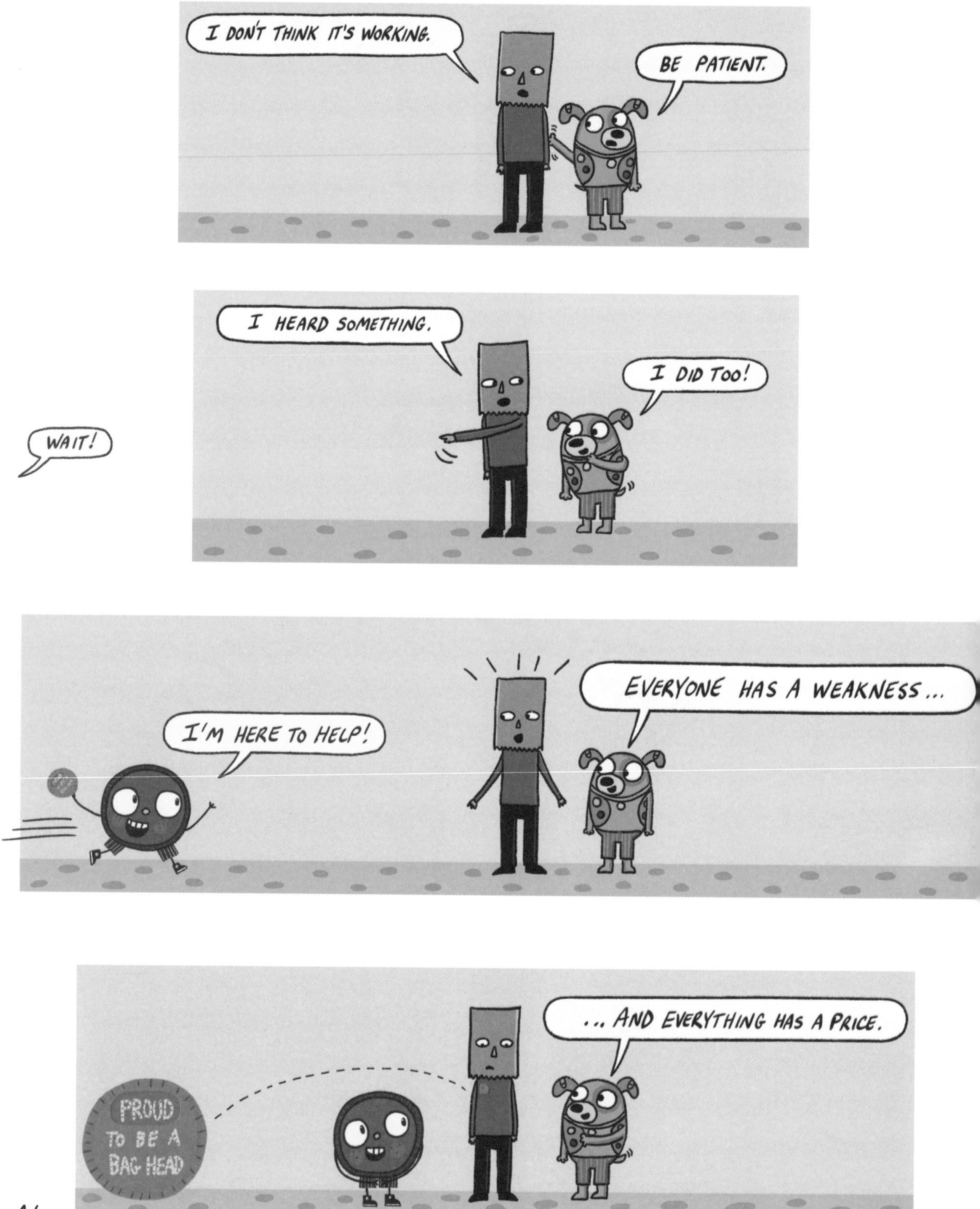

I DON'T THINK IT'S WORKING.
BE PATIENT.
I HEARD SOMETHING.
I DID TOO!
WAIT!
I'M HERE TO HELP!
EVERYONE HAS A WEAKNESS...
... AND EVERYTHING HAS A PRICE.
PROUD TO BE A BAG HEAD

4

BLUSHING

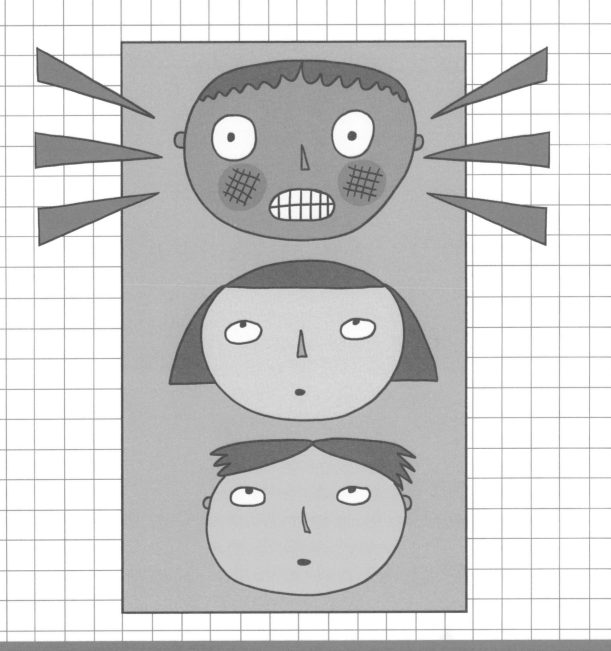

THIS HAPPENS NEXT

ROGER HAS JUST DONE SOMETHING EMBARRASSING, AND HE IS 100% SURE THAT EVERYONE SAW IT AND IS NOW WATCHING HIM.

THIS IS CALLED...

...THE SPOTLIGHT EFFECT.

PEOPLE AREN'T WATCHING YOU AS MUCH AS YOU THINK THEY ARE.

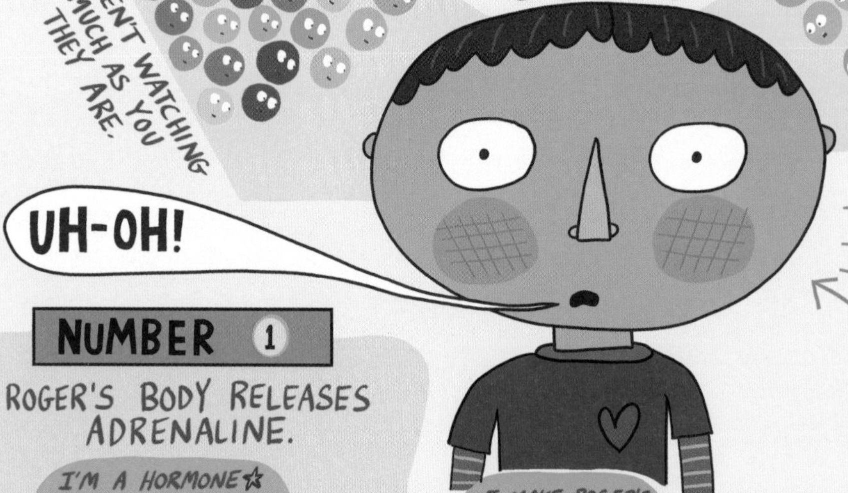
UH-OH!

WE SEE THIS AS BLUSHING.

NUMBER 1

ROGER'S BODY RELEASES ADRENALINE.

I'M A HORMONE☆ THAT IS RELEASED WHEN ROGER IS STRESSED.

I MAKE ROGER'S HEART BEAT FASTER.

I MAKE ROGER'S BLOOD PRESSURE GO UP.

NOW ROGER'S BLOOD MOVES FASTER THROUGH HIS BLOOD VESSELS.

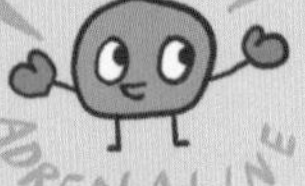
ADRENALINE

IT COMES FROM THE ADRENAL GLANDS

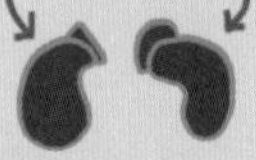

RIGHT ABOVE THE KIDNEYS.

NUMBER 2

ROGER'S BLOOD VESSELS SPRING INTO ACTION AND DILATE SO THEY CAN HANDLE THE INCREASED BLOOD FLOW.

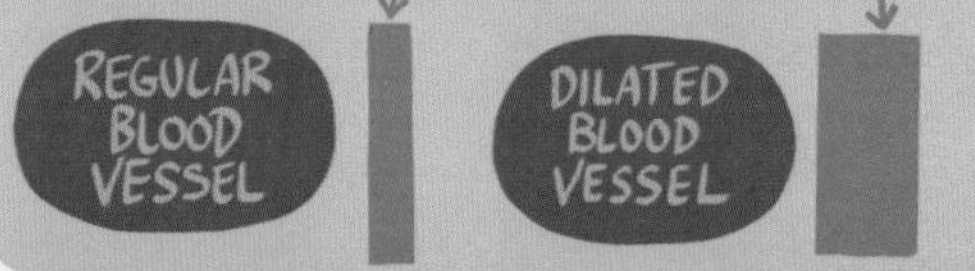
REGULAR BLOOD VESSEL
DILATED BLOOD VESSEL

NUMBER 3

THE CAPILLARIES (SMALL BLOOD VESSELS) THAT CARRY THE BLOOD TO THE NECK AND FACE ARE ESPECIALLY SENSITIVE TO THIS CHANGE AND THEY WIDEN. ROGER'S FACE NOW REDDENS.

☆ MORE ABOUT HORMONES ON PAGE 53

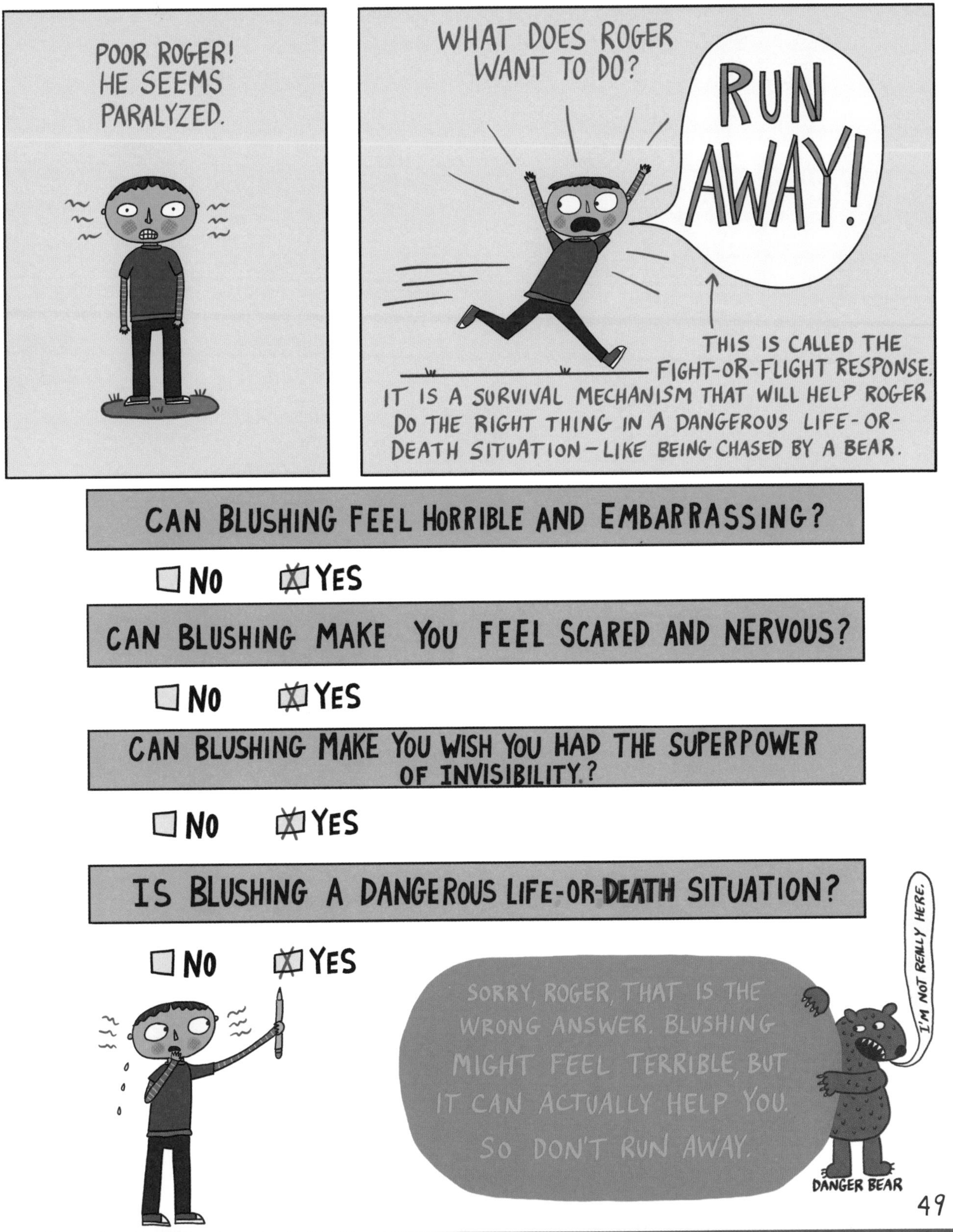
POOR ROGER! HE SEEMS PARALYZED.
WHAT DOES ROGER WANT TO DO?
RUN AWAY!
THIS IS CALLED THE FIGHT-OR-FLIGHT RESPONSE.
IT IS A SURVIVAL MECHANISM THAT WILL HELP ROGER DO THE RIGHT THING IN A DANGEROUS LIFE-OR-DEATH SITUATION—LIKE BEING CHASED BY A BEAR.
CAN BLUSHING FEEL HORRIBLE AND EMBARRASSING?
☐ NO ☒ YES
CAN BLUSHING MAKE YOU FEEL SCARED AND NERVOUS?
☐ NO ☒ YES
CAN BLUSHING MAKE YOU WISH YOU HAD THE SUPERPOWER OF INVISIBILITY?
☐ NO ☒ YES
IS BLUSHING A DANGEROUS LIFE-OR-DEATH SITUATION?
☐ NO ☒ YES
SORRY, ROGER, THAT IS THE WRONG ANSWER. BLUSHING MIGHT FEEL TERRIBLE, BUT IT CAN ACTUALLY HELP YOU. SO DON'T RUN AWAY.
I'M NOT REALLY HERE.
DANGER BEAR

IF ROGER DOES SOMETHING WRONG, PEOPLE ARE MORE LIKELY TO FORGIVE HIM AND EVEN LIKE HIM BETTER IF HE BLUSHES. IT'S HUMAN NATURE.

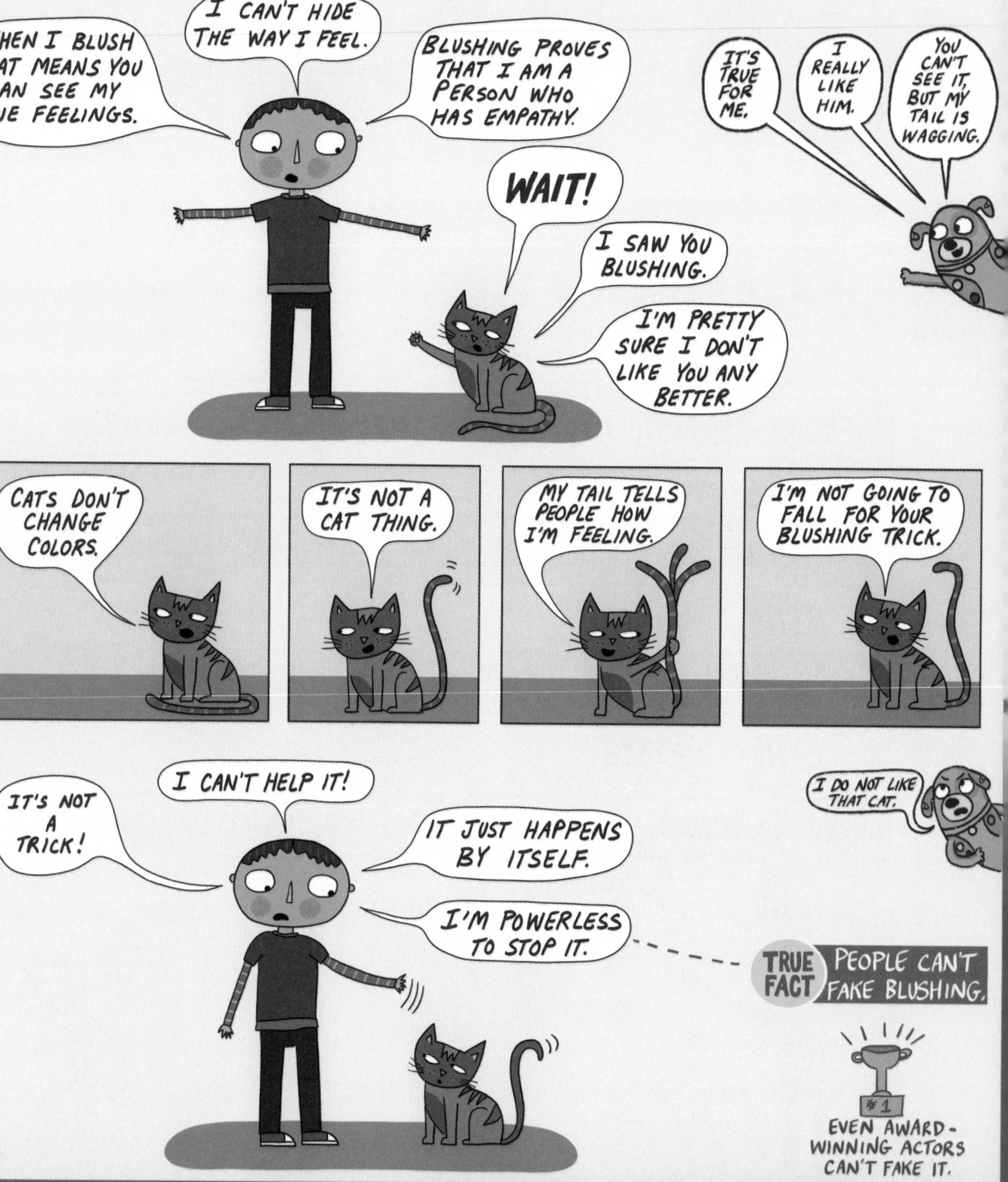
WHEN I BLUSH THAT MEANS YOU CAN SEE MY TRUE FEELINGS.
I CAN'T HIDE THE WAY I FEEL.
BLUSHING PROVES THAT I AM A PERSON WHO HAS EMPATHY.
IT'S TRUE FOR ME.
I REALLY LIKE HIM.
YOU CAN'T SEE IT, BUT MY TAIL IS WAGGING.
WAIT!
I SAW YOU BLUSHING.
I'M PRETTY SURE I DON'T LIKE YOU ANY BETTER.
CATS DON'T CHANGE COLORS.
IT'S NOT A CAT THING.
MY TAIL TELLS PEOPLE HOW I'M FEELING.
I'M NOT GOING TO FALL FOR YOUR BLUSHING TRICK.
IT'S NOT A TRICK!
I CAN'T HELP IT!
IT JUST HAPPENS BY ITSELF.
I'M POWERLESS TO STOP IT.
I DO NOT LIKE THAT CAT.
TRUE FACT PEOPLE CAN'T FAKE BLUSHING.
#1
EVEN AWARD-WINNING ACTORS CAN'T FAKE IT.

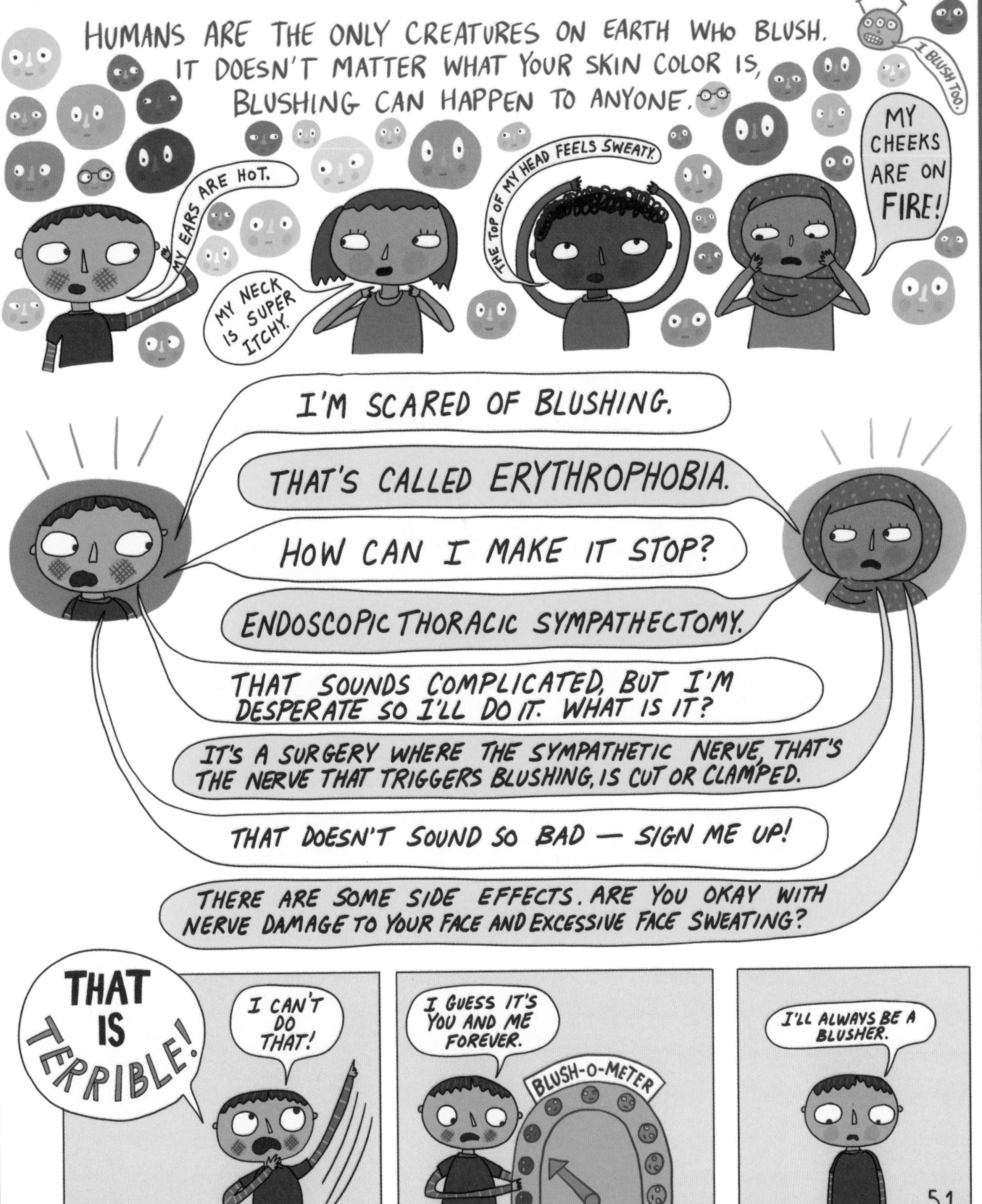
HUMANS ARE THE ONLY CREATURES ON EARTH WHO BLUSH. IT DOESN'T MATTER WHAT YOUR SKIN COLOR IS, BLUSHING CAN HAPPEN TO ANYONE.
I BLUSH TOO.
MY EARS ARE HOT.
MY NECK IS SUPER ITCHY.
THE TOP OF MY HEAD FEELS SWEATY.
MY CHEEKS ARE ON FIRE!
I'M SCARED OF BLUSHING.
THAT'S CALLED ERYTHROPHOBIA.
HOW CAN I MAKE IT STOP?
ENDOSCOPIC THORACIC SYMPATHECTOMY.
THAT SOUNDS COMPLICATED, BUT I'M DESPERATE SO I'LL DO IT. WHAT IS IT?
IT'S A SURGERY WHERE THE SYMPATHETIC NERVE, THAT'S THE NERVE THAT TRIGGERS BLUSHING, IS CUT OR CLAMPED.
THAT DOESN'T SOUND SO BAD — SIGN ME UP!
THERE ARE SOME SIDE EFFECTS. ARE YOU OKAY WITH NERVE DAMAGE TO YOUR FACE AND EXCESSIVE FACE SWEATING?
THAT IS TERRIBLE!
I CAN'T DO THAT!
I GUESS IT'S YOU AND ME FOREVER.
BLUSH-O-METER
I'LL ALWAYS BE A BLUSHER.

DON'T GIVE UP, ROGER. SPIN THE WHEEL.

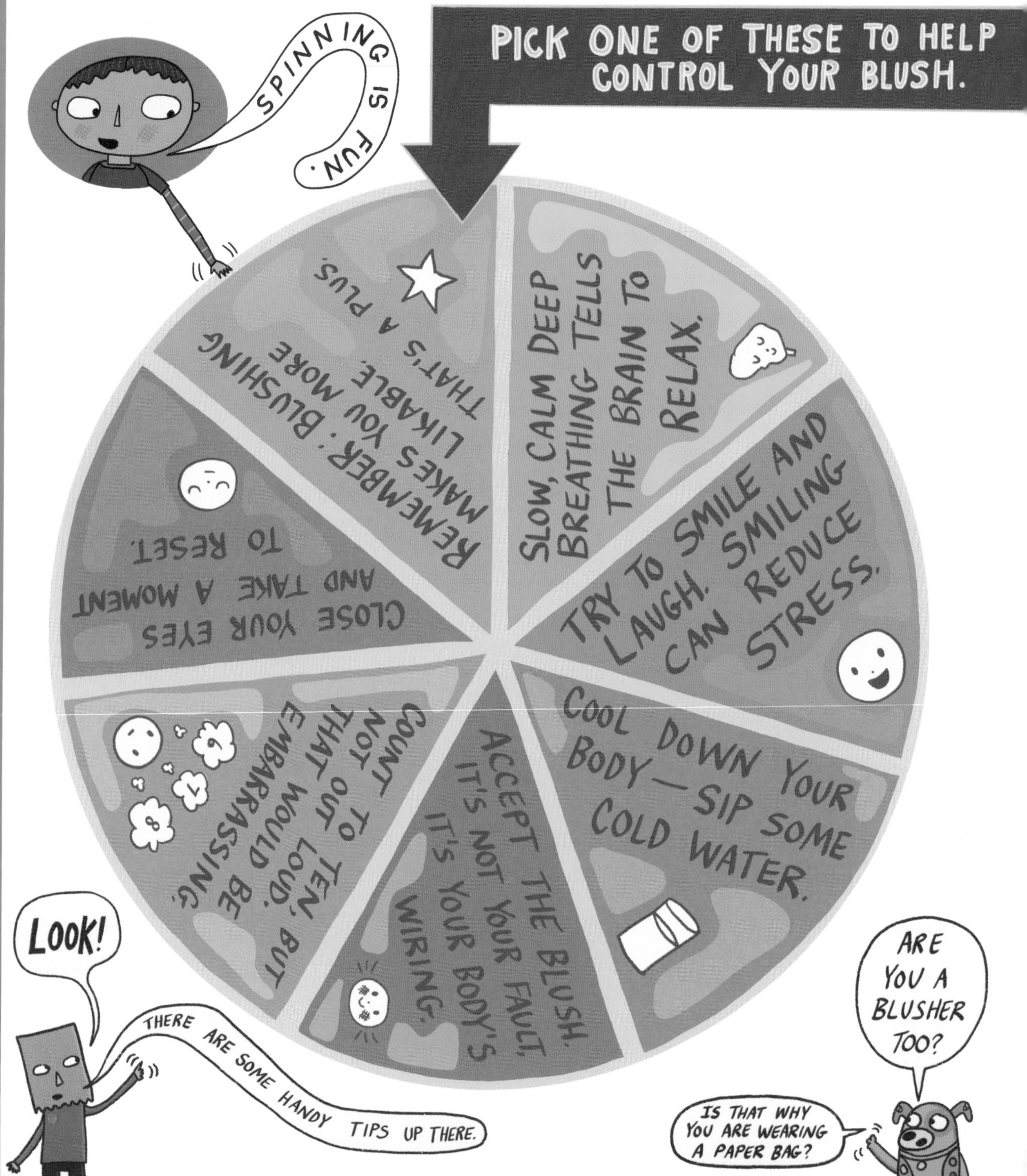

PICK ONE OF THESE TO HELP CONTROL YOUR BLUSH.
SPINNING IS FUN.
REMEMBER: BLUSHING MAKES YOU MORE LIKABLE. THAT'S A PLUS.
SLOW, CALM DEEP BREATHING TELLS THE BRAIN TO RELAX.
TRY TO SMILE AND LAUGH. SMILING CAN REDUCE STRESS.
COOL DOWN YOUR BODY—SIP SOME COLD WATER.
ACCEPT THE BLUSH. IT'S NOT YOUR FAULT. IT'S YOUR BODY'S WIRING.
COUNT TO TEN, NOT OUT LOUD. THAT WOULD BE EMBARRASSING, BUT
CLOSE YOUR EYES AND TAKE A MOMENT TO RESET.
LOOK!
THERE ARE SOME HANDY TIPS UP THERE.
ARE YOU A BLUSHER TOO?
IS THAT WHY YOU ARE WEARING A PAPER BAG?

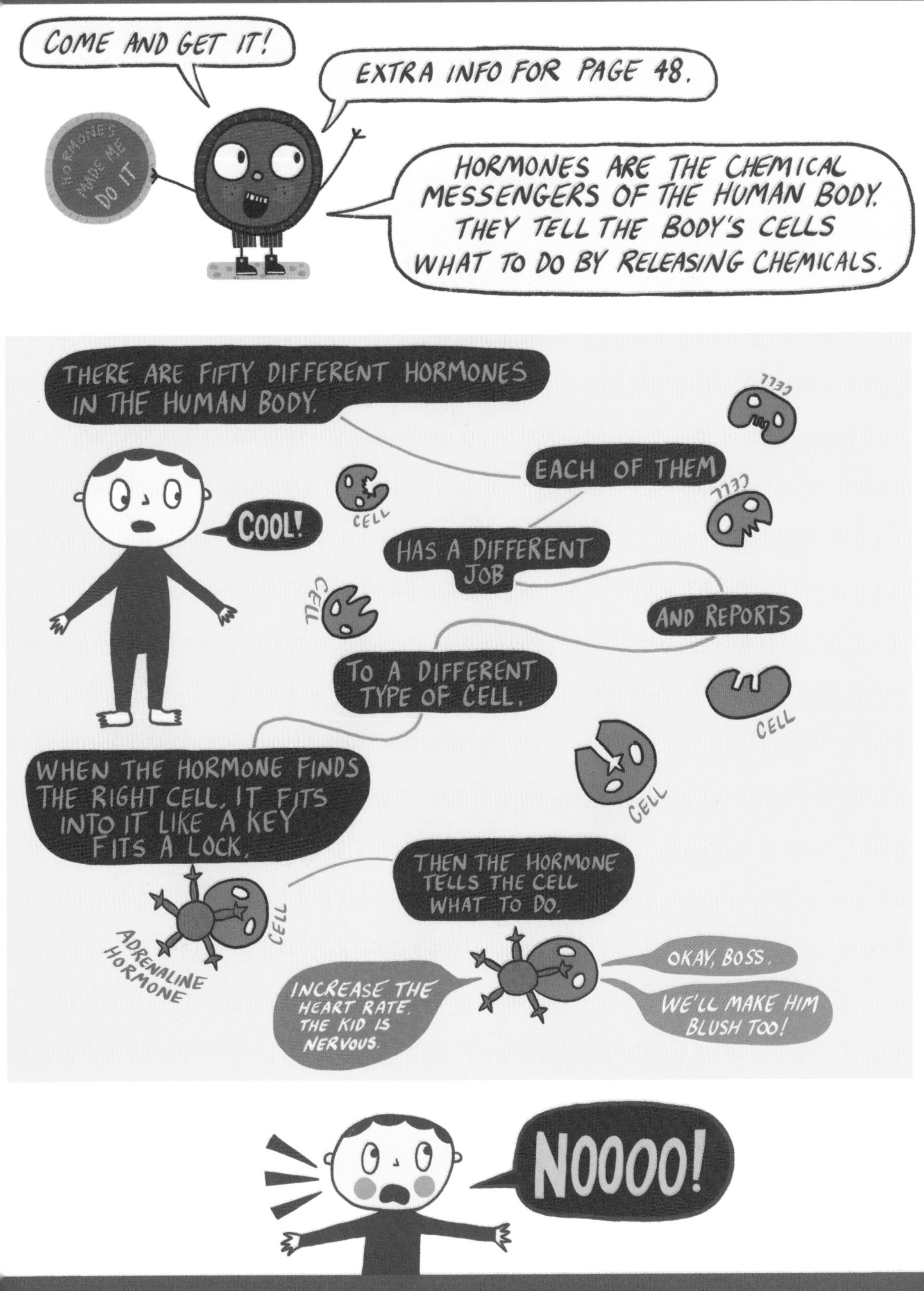

COME AND GET IT!
EXTRA INFO FOR PAGE 48.
HORMONES MADE ME DO IT
HORMONES ARE THE CHEMICAL MESSENGERS OF THE HUMAN BODY. THEY TELL THE BODY'S CELLS WHAT TO DO BY RELEASING CHEMICALS.
THERE ARE FIFTY DIFFERENT HORMONES IN THE HUMAN BODY.
EACH OF THEM
HAS A DIFFERENT JOB
AND REPORTS
TO A DIFFERENT TYPE OF CELL.
COOL!
CELL
CELL
CELL
CELL
CELL
CELL
WHEN THE HORMONE FINDS THE RIGHT CELL, IT FITS INTO IT LIKE A KEY FITS A LOCK.
THEN THE HORMONE TELLS THE CELL WHAT TO DO.
ADRENALINE HORMONE
CELL
INCREASE THE HEART RATE. THE KID IS NERVOUS.
OKAY, BOSS.
WE'LL MAKE HIM BLUSH TOO!
NOOOO!

DISCLAIMER: THESE ARE ARTISTIC REPRESENTATIONS OF CELLS AND HORMONES. AND ALSO: HORMONES AND CELLS DON'T REALLY TALK.

ROGER WASN'T THE ONLY ONE AFFECTED BY HIS BLUSHING.

EVERYONE WHO SAW HIM BLUSH WAS AFFECTED TOO.

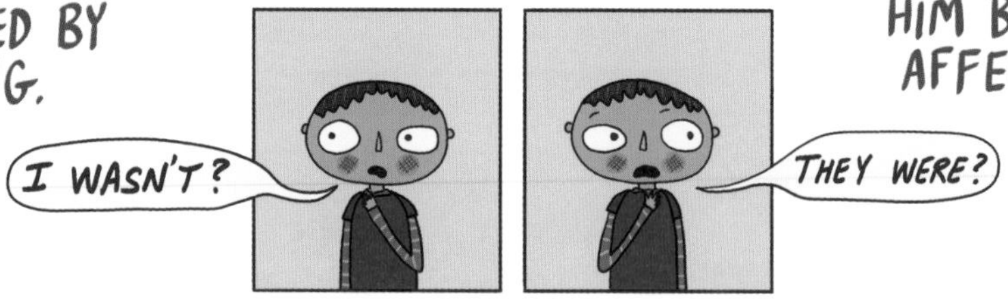

I WASN'T?
THEY WERE?

LET'S SEE HOW THEY FELT

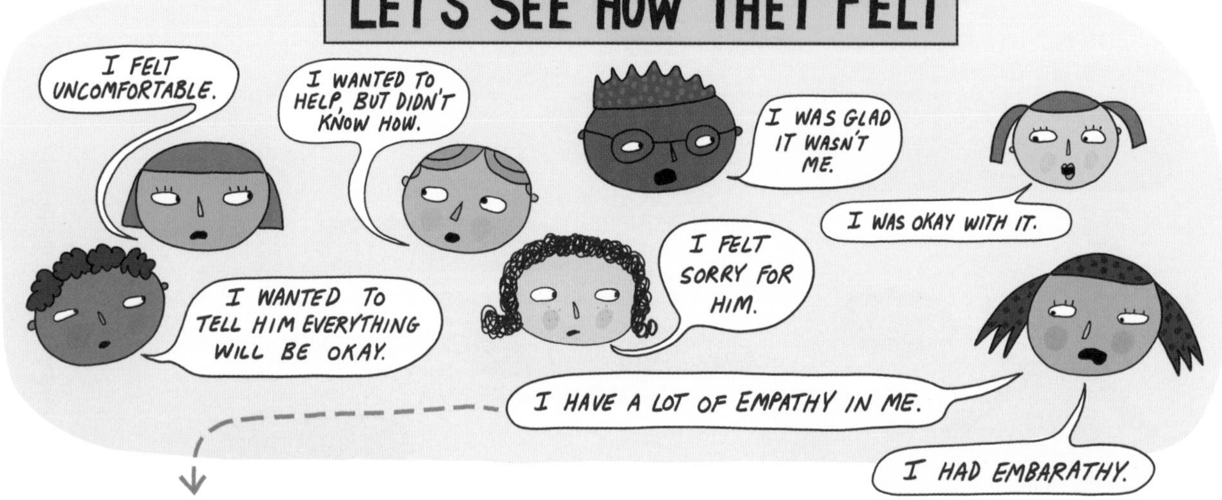

I FELT UNCOMFORTABLE.
I WANTED TO HELP, BUT DIDN'T KNOW HOW.
I WAS GLAD IT WASN'T ME.
I WAS OKAY WITH IT.
I WANTED TO TELL HIM EVERYTHING WILL BE OKAY.
I FELT SORRY FOR HIM.
I HAVE A LOT OF EMPATHY IN ME.
I HAD EMBARATHY.

EMPATHY (DICTIONARY)
THE ABILITY TO UNDERSTAND THE FEELINGS OF ANOTHER PERSON, TO BE TRULY SYMPATHETIC.

EMBARATHY (SLANG)
IS WHEN YOU FEEL EMBARRASSED, BECAUSE YOU ARE WITNESSING SOMEONE ELSE BEING EMBARRASSED.

EMBARATHY IN ACTION

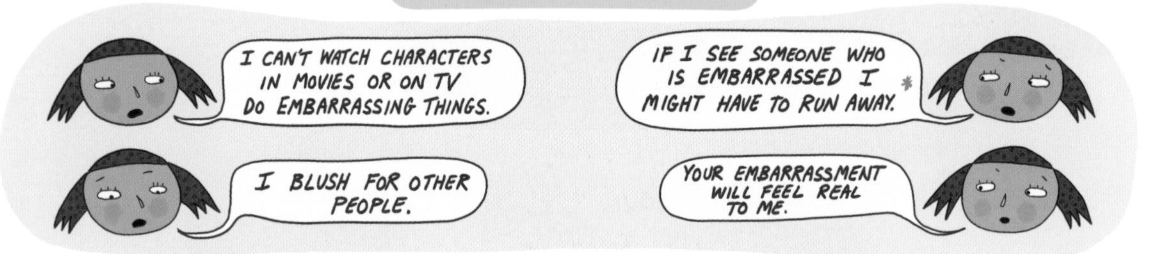

I CAN'T WATCH CHARACTERS IN MOVIES OR ON TV DO EMBARRASSING THINGS.
IF I SEE SOMEONE WHO IS EMBARRASSED I MIGHT HAVE TO RUN AWAY.*
I BLUSH FOR OTHER PEOPLE.
YOUR EMBARRASSMENT WILL FEEL REAL TO ME.

* FIGHT-OR-FLIGHT RESPONSE SEE PAGE 49

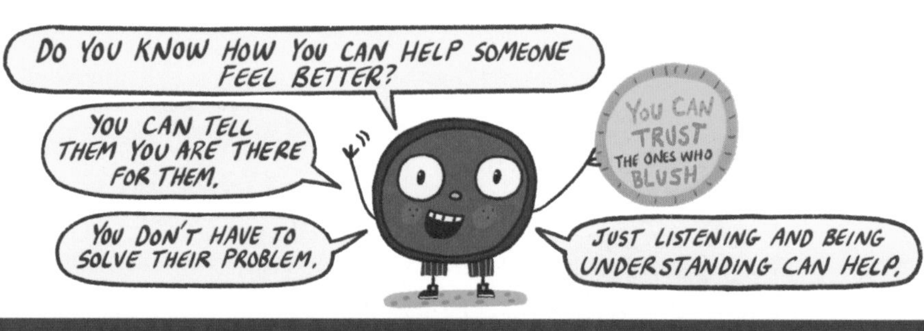

DO YOU KNOW HOW YOU CAN HELP SOMEONE FEEL BETTER?
YOU CAN TELL THEM YOU ARE THERE FOR THEM.
YOU CAN TRUST THE ONES WHO BLUSH
YOU DON'T HAVE TO SOLVE THEIR PROBLEM.
JUST LISTENING AND BEING UNDERSTANDING CAN HELP.

5

YOU DID IT WRONG

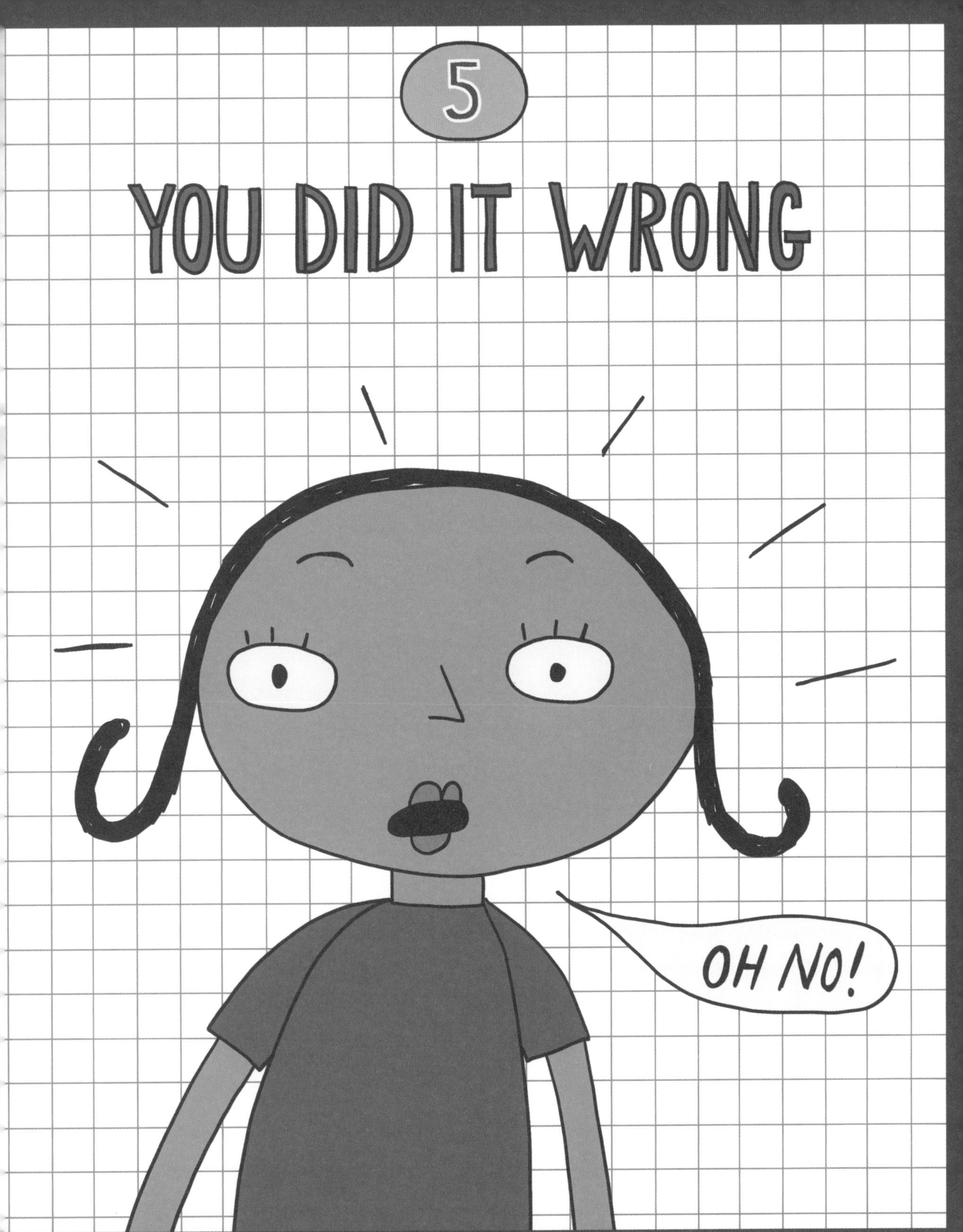
OH NO!

Let's Play

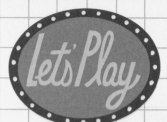

GUESS WHAT HAPPENED

NUMBER 1

ANSWERS ON PAGE 58

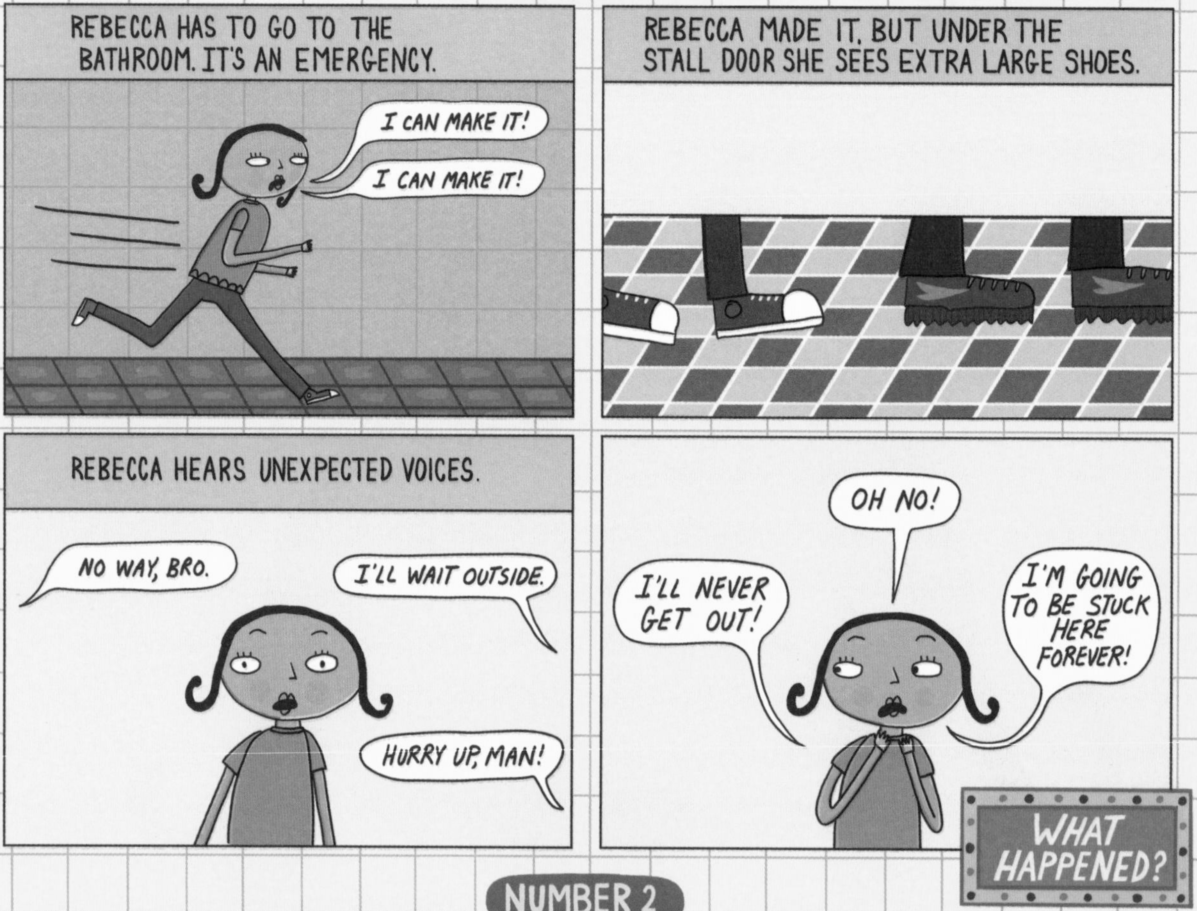
REBECCA HAS TO GO TO THE BATHROOM. IT'S AN EMERGENCY.
I CAN MAKE IT!
I CAN MAKE IT!
REBECCA MADE IT, BUT UNDER THE STALL DOOR SHE SEES EXTRA LARGE SHOES.
REBECCA HEARS UNEXPECTED VOICES.
NO WAY, BRO.
I'LL WAIT OUTSIDE.
HURRY UP, MAN!
OH NO!
I'LL NEVER GET OUT!
I'M GOING TO BE STUCK HERE FOREVER!
WHAT HAPPENED?

NUMBER 2

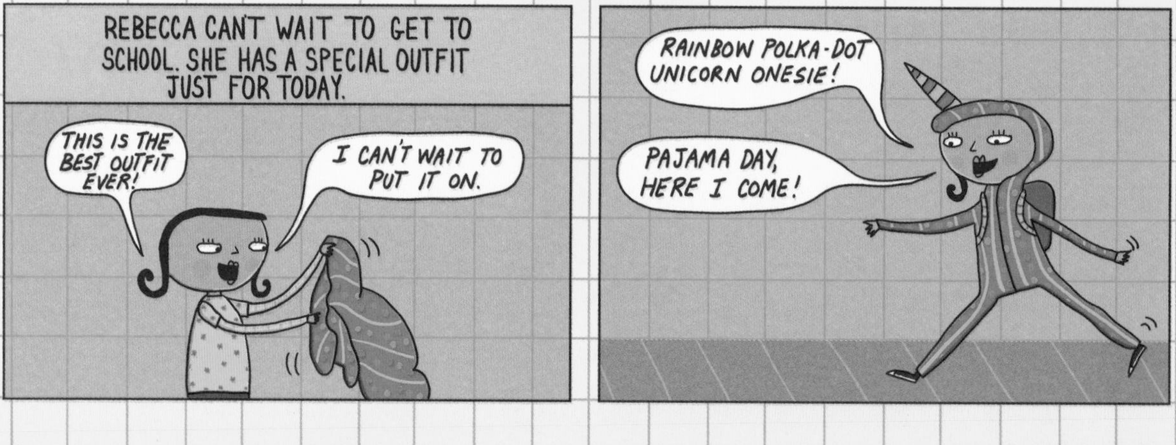
REBECCA CAN'T WAIT TO GET TO SCHOOL. SHE HAS A SPECIAL OUTFIT JUST FOR TODAY.
THIS IS THE BEST OUTFIT EVER!
I CAN'T WAIT TO PUT IT ON.
RAINBOW POLKA-DOT UNICORN ONESIE!
PAJAMA DAY, HERE I COME!

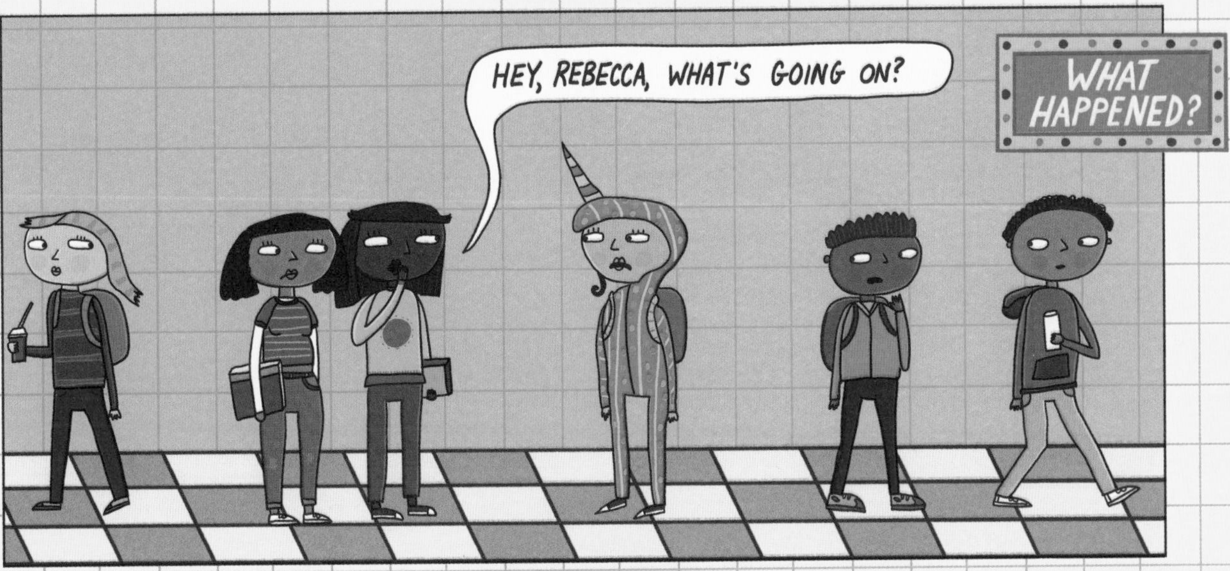
HEY, REBECCA, WHAT'S GOING ON?
WHAT HAPPENED?

NUMBER 3

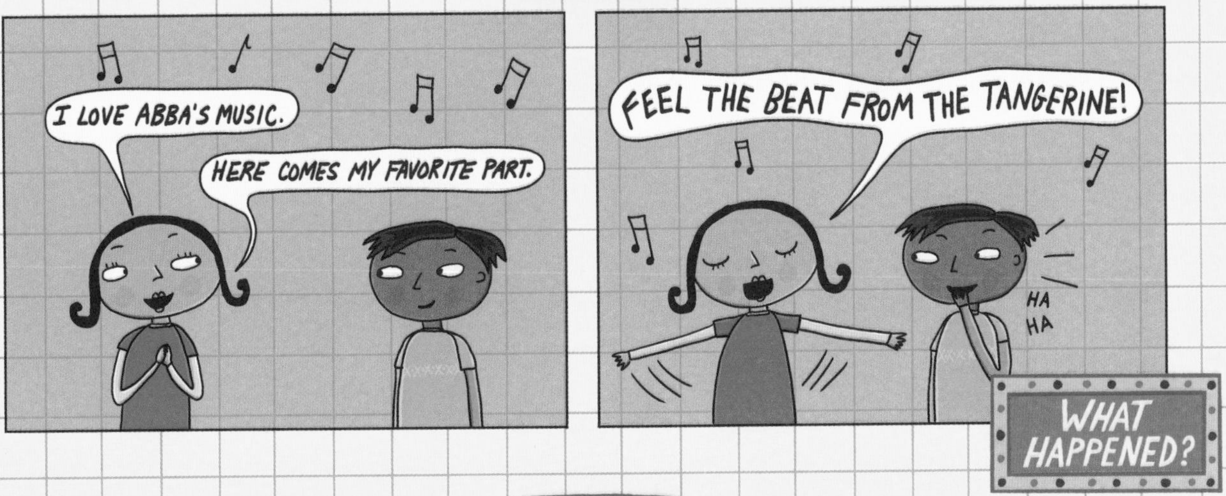
I LOVE ABBA'S MUSIC.
HERE COMES MY FAVORITE PART.
FEEL THE BEAT FROM THE TANGERINE!
HA HA
WHAT HAPPENED?

NUMBER 4

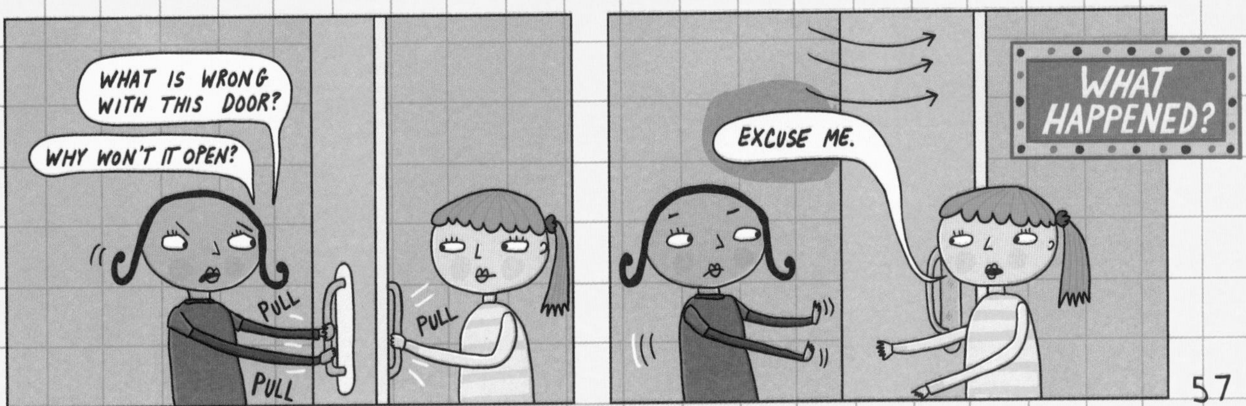
WHAT IS WRONG WITH THIS DOOR?
WHY WON'T IT OPEN?
PULL
PULL
PULL
EXCUSE ME.
WHAT HAPPENED?

NUMBER 5

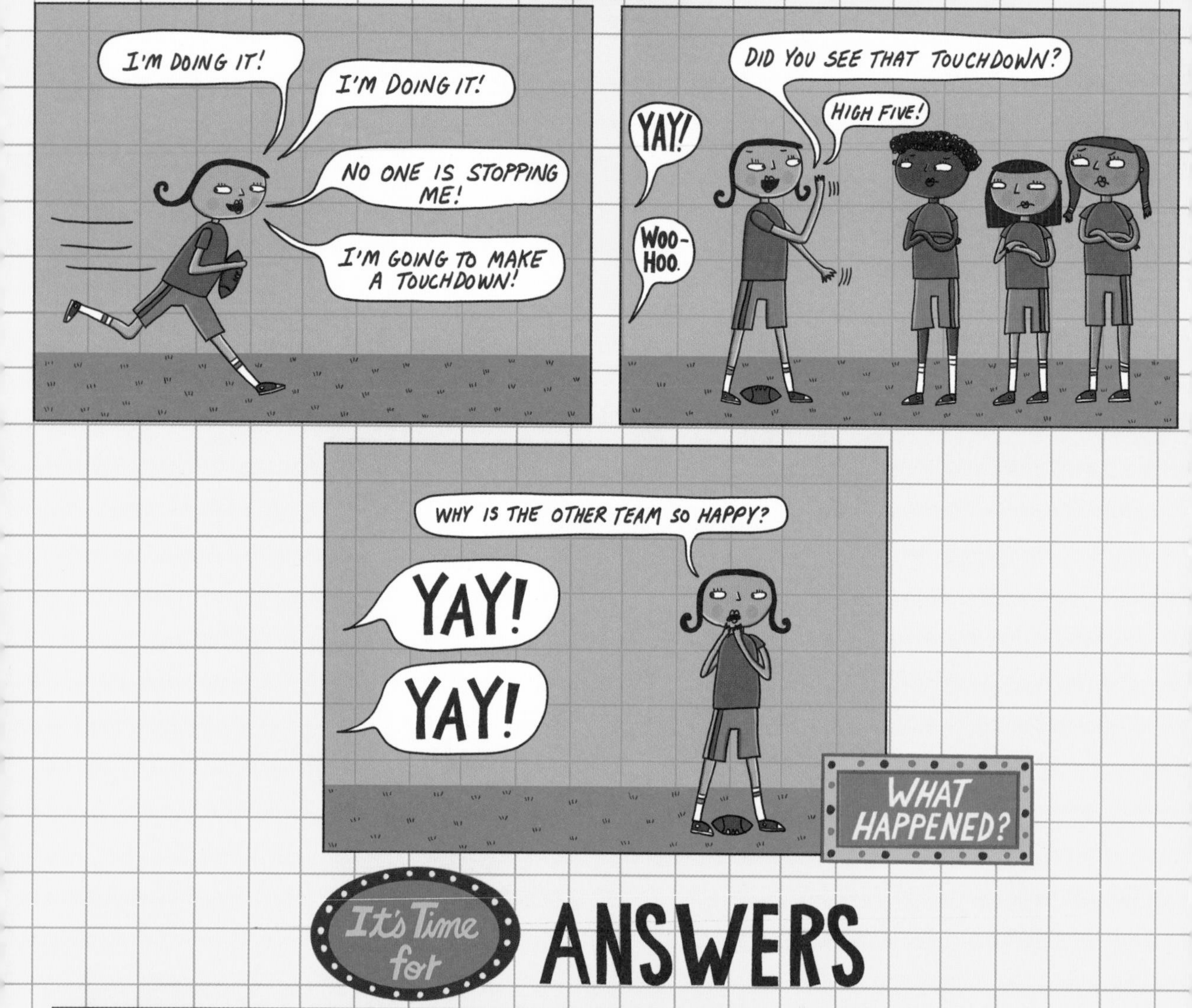

I'M DOING IT!
I'M DOING IT!
NO ONE IS STOPPING ME!
I'M GOING TO MAKE A TOUCHDOWN!
DID YOU SEE THAT TOUCHDOWN?
HIGH FIVE!
YAY!
WOO-HOO.
WHY IS THE OTHER TEAM SO HAPPY?
YAY!
YAY!
WHAT HAPPENED?

It's Time for ANSWERS

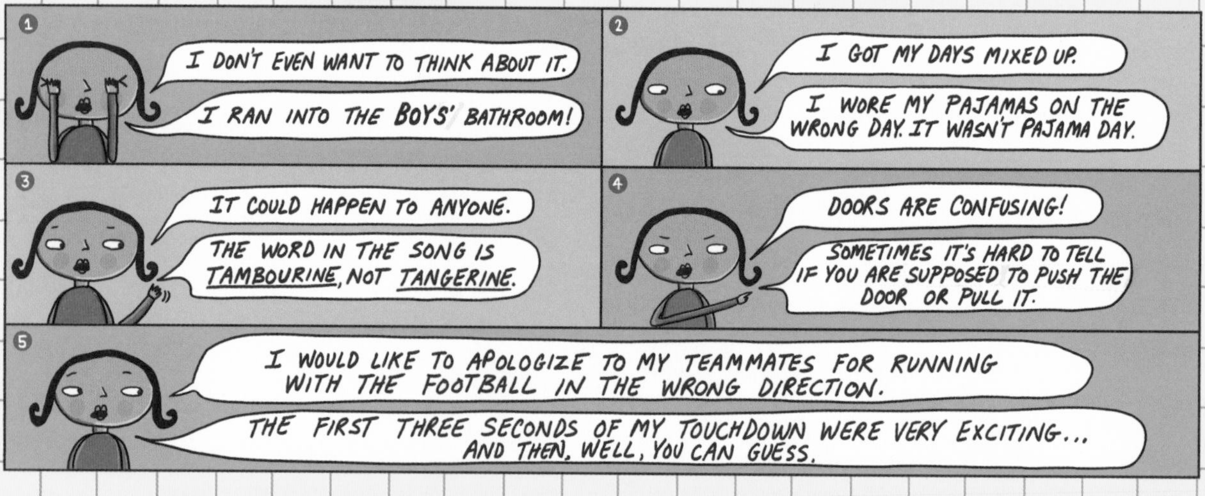

1
I DON'T EVEN WANT TO THINK ABOUT IT.
I RAN INTO THE BOYS' BATHROOM!
2
I GOT MY DAYS MIXED UP.
I WORE MY PAJAMAS ON THE WRONG DAY. IT WASN'T PAJAMA DAY.
3
IT COULD HAPPEN TO ANYONE.
THE WORD IN THE SONG IS TAMBOURINE, NOT TANGERINE.
4
DOORS ARE CONFUSING!
SOMETIMES IT'S HARD TO TELL IF YOU ARE SUPPOSED TO PUSH THE DOOR OR PULL IT.
5
I WOULD LIKE TO APOLOGIZE TO MY TEAMMATES FOR RUNNING WITH THE FOOTBALL IN THE WRONG DIRECTION.
THE FIRST THREE SECONDS OF MY TOUCHDOWN WERE VERY EXCITING... AND THEN, WELL, YOU CAN GUESS.

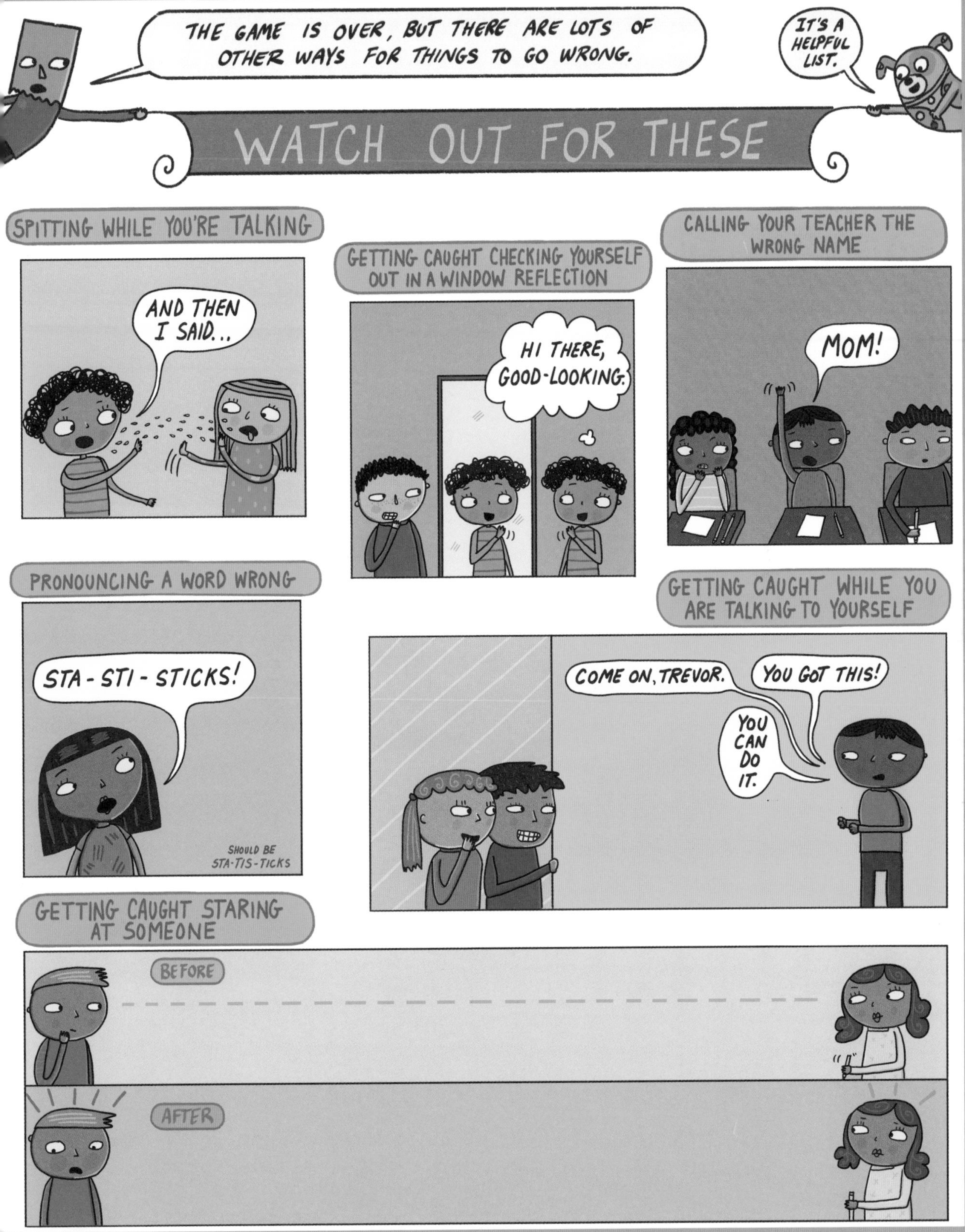
THE GAME IS OVER, BUT THERE ARE LOTS OF OTHER WAYS FOR THINGS TO GO WRONG.
IT'S A HELPFUL LIST.
WATCH OUT FOR THESE
SPITTING WHILE YOU'RE TALKING
AND THEN I SAID...
GETTING CAUGHT CHECKING YOURSELF OUT IN A WINDOW REFLECTION
HI THERE, GOOD-LOOKING.
CALLING YOUR TEACHER THE WRONG NAME
MOM!
PRONOUNCING A WORD WRONG
STA-STI-STICKS!
SHOULD BE STA-TIS-TICKS
GETTING CAUGHT WHILE YOU ARE TALKING TO YOURSELF
COME ON, TREVOR.
YOU GOT THIS!
YOU CAN DO IT.
GETTING CAUGHT STARING AT SOMEONE
BEFORE
AFTER

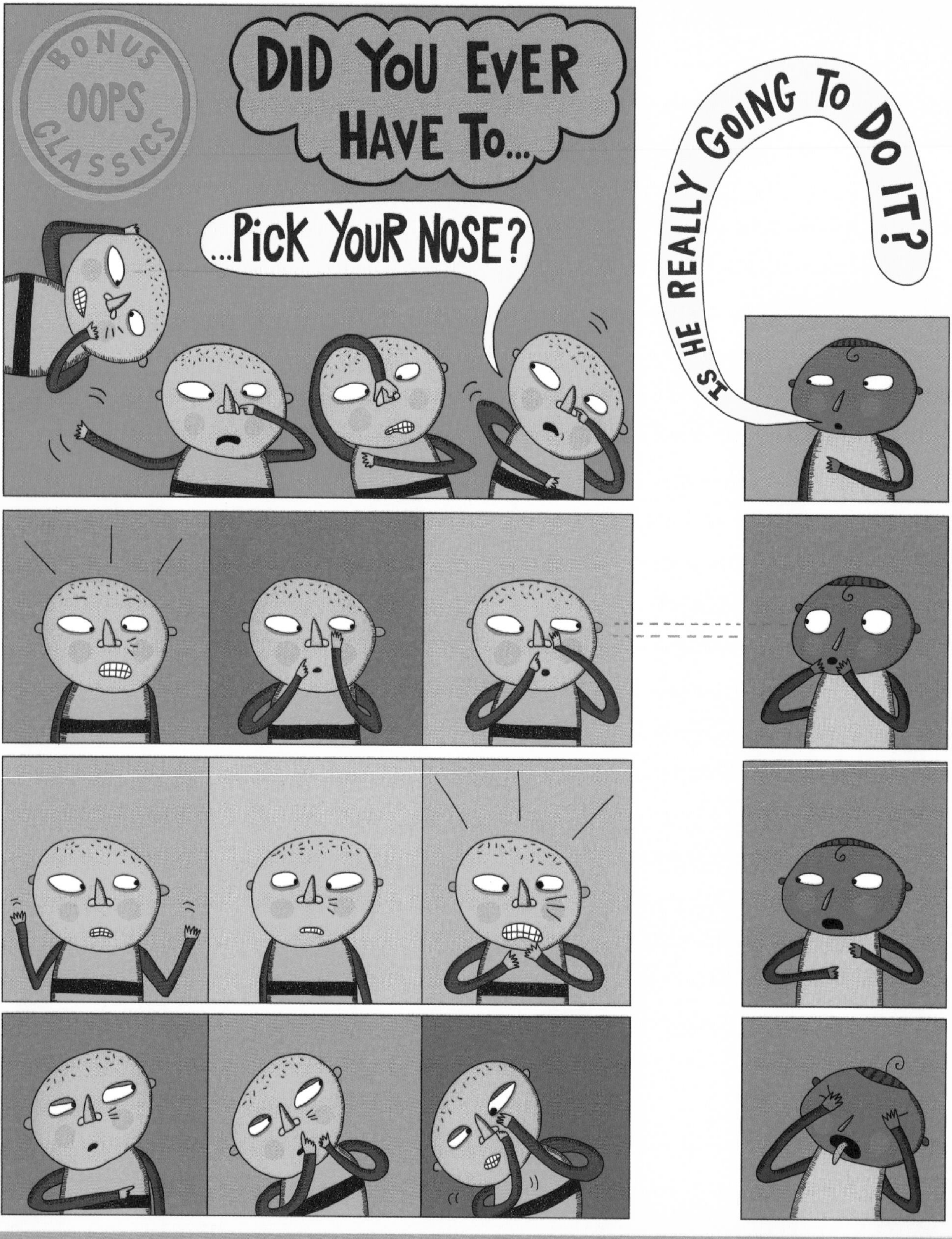
BONUS OOPS CLASSICS
DID YOU EVER HAVE TO...
...PICK YOUR NOSE?
IS HE REALLY GOING TO DO IT?

THIS IS 100% EMBARRASSING

THAT IS DISGUSTING!

UNLESS

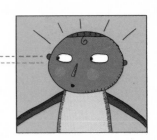

THAT IS AMAZING!

TRUE FACT — A 1995 STUDY FOUND THAT 90% OF ADULTS ADMITTED THAT THEY PICK THEIR NOSE.

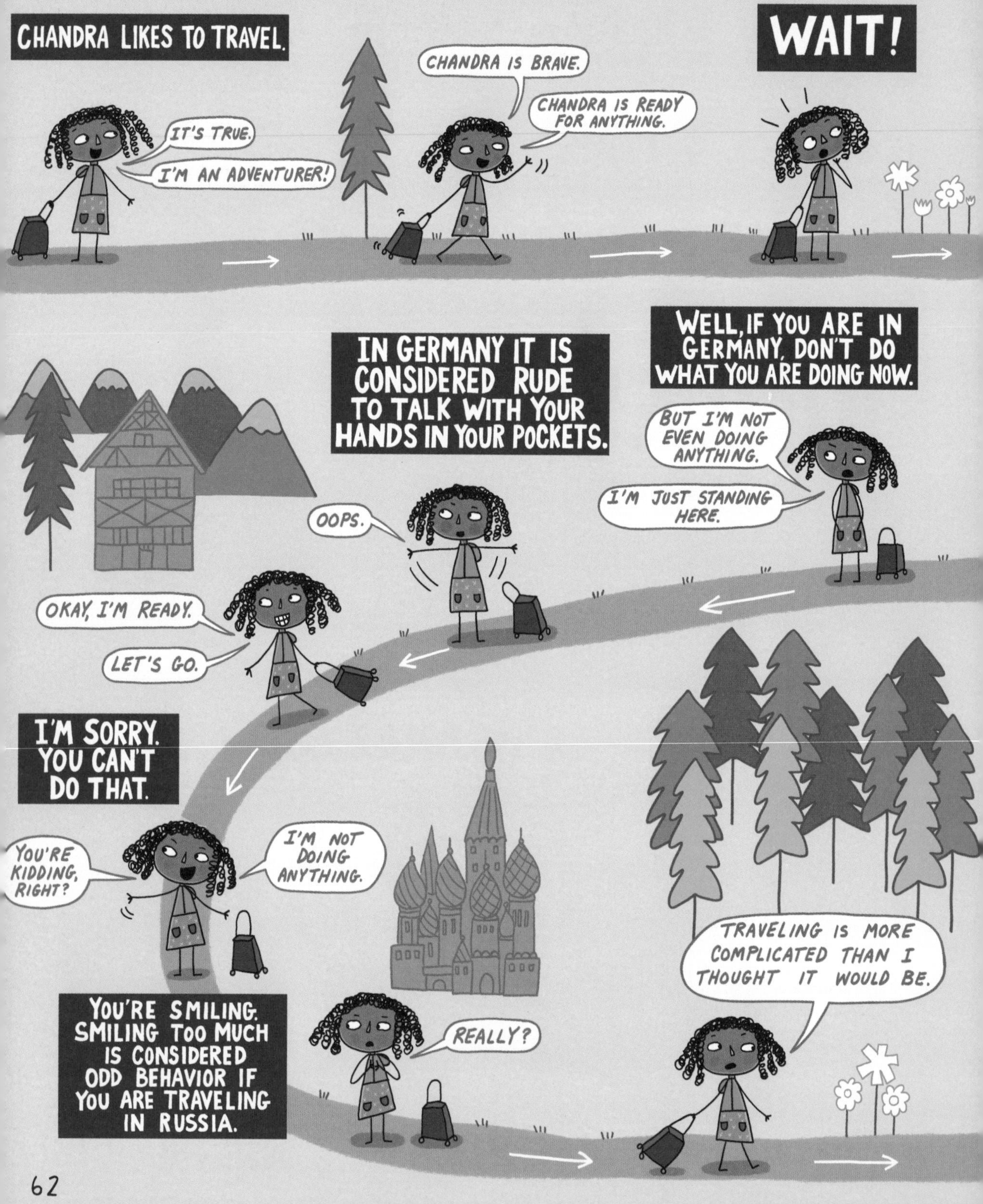

CHANDRA LIKES TO TRAVEL.
IT'S TRUE.
I'M AN ADVENTURER!
CHANDRA IS BRAVE.
CHANDRA IS READY FOR ANYTHING.
WAIT!
IN GERMANY IT IS CONSIDERED RUDE TO TALK WITH YOUR HANDS IN YOUR POCKETS.
WELL, IF YOU ARE IN GERMANY, DON'T DO WHAT YOU ARE DOING NOW.
BUT I'M NOT EVEN DOING ANYTHING.
I'M JUST STANDING HERE.
OOPS.
OKAY, I'M READY.
LET'S GO.
I'M SORRY. YOU CAN'T DO THAT.
YOU'RE KIDDING, RIGHT?
I'M NOT DOING ANYTHING.
YOU'RE SMILING. SMILING TOO MUCH IS CONSIDERED ODD BEHAVIOR IF YOU ARE TRAVELING IN RUSSIA.
REALLY?
TRAVELING IS MORE COMPLICATED THAN I THOUGHT IT WOULD BE.

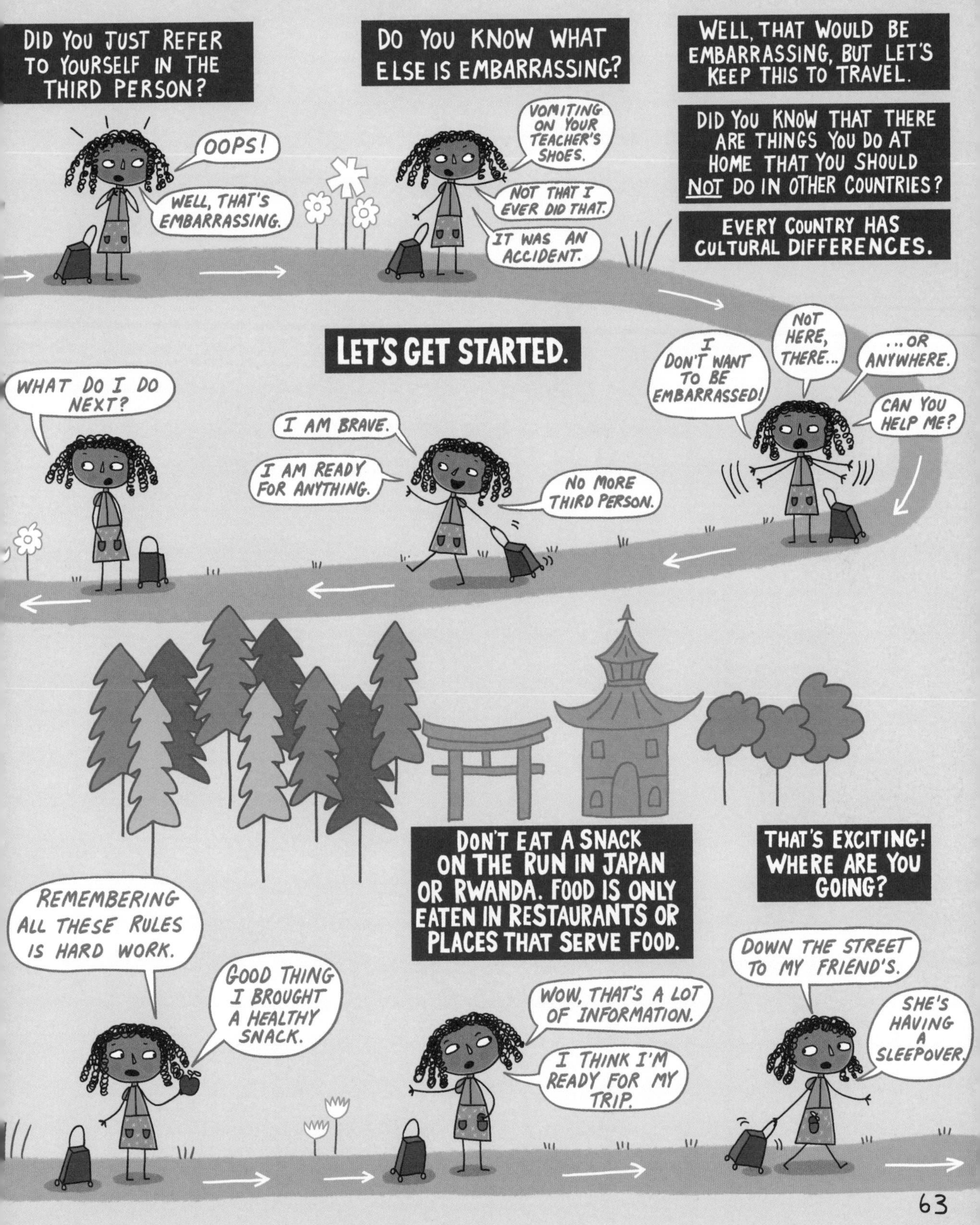

DID YOU JUST REFER TO YOURSELF IN THE THIRD PERSON?
OOPS!
WELL, THAT'S EMBARRASSING.
DO YOU KNOW WHAT ELSE IS EMBARRASSING?
VOMITING ON YOUR TEACHER'S SHOES.
NOT THAT I EVER DID THAT.
IT WAS AN ACCIDENT.
WELL, THAT WOULD BE EMBARRASSING, BUT LET'S KEEP THIS TO TRAVEL.
DID YOU KNOW THAT THERE ARE THINGS YOU DO AT HOME THAT YOU SHOULD NOT DO IN OTHER COUNTRIES?
EVERY COUNTRY HAS CULTURAL DIFFERENCES.
I DON'T WANT TO BE EMBARRASSED!
NOT HERE, THERE...
...OR ANYWHERE.
CAN YOU HELP ME?
LET'S GET STARTED.
I AM BRAVE.
I AM READY FOR ANYTHING.
NO MORE THIRD PERSON.
WHAT DO I DO NEXT?
REMEMBERING ALL THESE RULES IS HARD WORK.
GOOD THING I BROUGHT A HEALTHY SNACK.
DON'T EAT A SNACK ON THE RUN IN JAPAN OR RWANDA. FOOD IS ONLY EATEN IN RESTAURANTS OR PLACES THAT SERVE FOOD.
WOW, THAT'S A LOT OF INFORMATION.
I THINK I'M READY FOR MY TRIP.
THAT'S EXCITING! WHERE ARE YOU GOING?
DOWN THE STREET TO MY FRIEND'S.
SHE'S HAVING A SLEEPOVER.

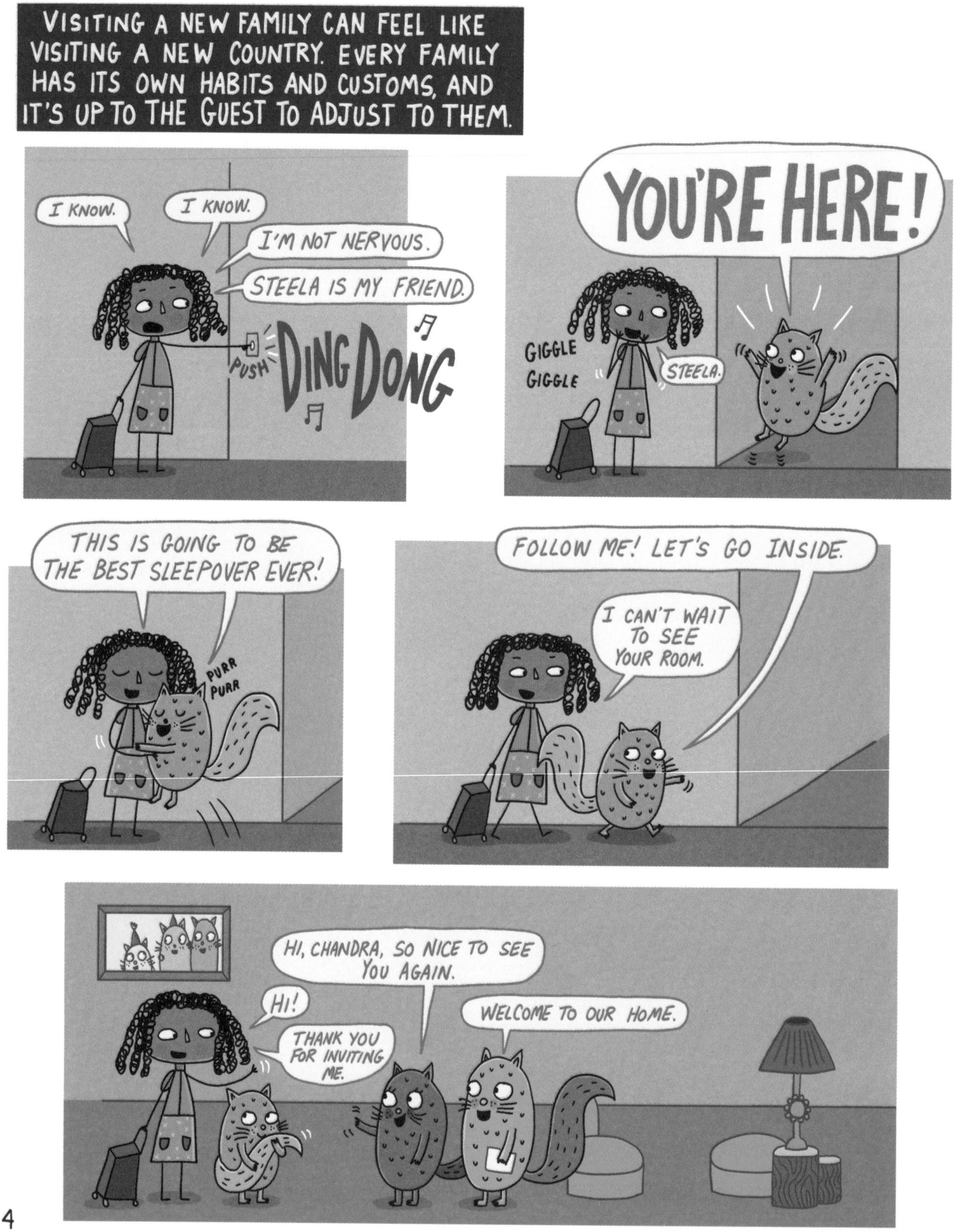
VISITING A NEW FAMILY CAN FEEL LIKE VISITING A NEW COUNTRY. EVERY FAMILY HAS ITS OWN HABITS AND CUSTOMS, AND IT'S UP TO THE GUEST TO ADJUST TO THEM.
I KNOW.
I KNOW.
I'M NOT NERVOUS.
STEELA IS MY FRIEND.
PUSH
DING DONG
YOU'RE HERE!
GIGGLE GIGGLE
STEELA.
THIS IS GOING TO BE THE BEST SLEEPOVER EVER!
PURR PURR
FOLLOW ME! LET'S GO INSIDE.
I CAN'T WAIT TO SEE YOUR ROOM.
HI, CHANDRA, SO NICE TO SEE YOU AGAIN.
HI!
THANK YOU FOR INVITING ME.
WELCOME TO OUR HOME.

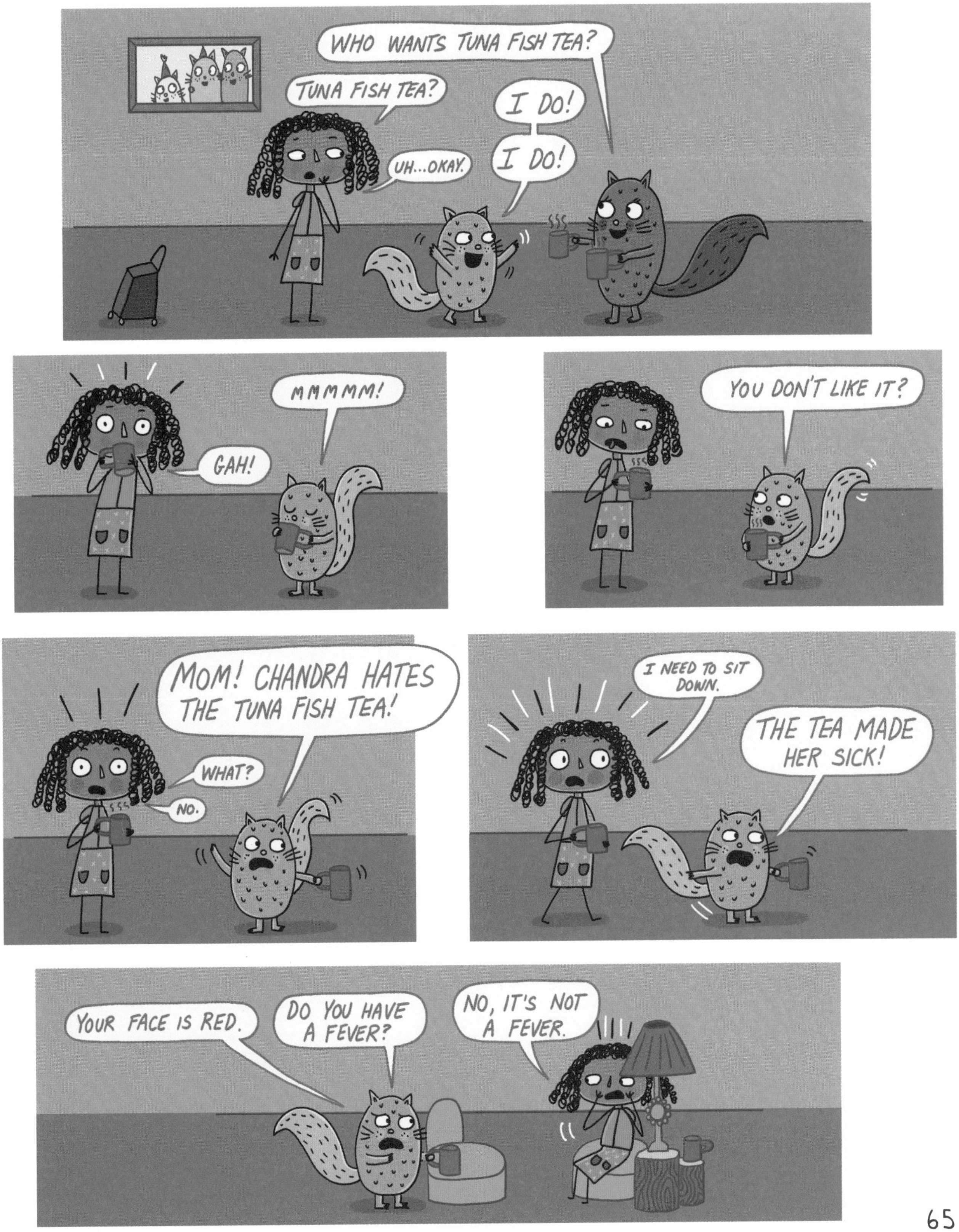
WHO WANTS TUNA FISH TEA?
TUNA FISH TEA?
I DO!
I DO!
UH...OKAY.
MMMMM!
GAH!
YOU DON'T LIKE IT?
MOM! CHANDRA HATES THE TUNA FISH TEA!
WHAT?
NO.
I NEED TO SIT DOWN.
THE TEA MADE HER SICK!
YOUR FACE IS RED.
DO YOU HAVE A FEVER?
NO, IT'S NOT A FEVER.

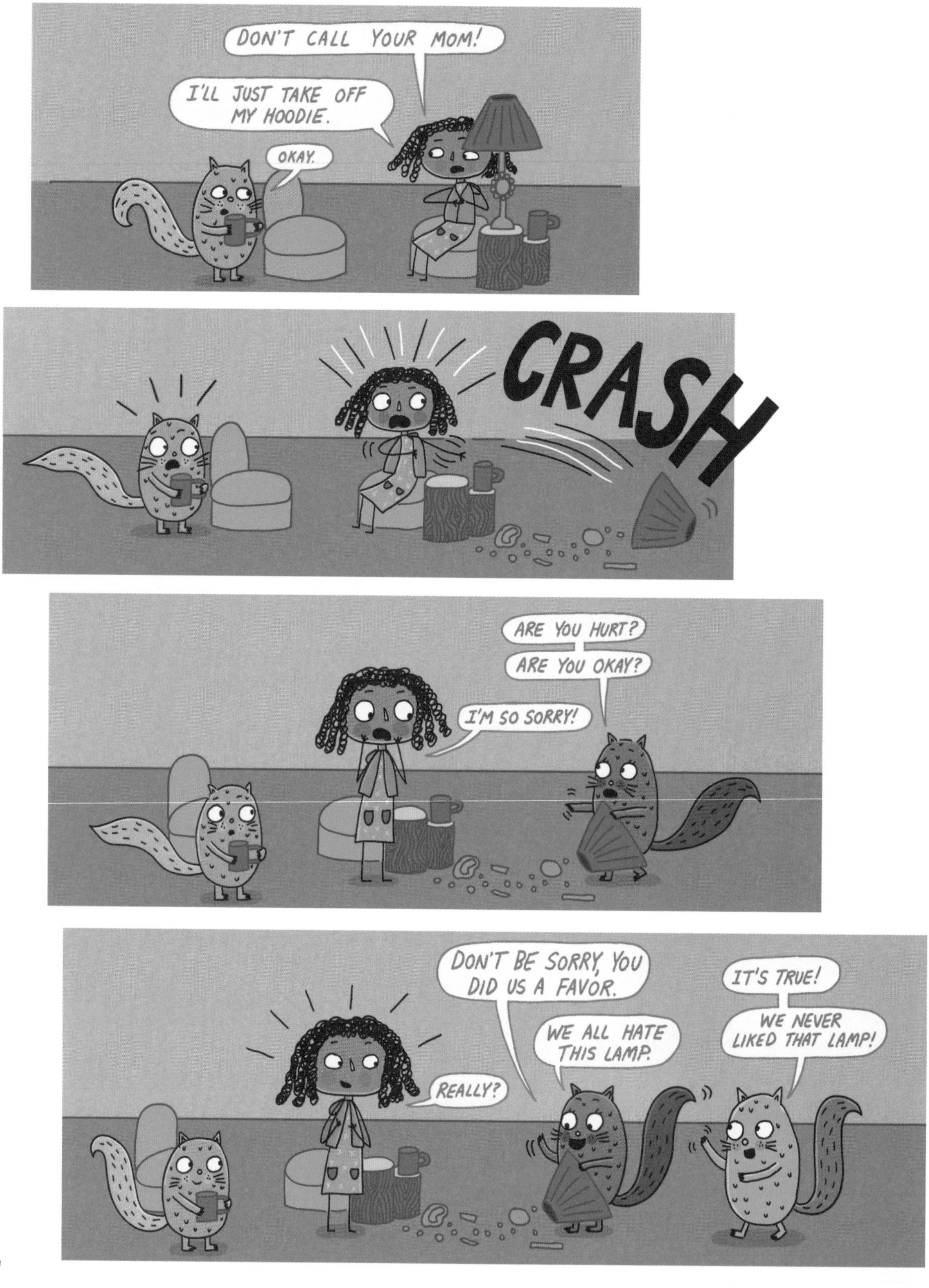
DON'T CALL YOUR MOM!
I'LL JUST TAKE OFF MY HOODIE.
OKAY.
CRASH
ARE YOU HURT?
ARE YOU OKAY?
I'M SO SORRY!
DON'T BE SORRY, YOU DID US A FAVOR.
WE ALL HATE THIS LAMP.
IT'S TRUE!
WE NEVER LIKED THAT LAMP!
REALLY?

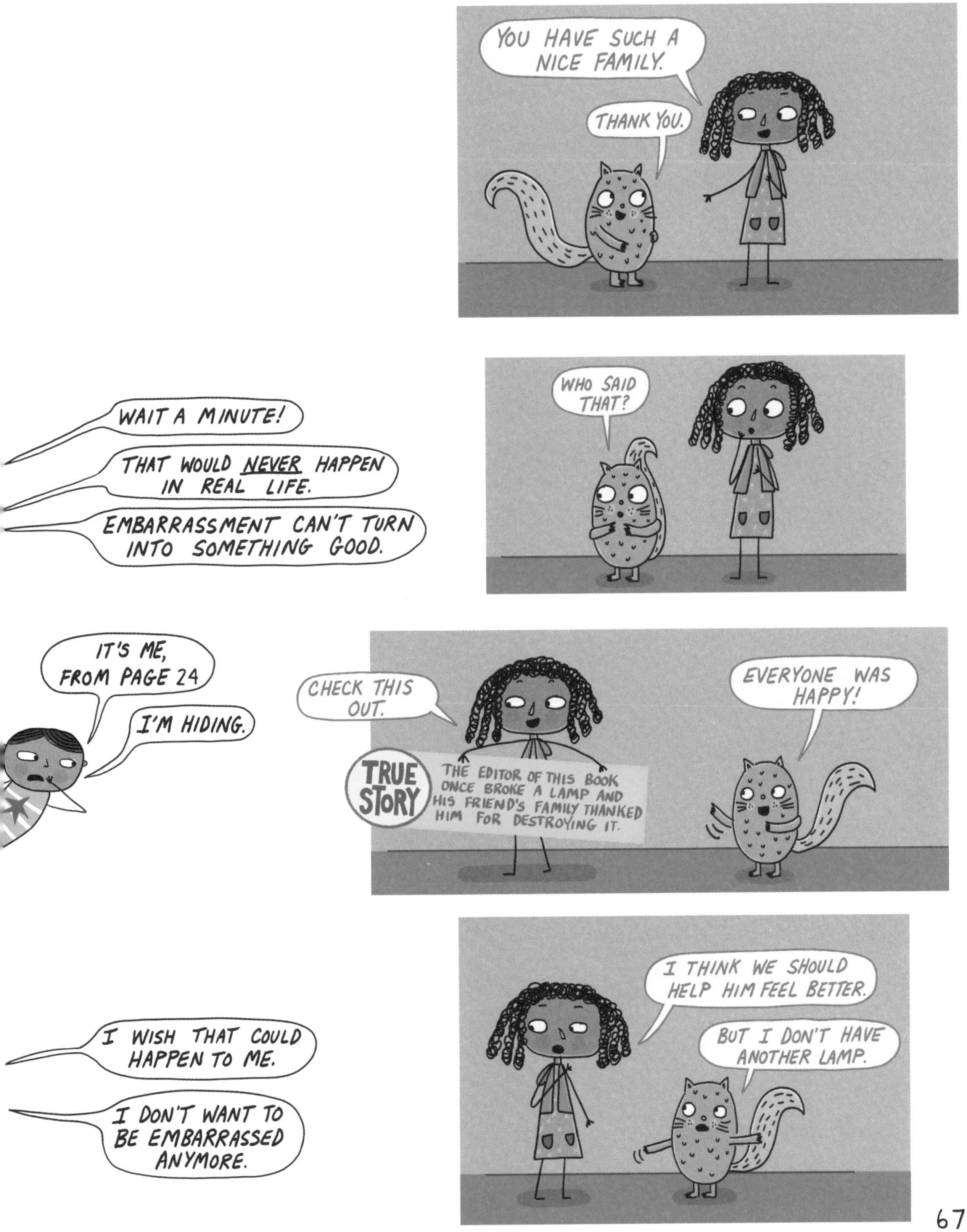

YOU HAVE SUCH A NICE FAMILY.
THANK YOU.
WAIT A MINUTE!
THAT WOULD NEVER HAPPEN IN REAL LIFE.
EMBARRASSMENT CAN'T TURN INTO SOMETHING GOOD.
WHO SAID THAT?
IT'S ME, FROM PAGE 24
I'M HIDING.
CHECK THIS OUT.
TRUE STORY
THE EDITOR OF THIS BOOK ONCE BROKE A LAMP AND HIS FRIEND'S FAMILY THANKED HIM FOR DESTROYING IT.
EVERYONE WAS HAPPY!
I WISH THAT COULD HAPPEN TO ME.
I DON'T WANT TO BE EMBARRASSED ANYMORE.
I THINK WE SHOULD HELP HIM FEEL BETTER.
BUT I DON'T HAVE ANOTHER LAMP.

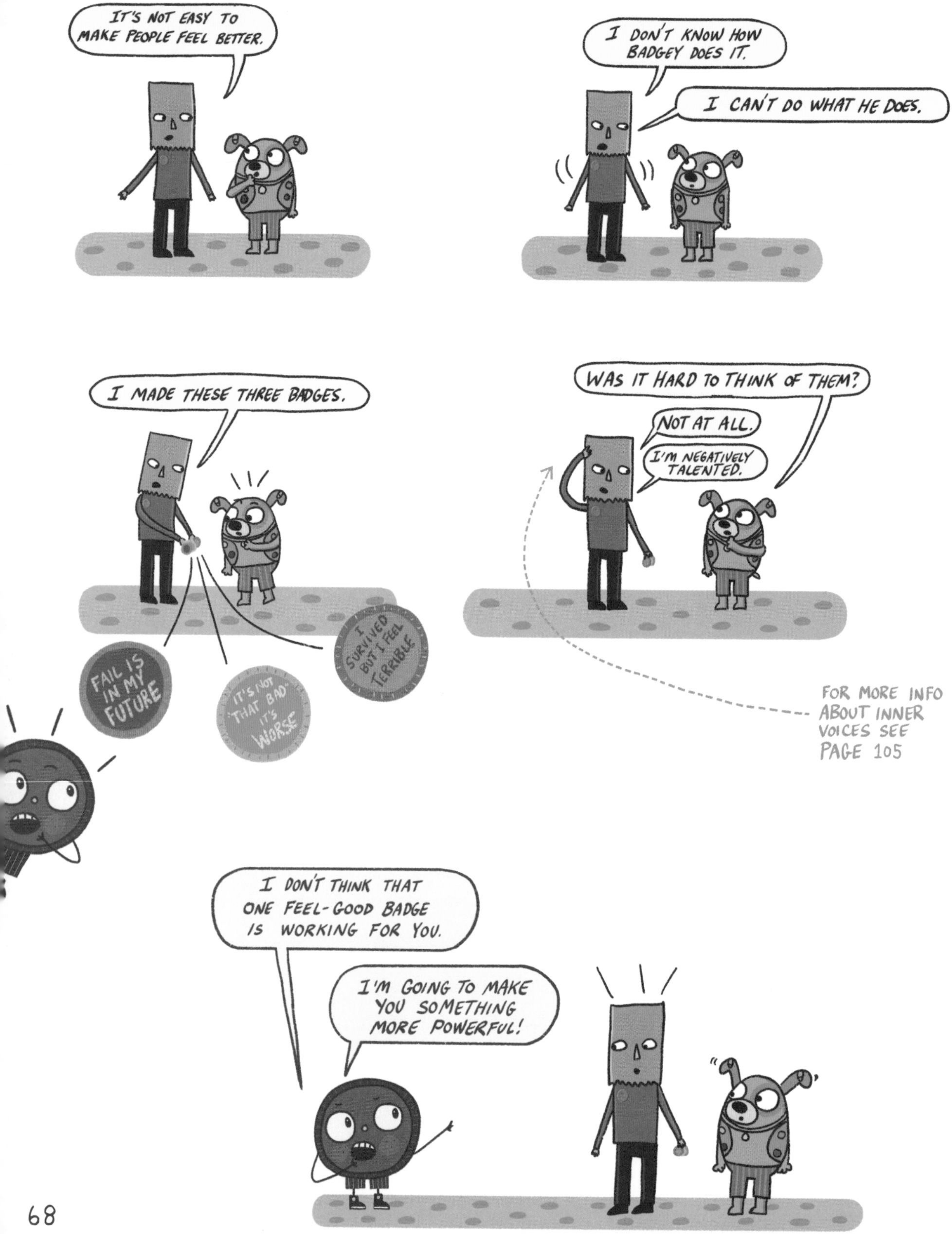
IT'S NOT EASY TO MAKE PEOPLE FEEL BETTER.
I DON'T KNOW HOW BADGEY DOES IT.
I CAN'T DO WHAT HE DOES.
I MADE THESE THREE BADGES.
FAIL IS IN MY FUTURE
IT'S NOT "THAT BAD" IT'S WORSE
I SURVIVED BUT I FEEL TERRIBLE
WAS IT HARD TO THINK OF THEM?
NOT AT ALL.
I'M NEGATIVELY TALENTED.
I DON'T THINK THAT ONE FEEL-GOOD BADGE IS WORKING FOR YOU.
I'M GOING TO MAKE YOU SOMETHING MORE POWERFUL!

FOR MORE INFO ABOUT INNER VOICES SEE PAGE 105

6

DANGER ZONE—PIP

PARENTS IN PUBLIC

WARNING

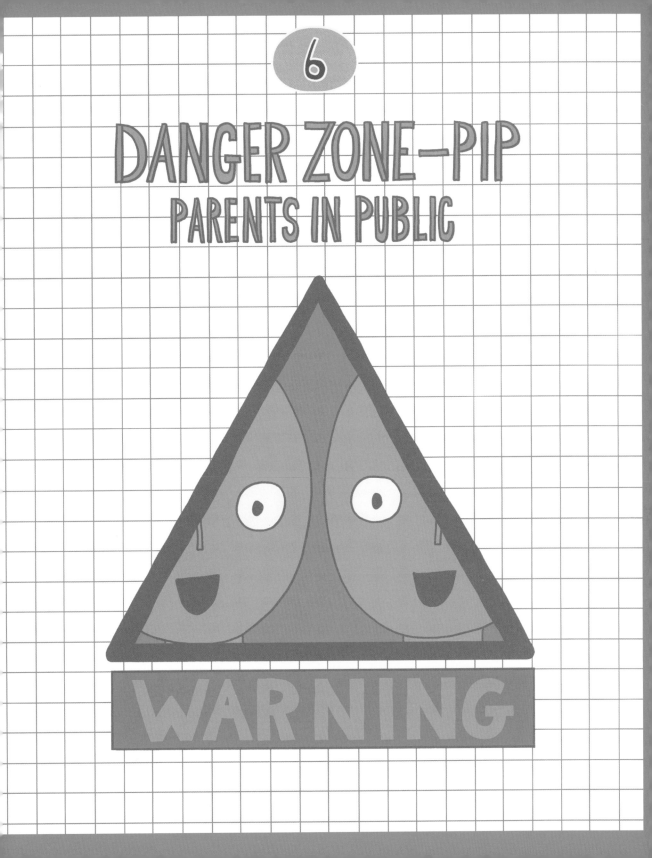

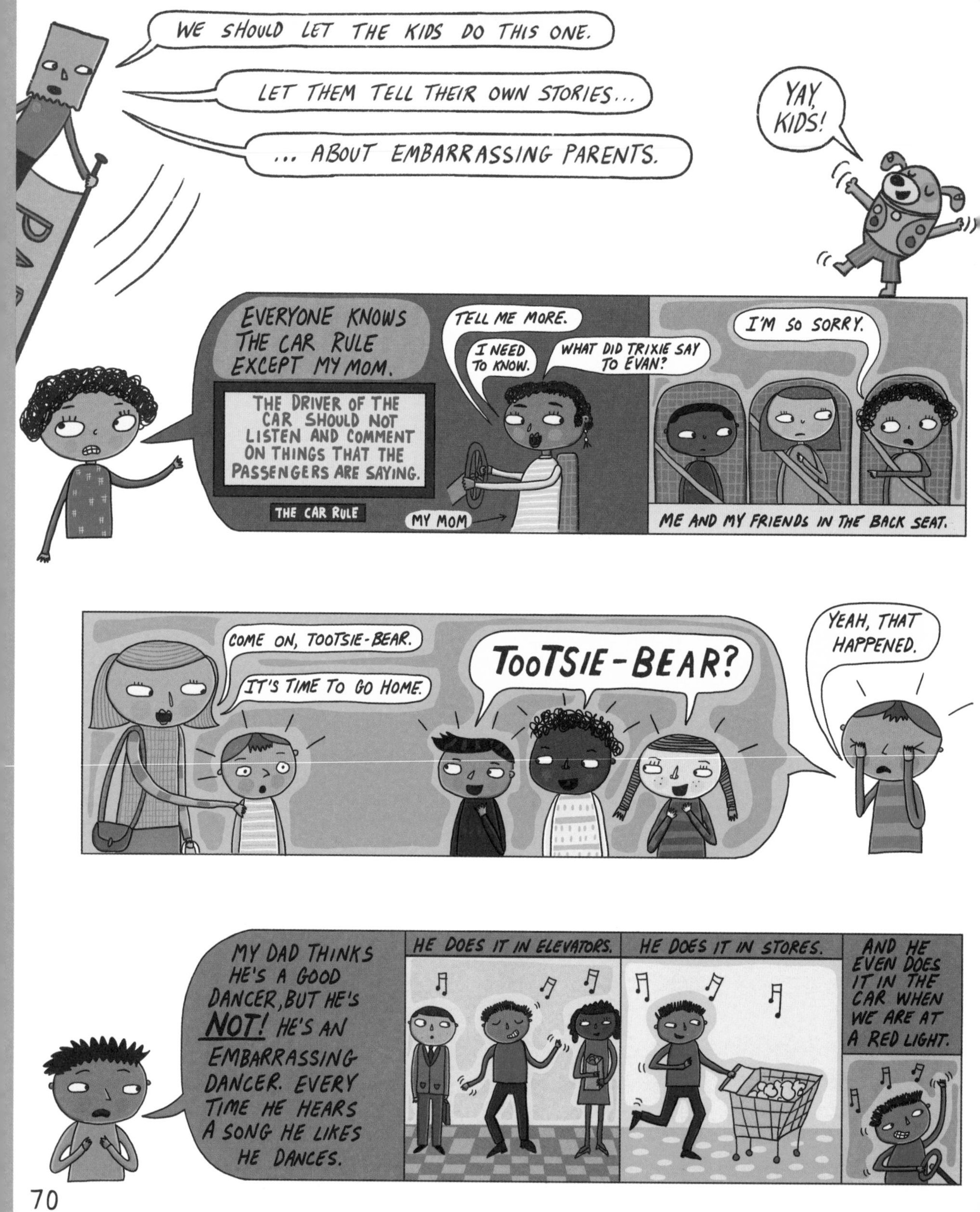

WE SHOULD LET THE KIDS DO THIS ONE.
LET THEM TELL THEIR OWN STORIES...
... ABOUT EMBARRASSING PARENTS.
YAY, KIDS!
EVERYONE KNOWS THE CAR RULE EXCEPT MY MOM.
THE DRIVER OF THE CAR SHOULD NOT LISTEN AND COMMENT ON THINGS THAT THE PASSENGERS ARE SAYING.
THE CAR RULE
TELL ME MORE.
I NEED TO KNOW.
WHAT DID TRIXIE SAY TO EVAN?
MY MOM
I'M SO SORRY.
ME AND MY FRIENDS IN THE BACK SEAT.
COME ON, TOOTSIE-BEAR.
IT'S TIME TO GO HOME.
TOOTSIE-BEAR?
YEAH, THAT HAPPENED.
MY DAD THINKS HE'S A GOOD DANCER, BUT HE'S NOT! HE'S AN EMBARRASSING DANCER. EVERY TIME HE HEARS A SONG HE LIKES HE DANCES.
HE DOES IT IN ELEVATORS.
HE DOES IT IN STORES.
AND HE EVEN DOES IT IN THE CAR WHEN WE ARE AT A RED LIGHT.

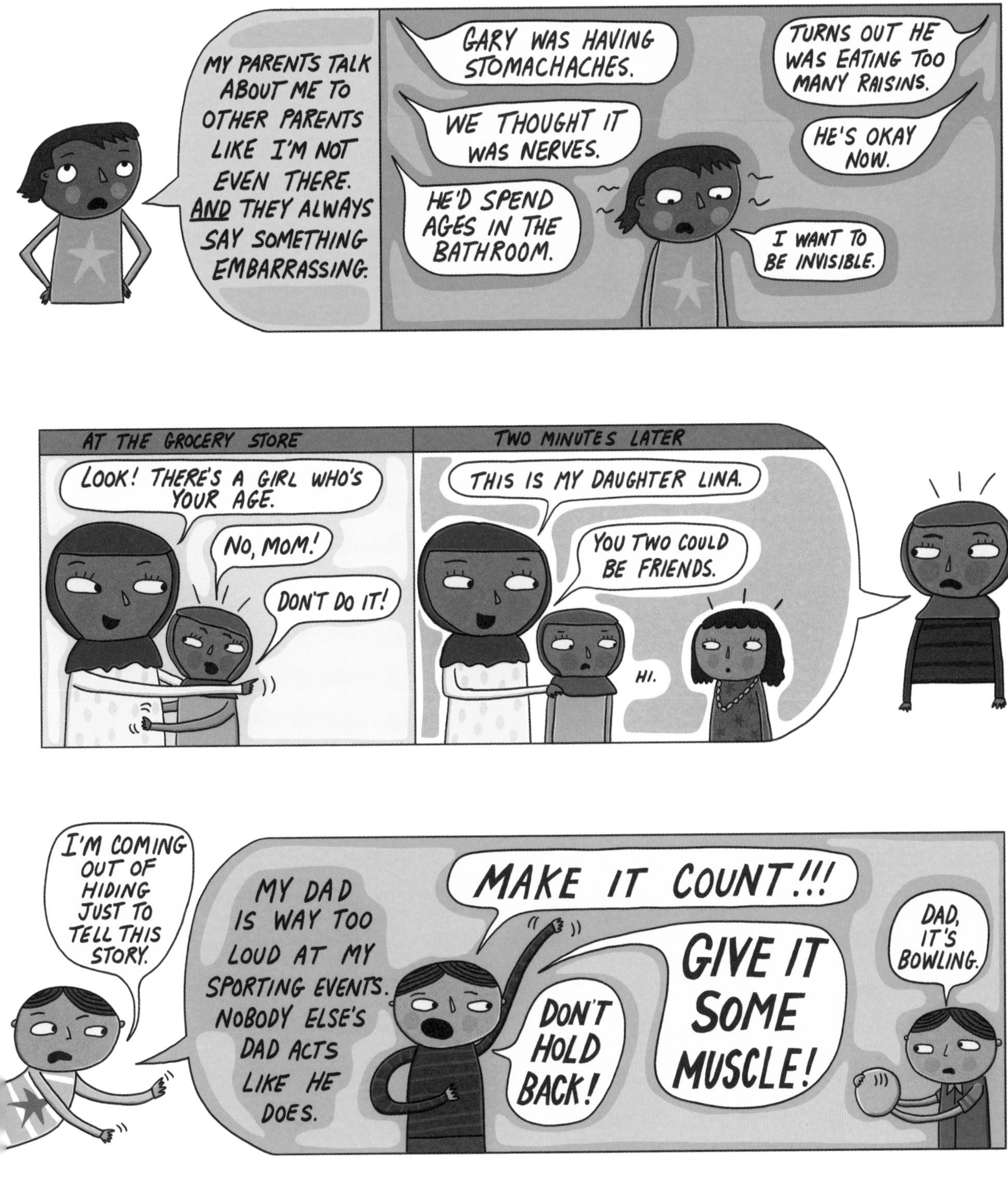
MY PARENTS TALK ABOUT ME TO OTHER PARENTS LIKE I'M NOT EVEN THERE. AND THEY ALWAYS SAY SOMETHING EMBARRASSING.
GARY WAS HAVING STOMACHACHES.
WE THOUGHT IT WAS NERVES.
HE'D SPEND AGES IN THE BATHROOM.
TURNS OUT HE WAS EATING TOO MANY RAISINS.
HE'S OKAY NOW.
I WANT TO BE INVISIBLE.
AT THE GROCERY STORE
LOOK! THERE'S A GIRL WHO'S YOUR AGE.
NO, MOM!
DON'T DO IT!
TWO MINUTES LATER
THIS IS MY DAUGHTER LINA.
YOU TWO COULD BE FRIENDS.
HI.
I'M COMING OUT OF HIDING JUST TO TELL THIS STORY.
MY DAD IS WAY TOO LOUD AT MY SPORTING EVENTS. NOBODY ELSE'S DAD ACTS LIKE HE DOES.
MAKE IT COUNT!!!
DON'T HOLD BACK!
GIVE IT SOME MUSCLE!
DAD, IT'S BOWLING.

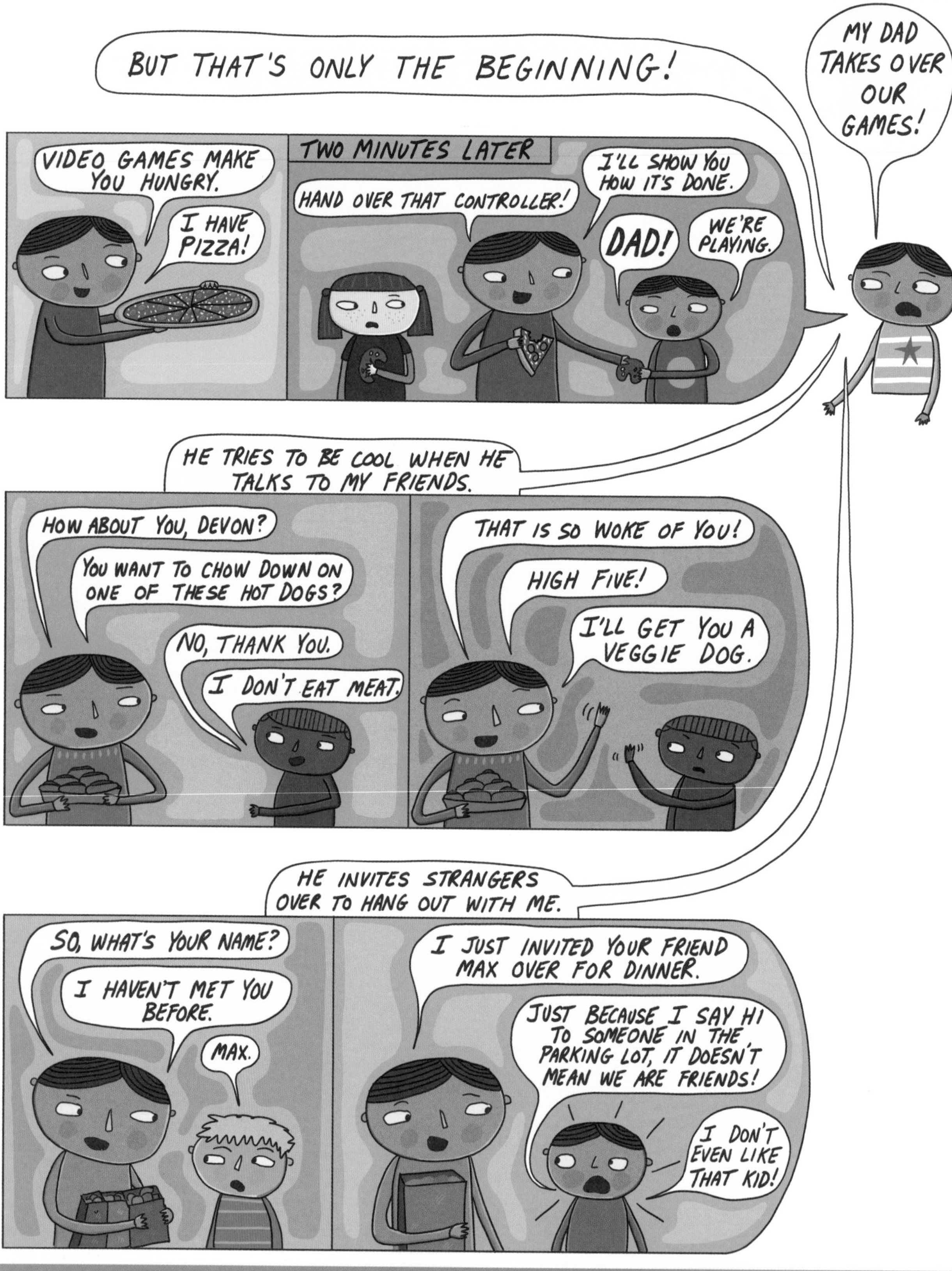
BUT THAT'S ONLY THE BEGINNING!
MY DAD TAKES OVER OUR GAMES!
VIDEO GAMES MAKE YOU HUNGRY.
I HAVE PIZZA!
TWO MINUTES LATER
HAND OVER THAT CONTROLLER!
I'LL SHOW YOU HOW IT'S DONE.
DAD!
WE'RE PLAYING.
HE TRIES TO BE COOL WHEN HE TALKS TO MY FRIENDS.
HOW ABOUT YOU, DEVON?
YOU WANT TO CHOW DOWN ON ONE OF THESE HOT DOGS?
NO, THANK YOU.
I DON'T EAT MEAT.
THAT IS SO WOKE OF YOU!
HIGH FIVE!
I'LL GET YOU A VEGGIE DOG.
HE INVITES STRANGERS OVER TO HANG OUT WITH ME.
SO, WHAT'S YOUR NAME?
I HAVEN'T MET YOU BEFORE.
MAX.
I JUST INVITED YOUR FRIEND MAX OVER FOR DINNER.
JUST BECAUSE I SAY HI TO SOMEONE IN THE PARKING LOT, IT DOESN'T MEAN WE ARE FRIENDS!
I DON'T EVEN LIKE THAT KID!

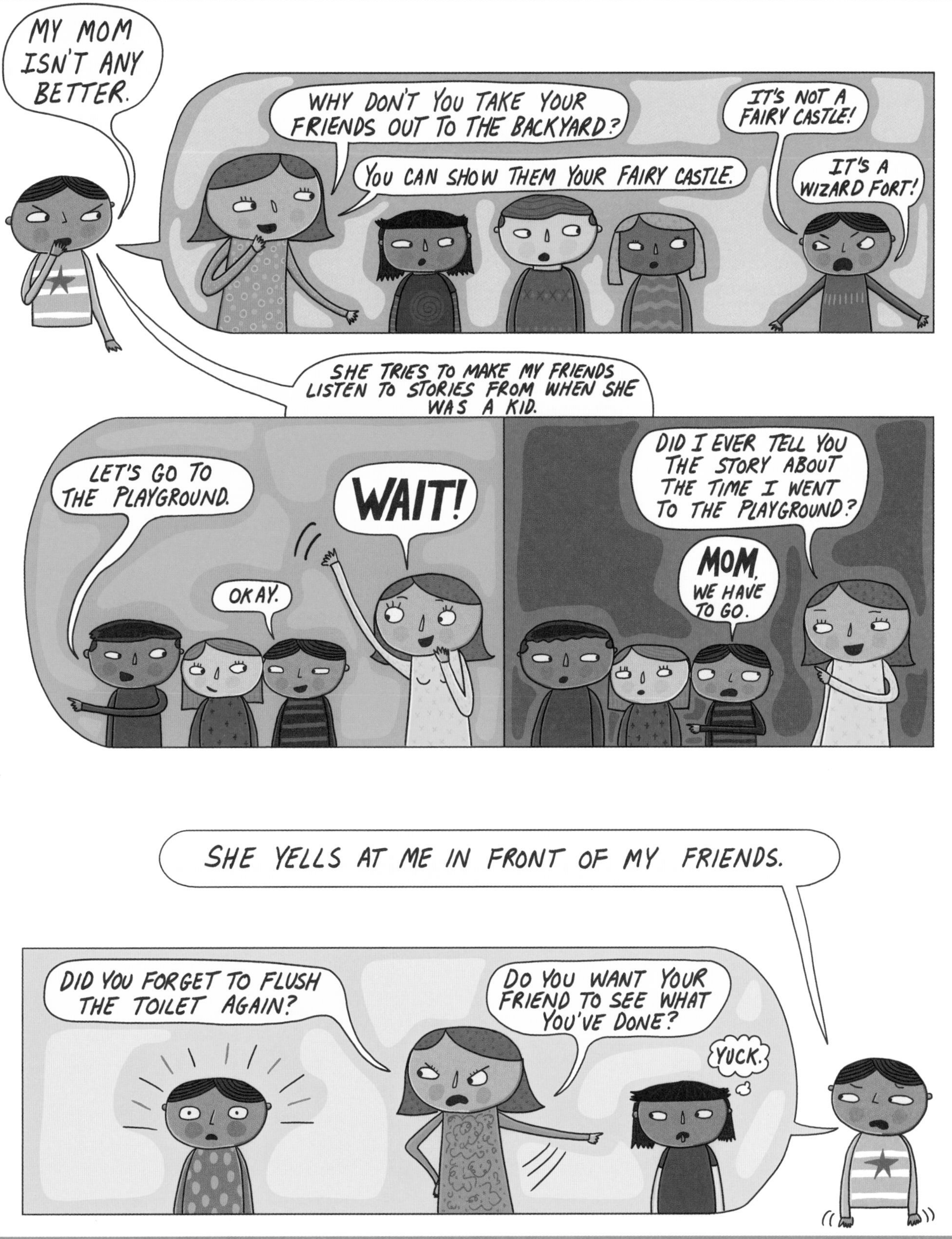
MY MOM ISN'T ANY BETTER.
WHY DON'T YOU TAKE YOUR FRIENDS OUT TO THE BACKYARD?
YOU CAN SHOW THEM YOUR FAIRY CASTLE.
IT'S NOT A FAIRY CASTLE!
IT'S A WIZARD FORT!
SHE TRIES TO MAKE MY FRIENDS LISTEN TO STORIES FROM WHEN SHE WAS A KID.
LET'S GO TO THE PLAYGROUND.
OKAY.
WAIT!
DID I EVER TELL YOU THE STORY ABOUT THE TIME I WENT TO THE PLAYGROUND?
MOM, WE HAVE TO GO.
SHE YELLS AT ME IN FRONT OF MY FRIENDS.
DID YOU FORGET TO FLUSH THE TOILET AGAIN?
DO YOU WANT YOUR FRIEND TO SEE WHAT YOU'VE DONE?
YUCK.

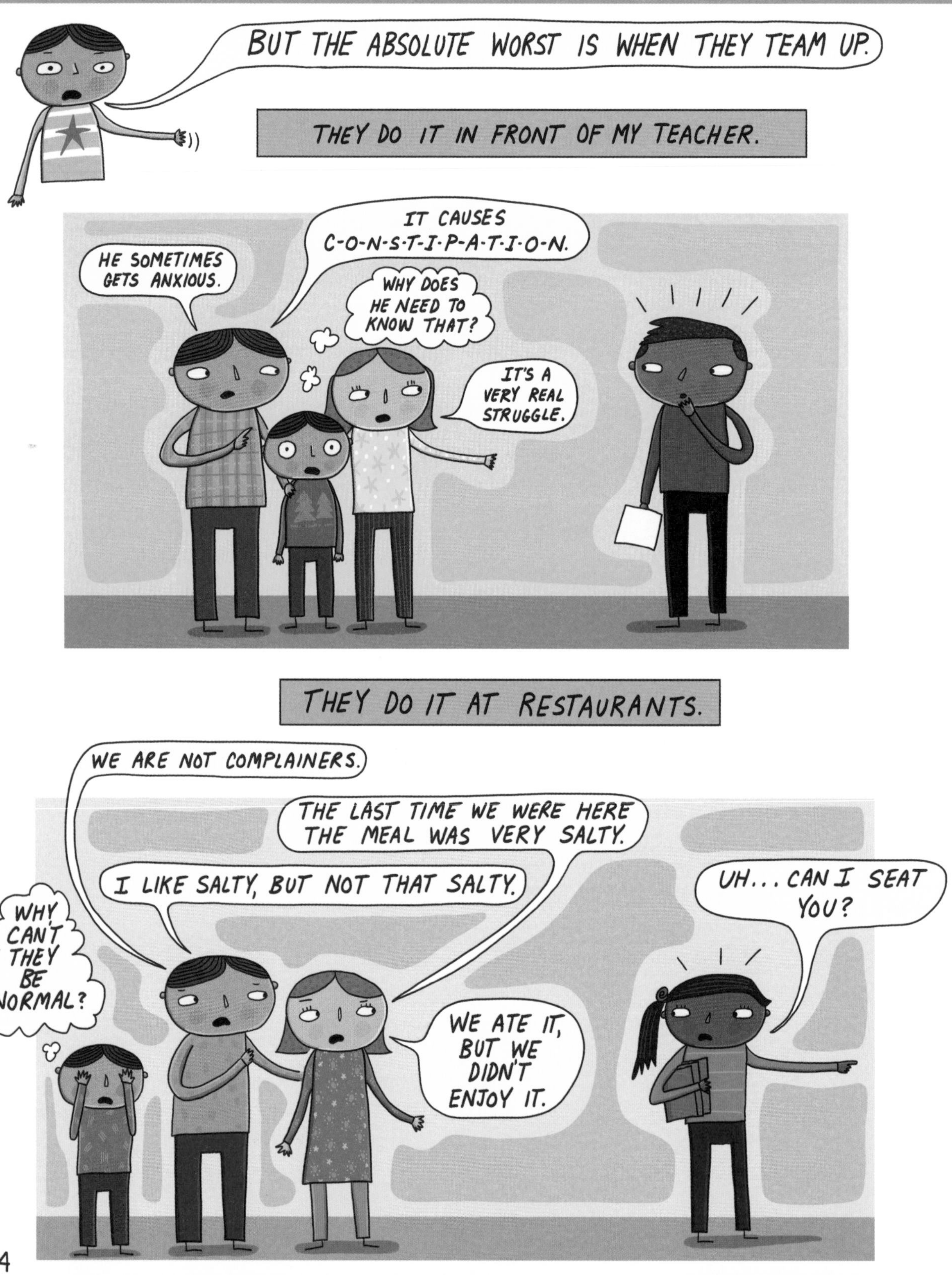
BUT THE ABSOLUTE WORST IS WHEN THEY TEAM UP.
THEY DO IT IN FRONT OF MY TEACHER.
HE SOMETIMES GETS ANXIOUS.
IT CAUSES C-O-N-S-T-I-P-A-T-I-O-N.
WHY DOES HE NEED TO KNOW THAT?
IT'S A VERY REAL STRUGGLE.
THEY DO IT AT RESTAURANTS.
WE ARE NOT COMPLAINERS.
THE LAST TIME WE WERE HERE THE MEAL WAS VERY SALTY.
I LIKE SALTY, BUT NOT THAT SALTY.
WHY CAN'T THEY BE NORMAL?
WE ATE IT, BUT WE DIDN'T ENJOY IT.
UH... CAN I SEAT YOU?

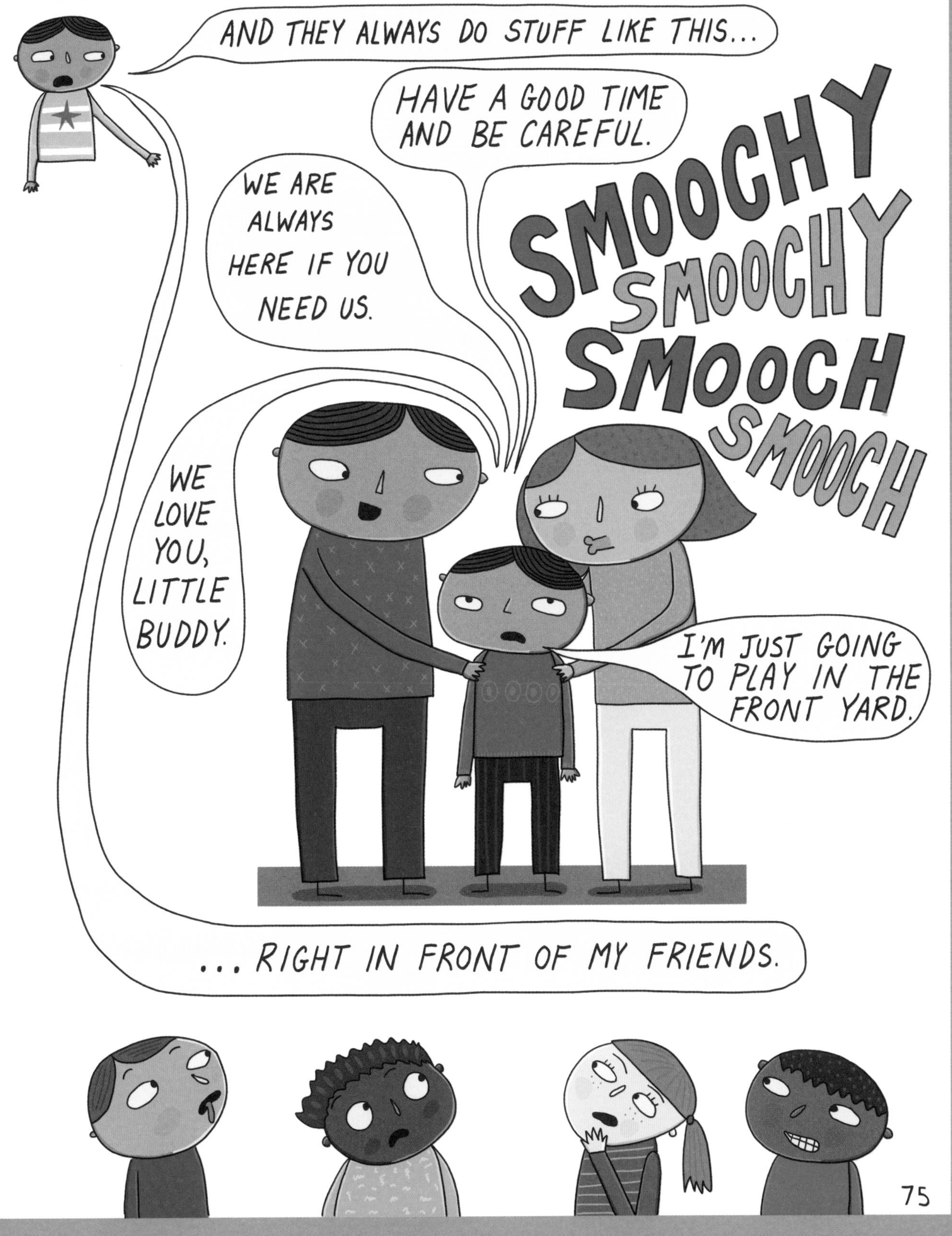
AND THEY ALWAYS DO STUFF LIKE THIS...
HAVE A GOOD TIME AND BE CAREFUL.
WE ARE ALWAYS HERE IF YOU NEED US.
WE LOVE YOU, LITTLE BUDDY.
SMOOCHY SMOOCHY SMOOCH SMOOCH
I'M JUST GOING TO PLAY IN THE FRONT YARD.
... RIGHT IN FRONT OF MY FRIENDS.

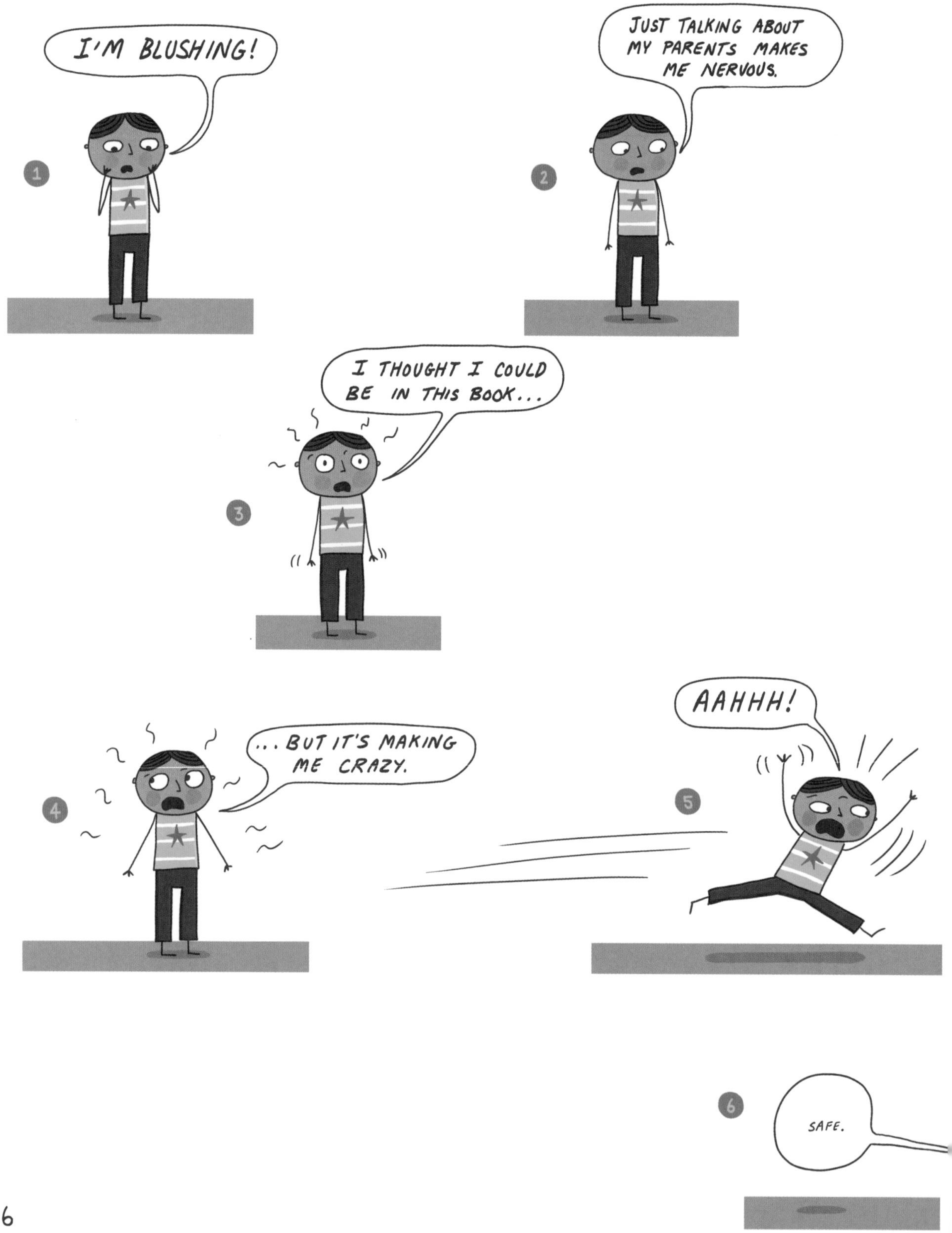
1
I'M BLUSHING!
2
JUST TALKING ABOUT MY PARENTS MAKES ME NERVOUS.
3
I THOUGHT I COULD BE IN THIS BOOK...
4
...BUT IT'S MAKING ME CRAZY.
5
AAHHH!
6
SAFE.

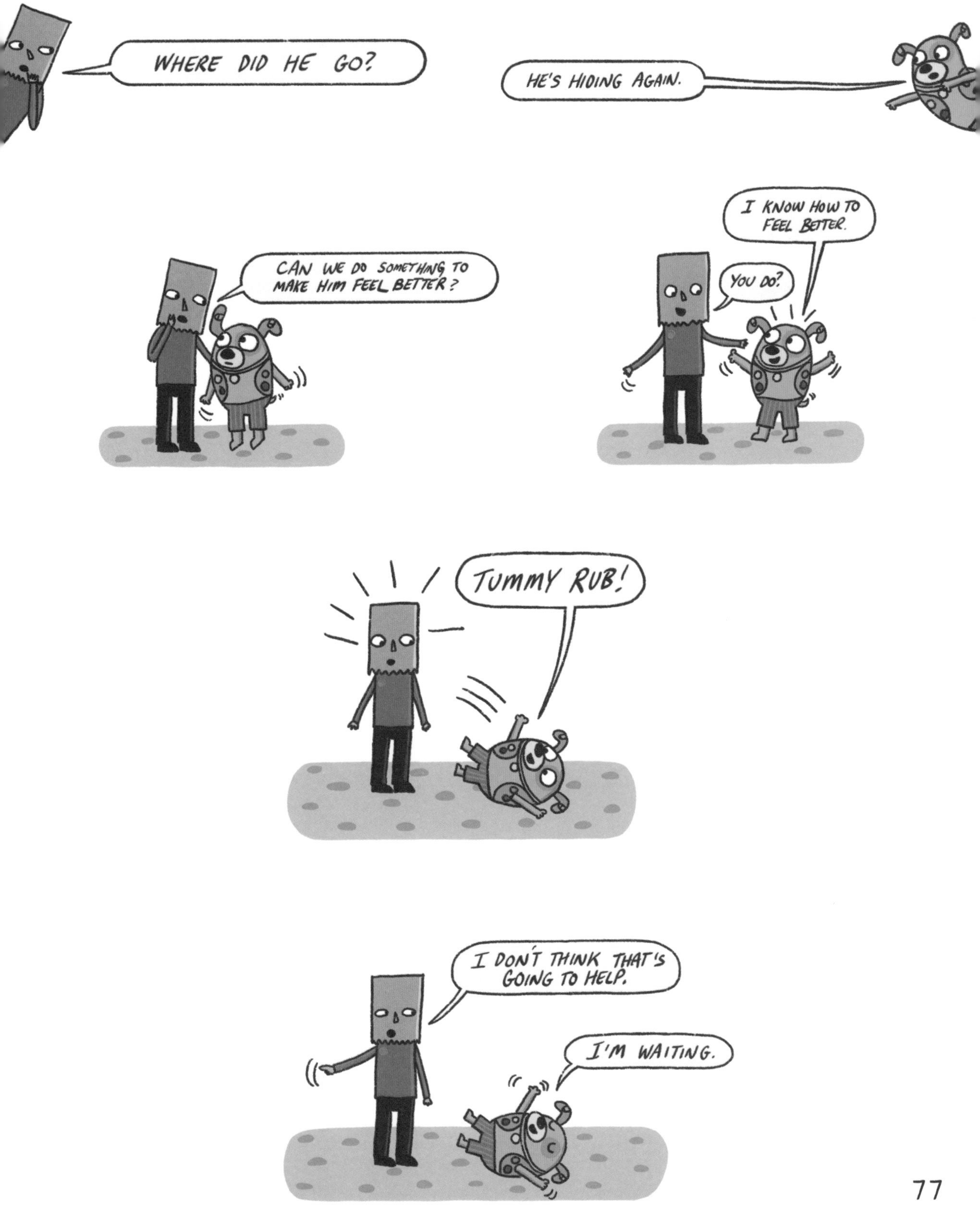
WHERE DID HE GO?
HE'S HIDING AGAIN.
CAN WE DO SOMETHING TO MAKE HIM FEEL BETTER?
I KNOW HOW TO FEEL BETTER.
YOU DO?
TUMMY RUB!
I DON'T THINK THAT'S GOING TO HELP.
I'M WAITING.

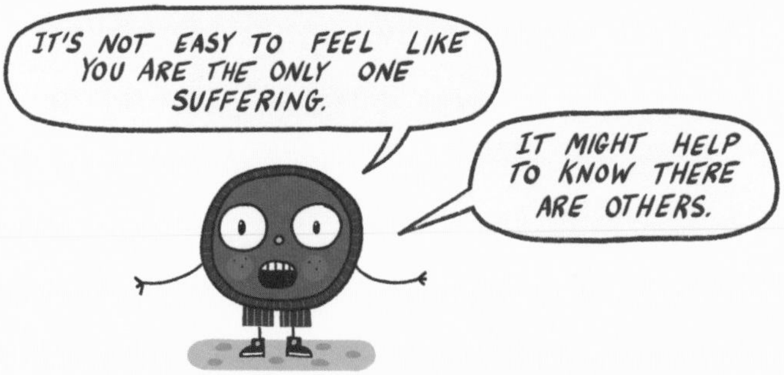
IT'S NOT EASY TO FEEL LIKE YOU ARE THE ONLY ONE SUFFERING.
IT MIGHT HELP TO KNOW THERE ARE OTHERS.

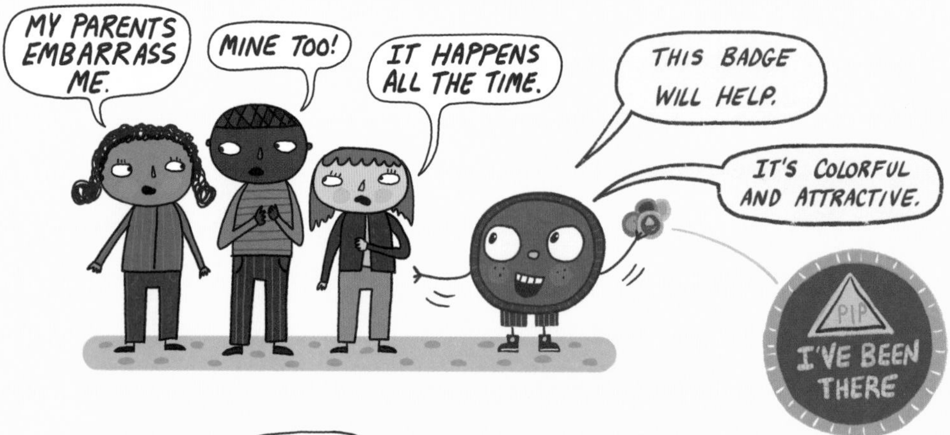
MY PARENTS EMBARRASS ME.
MINE TOO!
IT HAPPENS ALL THE TIME.
THIS BADGE WILL HELP.
IT'S COLORFUL AND ATTRACTIVE.
PIP
I'VE BEEN THERE

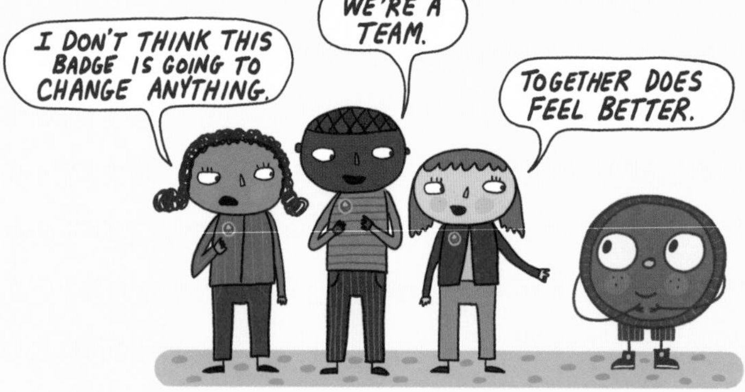
I DON'T THINK THIS BADGE IS GOING TO CHANGE ANYTHING.
WE'RE A TEAM.
TOGETHER DOES FEEL BETTER.

TRUE FACT SHARING YOUR EXPERIENCES WITH OTHERS WHO ARE FACING SIMILAR CHALLENGES CAN INCREASE YOUR OWN ABILITY TO HANDLE THINGS.

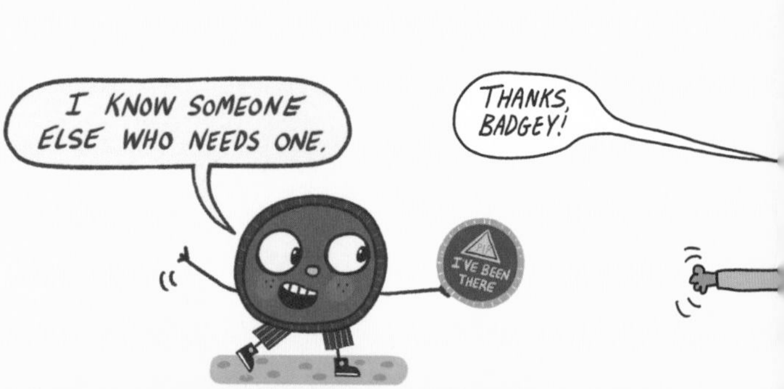
I KNOW SOMEONE ELSE WHO NEEDS ONE.
THANKS, BADGEY!
I'VE BEEN THERE

 THIS PAGE WAS PAID FOR AND APPROVED BY BADGEY BADGES.

7

THE SECRET IS OUT

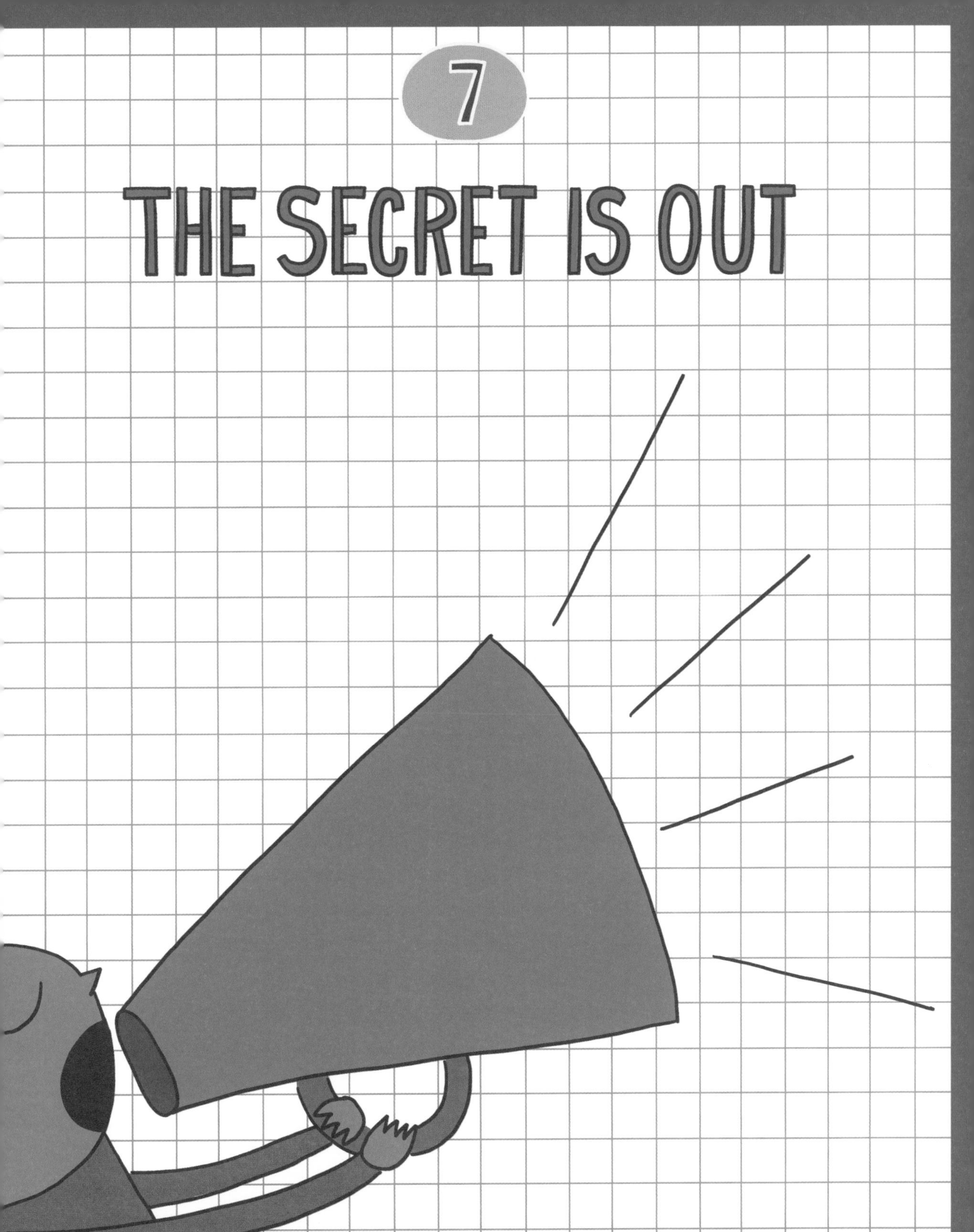

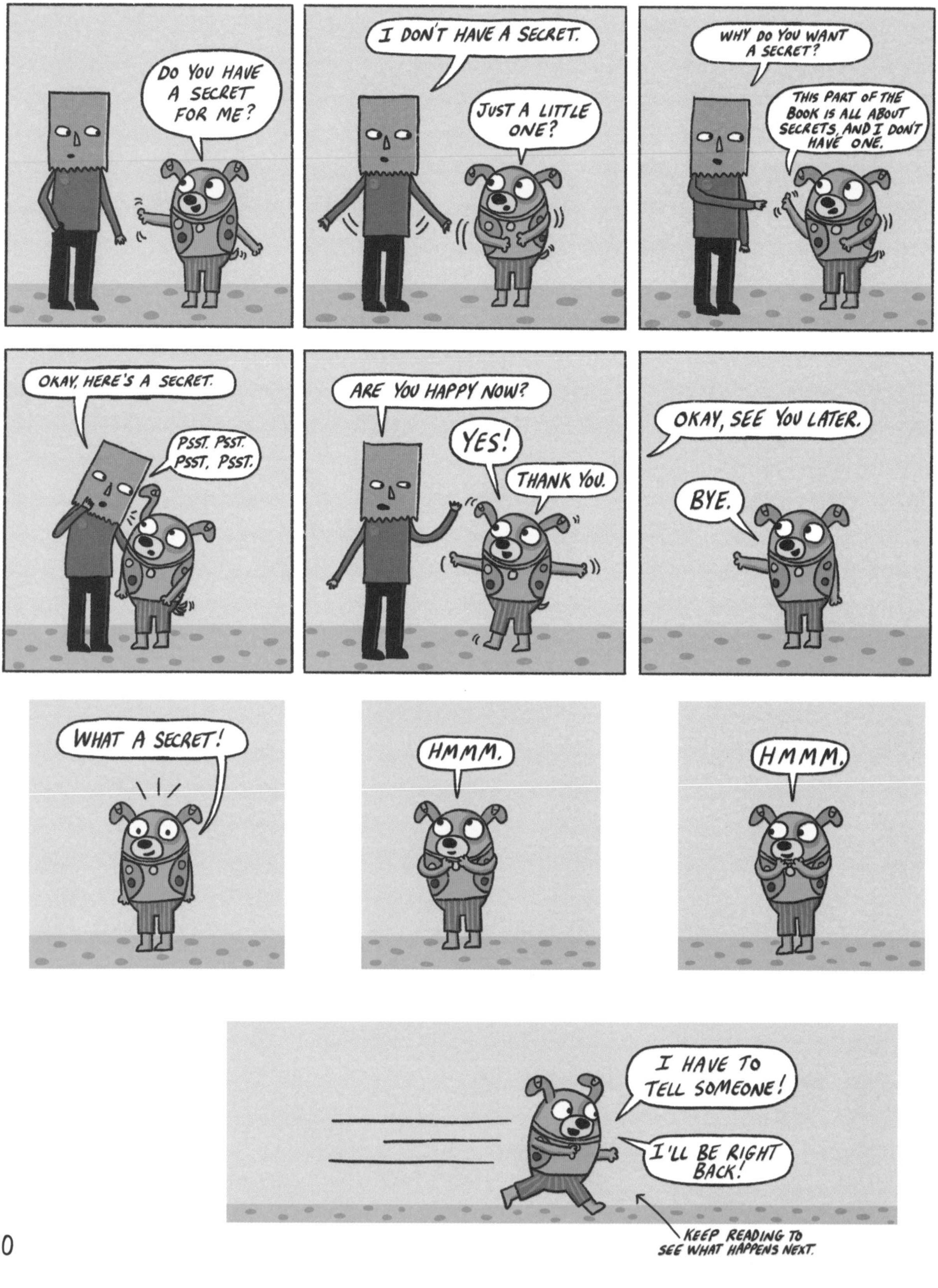
DO YOU HAVE A SECRET FOR ME?
I DON'T HAVE A SECRET.
JUST A LITTLE ONE?
WHY DO YOU WANT A SECRET?
THIS PART OF THE BOOK IS ALL ABOUT SECRETS, AND I DON'T HAVE ONE.
OKAY, HERE'S A SECRET.
PSST. PSST. PSST, PSST.
ARE YOU HAPPY NOW?
YES!
THANK YOU.
OKAY, SEE YOU LATER.
BYE.
WHAT A SECRET!
HMMM.
HMMM.
I HAVE TO TELL SOMEONE!
I'LL BE RIGHT BACK!
KEEP READING TO SEE WHAT HAPPENS NEXT.

A SECRET WARNING

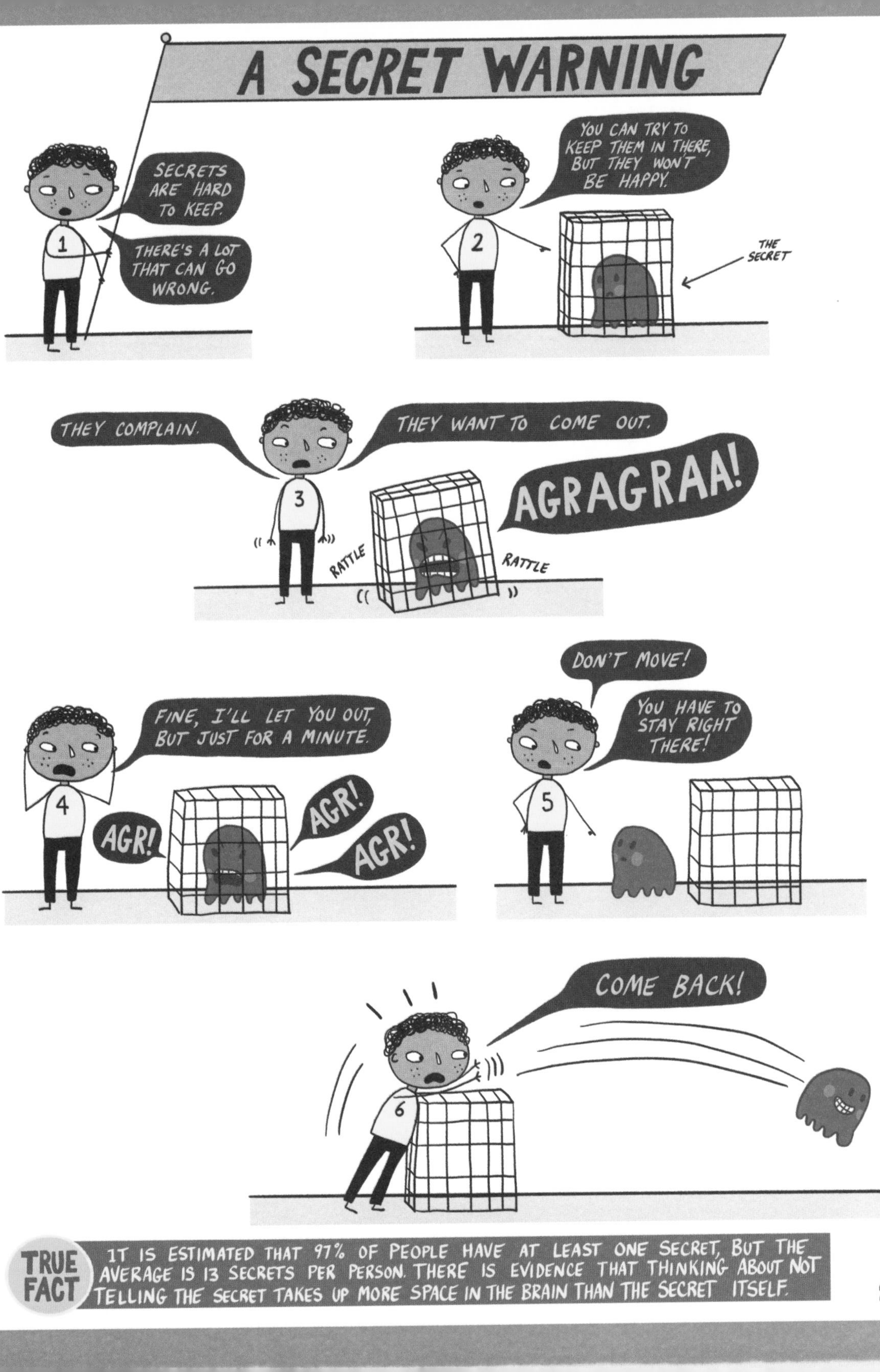
SECRETS ARE HARD TO KEEP.
THERE'S A LOT THAT CAN GO WRONG.
1
YOU CAN TRY TO KEEP THEM IN THERE, BUT THEY WON'T BE HAPPY.
2
THE SECRET
THEY COMPLAIN.
THEY WANT TO COME OUT.
3
AGRAGRAA!
RATTLE
RATTLE
FINE, I'LL LET YOU OUT, BUT JUST FOR A MINUTE.
4
AGR!
AGR!
AGR!
DON'T MOVE!
YOU HAVE TO STAY RIGHT THERE!
5
COME BACK!
6

TRUE FACT IT IS ESTIMATED THAT 97% OF PEOPLE HAVE AT LEAST ONE SECRET, BUT THE AVERAGE IS 13 SECRETS PER PERSON. THERE IS EVIDENCE THAT THINKING ABOUT NOT TELLING THE SECRET TAKES UP MORE SPACE IN THE BRAIN THAN THE SECRET ITSELF.

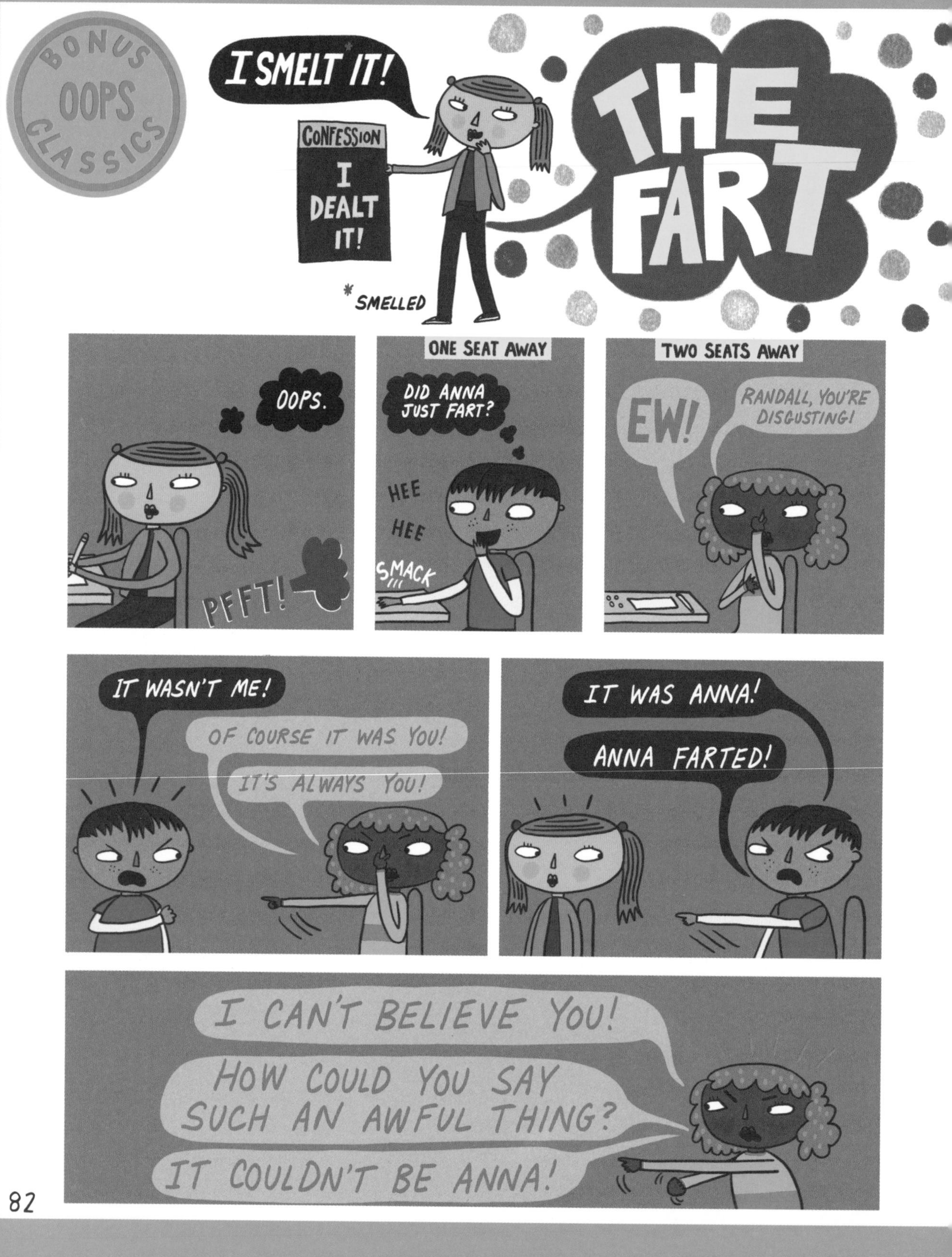

BONUS OOPS CLASSICS
I SMELT* IT!
CONFESSION
I DEALT IT!
*SMELLED
THE FART
OOPS.
PFFT!
ONE SEAT AWAY
DID ANNA JUST FART?
HEE
HEE
SMACK
TWO SEATS AWAY
EW!
RANDALL, YOU'RE DISGUSTING!
IT WASN'T ME!
OF COURSE IT WAS YOU!
IT'S ALWAYS YOU!
IT WAS ANNA!
ANNA FARTED!
I CAN'T BELIEVE YOU!
HOW COULD YOU SAY SUCH AN AWFUL THING?
IT COULDN'T BE ANNA!

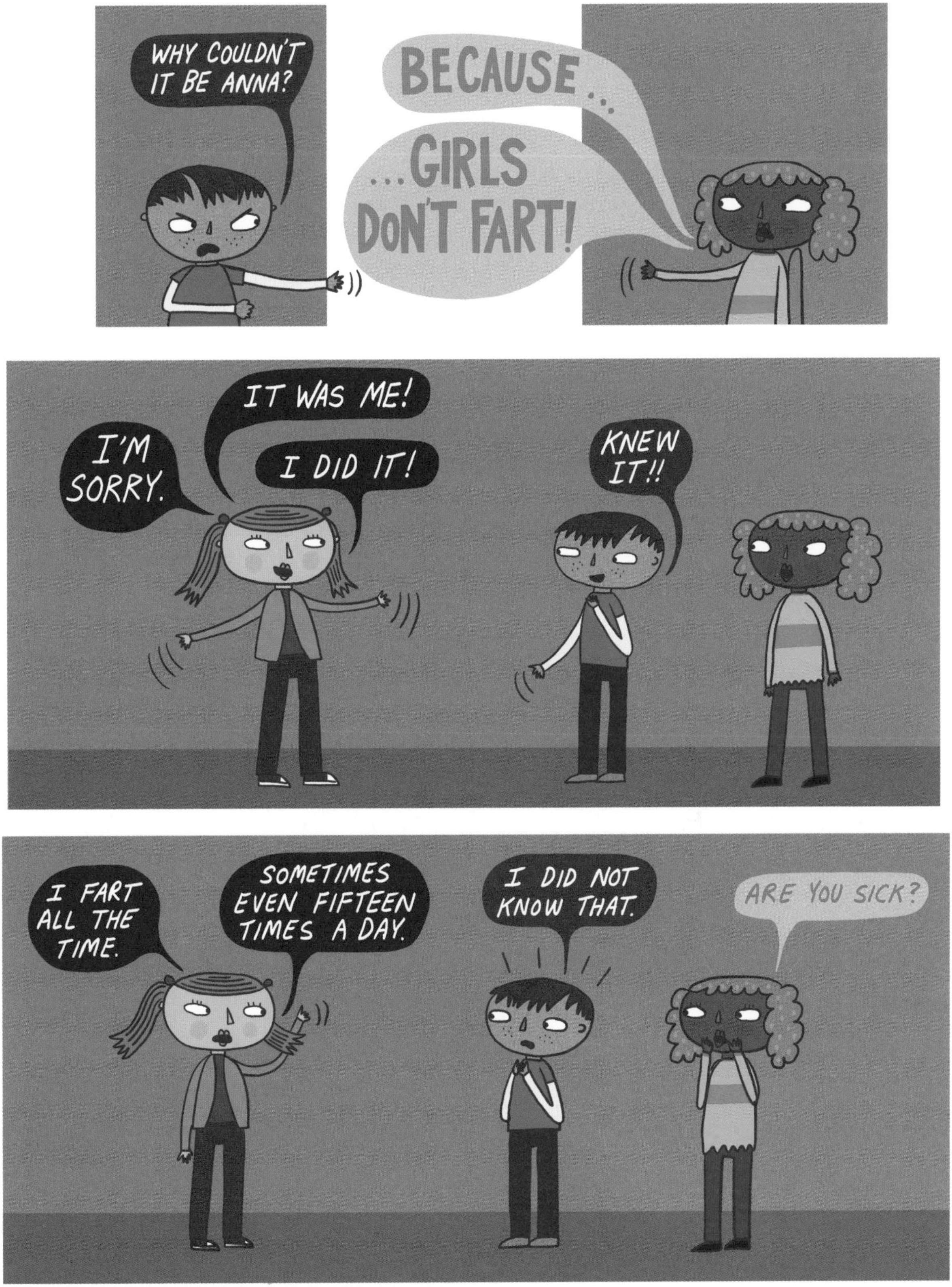
WHY COULDN'T IT BE ANNA?
BECAUSE...
...GIRLS DON'T FART!
I'M SORRY.
IT WAS ME!
I DID IT!
KNEW IT!!
I FART ALL THE TIME.
SOMETIMES EVEN FIFTEEN TIMES A DAY.
I DID NOT KNOW THAT.
ARE YOU SICK?

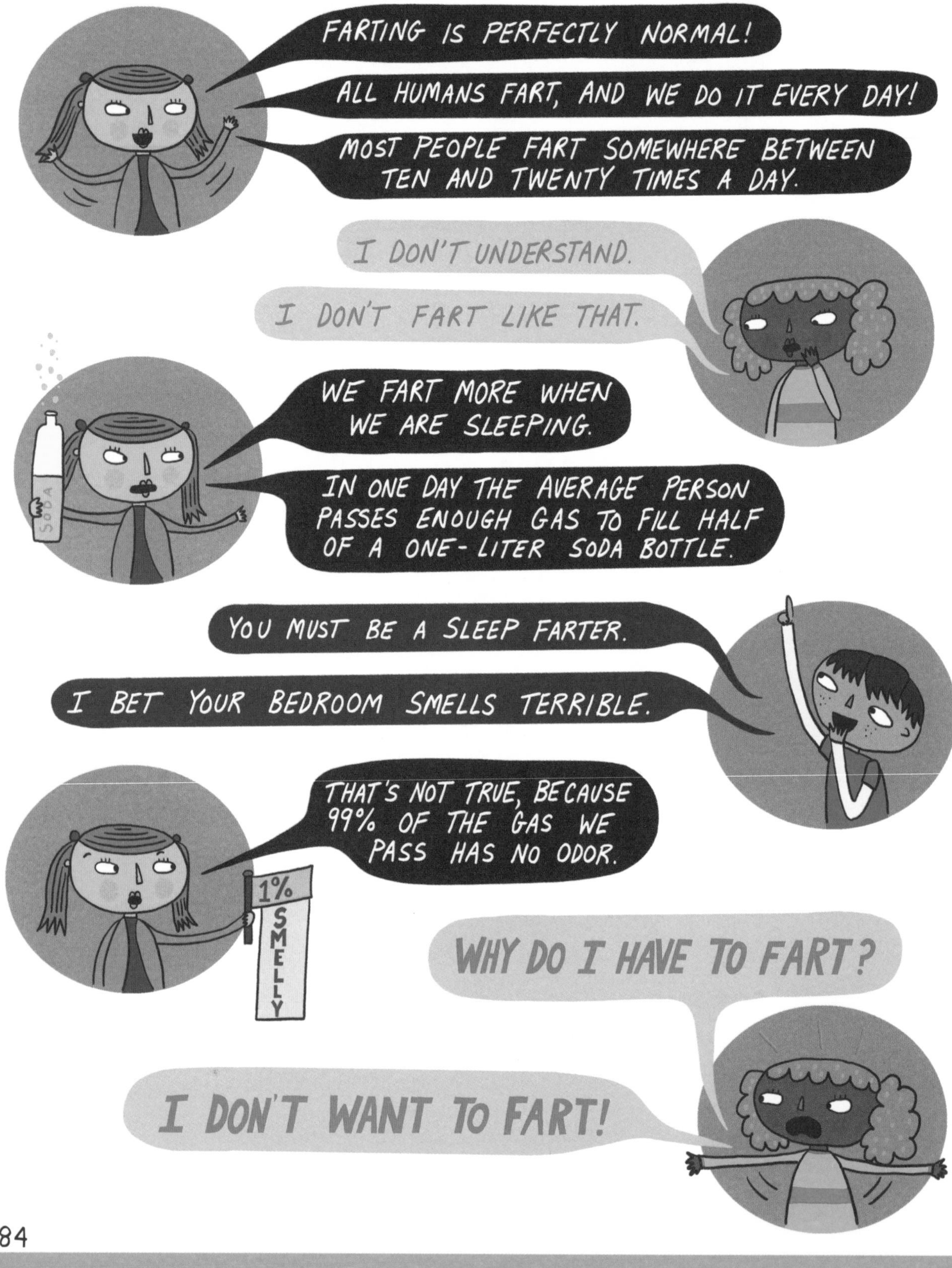
FARTING IS PERFECTLY NORMAL!
ALL HUMANS FART, AND WE DO IT EVERY DAY!
MOST PEOPLE FART SOMEWHERE BETWEEN TEN AND TWENTY TIMES A DAY.
I DON'T UNDERSTAND.
I DON'T FART LIKE THAT.
WE FART MORE WHEN WE ARE SLEEPING.
SODA
IN ONE DAY THE AVERAGE PERSON PASSES ENOUGH GAS TO FILL HALF OF A ONE-LITER SODA BOTTLE.
YOU MUST BE A SLEEP FARTER.
I BET YOUR BEDROOM SMELLS TERRIBLE.
THAT'S NOT TRUE, BECAUSE 99% OF THE GAS WE PASS HAS NO ODOR.
1%
SMELLY
WHY DO I HAVE TO FART?
I DON'T WANT TO FART!

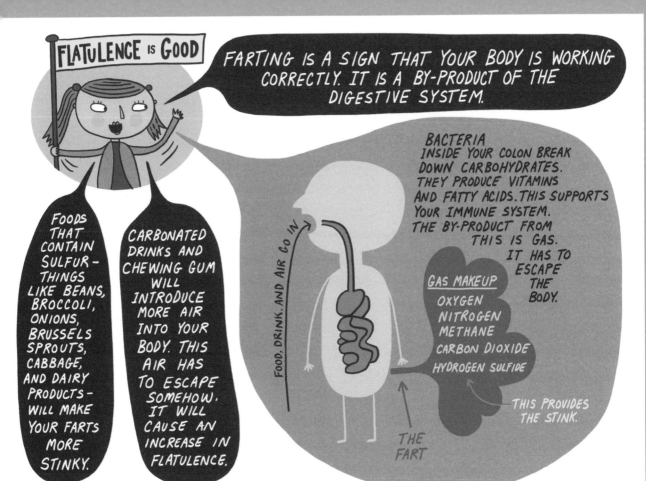

FLATULENCE IS GOOD

FARTING IS A SIGN THAT YOUR BODY IS WORKING CORRECTLY. IT IS A BY-PRODUCT OF THE DIGESTIVE SYSTEM.

FOODS THAT CONTAIN SULFUR—THINGS LIKE BEANS, BROCCOLI, ONIONS, BRUSSELS SPROUTS, CABBAGE, AND DAIRY PRODUCTS—WILL MAKE YOUR FARTS MORE STINKY.

CARBONATED DRINKS AND CHEWING GUM WILL INTRODUCE MORE AIR INTO YOUR BODY. THIS AIR HAS TO ESCAPE SOMEHOW. IT WILL CAUSE AN INCREASE IN FLATULENCE.

FOOD, DRINK, AND AIR GO IN

BACTERIA INSIDE YOUR COLON BREAK DOWN CARBOHYDRATES. THEY PRODUCE VITAMINS AND FATTY ACIDS. THIS SUPPORTS YOUR IMMUNE SYSTEM. THE BY-PRODUCT FROM THIS IS GAS. IT HAS TO ESCAPE THE BODY.

<u>GAS MAKEUP</u>
OXYGEN
NITROGEN
METHANE
CARBON DIOXIDE
HYDROGEN SULFIDE

THIS PROVIDES THE STINK.

THE FART

PRETTY GREAT, RIGHT?

OUR BODIES ARE AMAZING.

SOME PEOPLE DON'T DESERVE TO KNOW SCIENCE.

THANK YOU, BACTERIA

MY BUTT IS GOING TO DO AMAZING THINGS.

SODA

GUM GUM GUM

BEANS

MILK CABBAGE

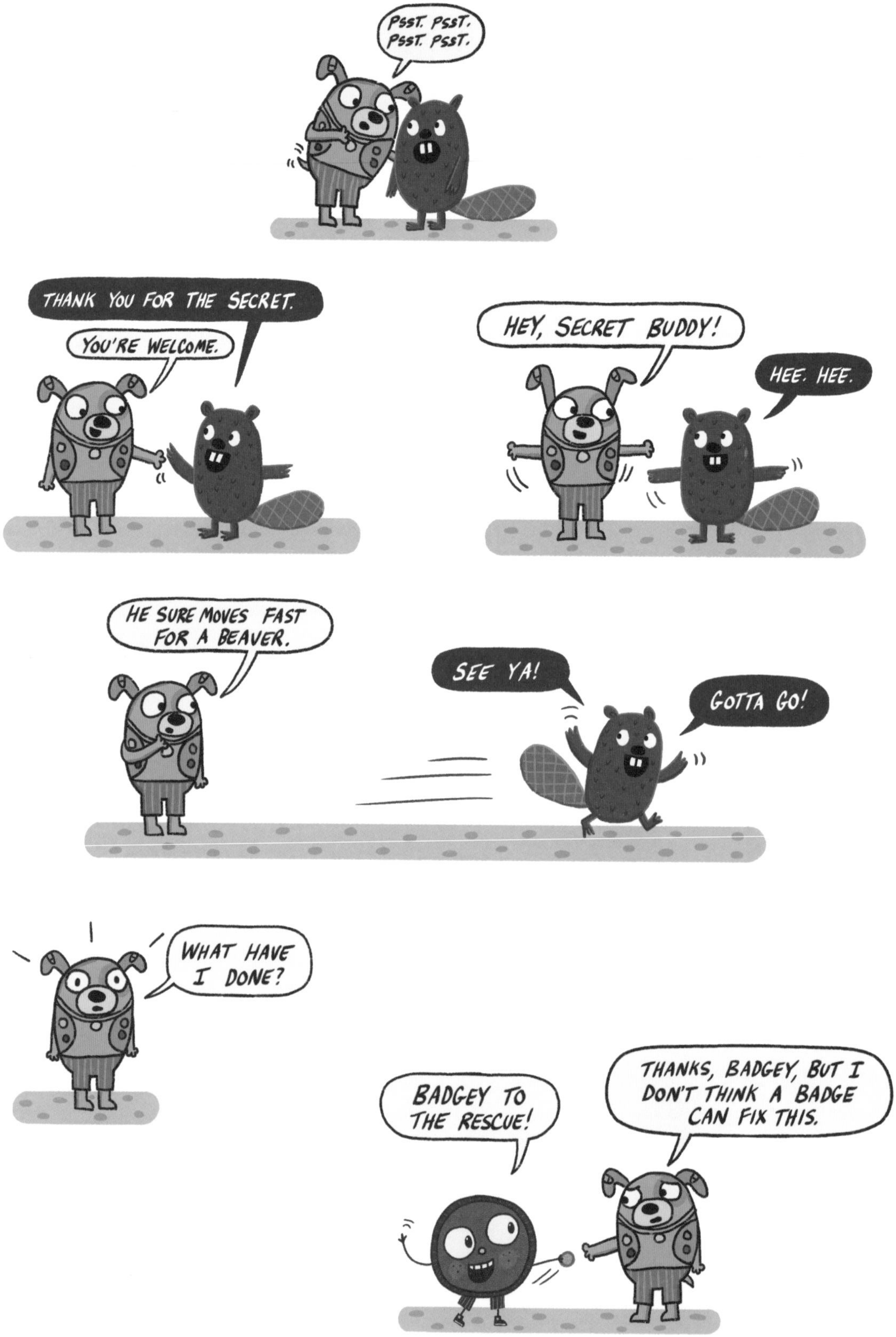
PSST. PSST.
PSST. PSST.
THANK YOU FOR THE SECRET.
YOU'RE WELCOME.
HEY, SECRET BUDDY!
HEE. HEE.
HE SURE MOVES FAST FOR A BEAVER.
SEE YA!
GOTTA GO!
WHAT HAVE I DONE?
BADGEY TO THE RESCUE!
THANKS, BADGEY, BUT I DON'T THINK A BADGE CAN FIX THIS.

8

ADVICE

THE OKAY, THE BAD, THE TERRIBLE

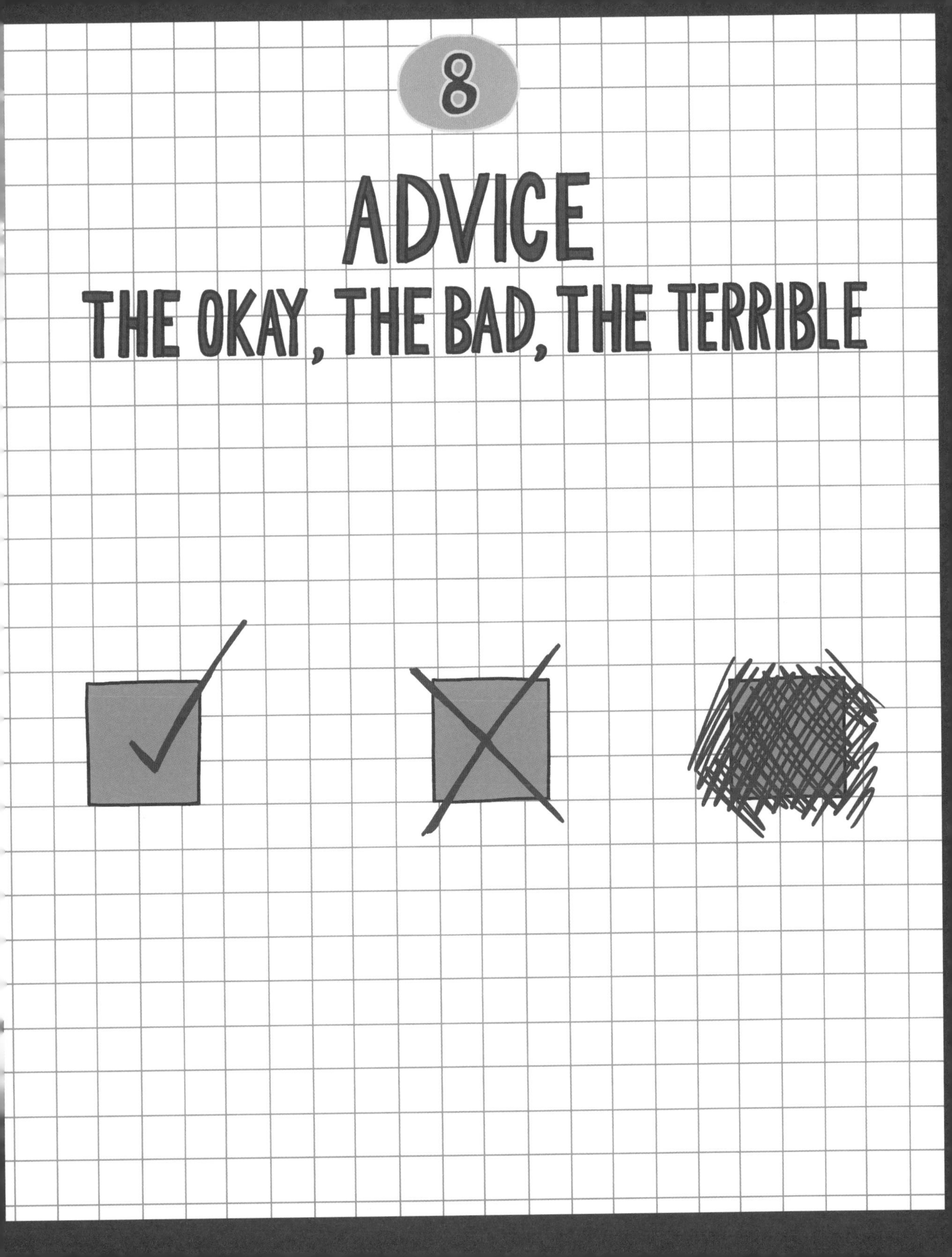

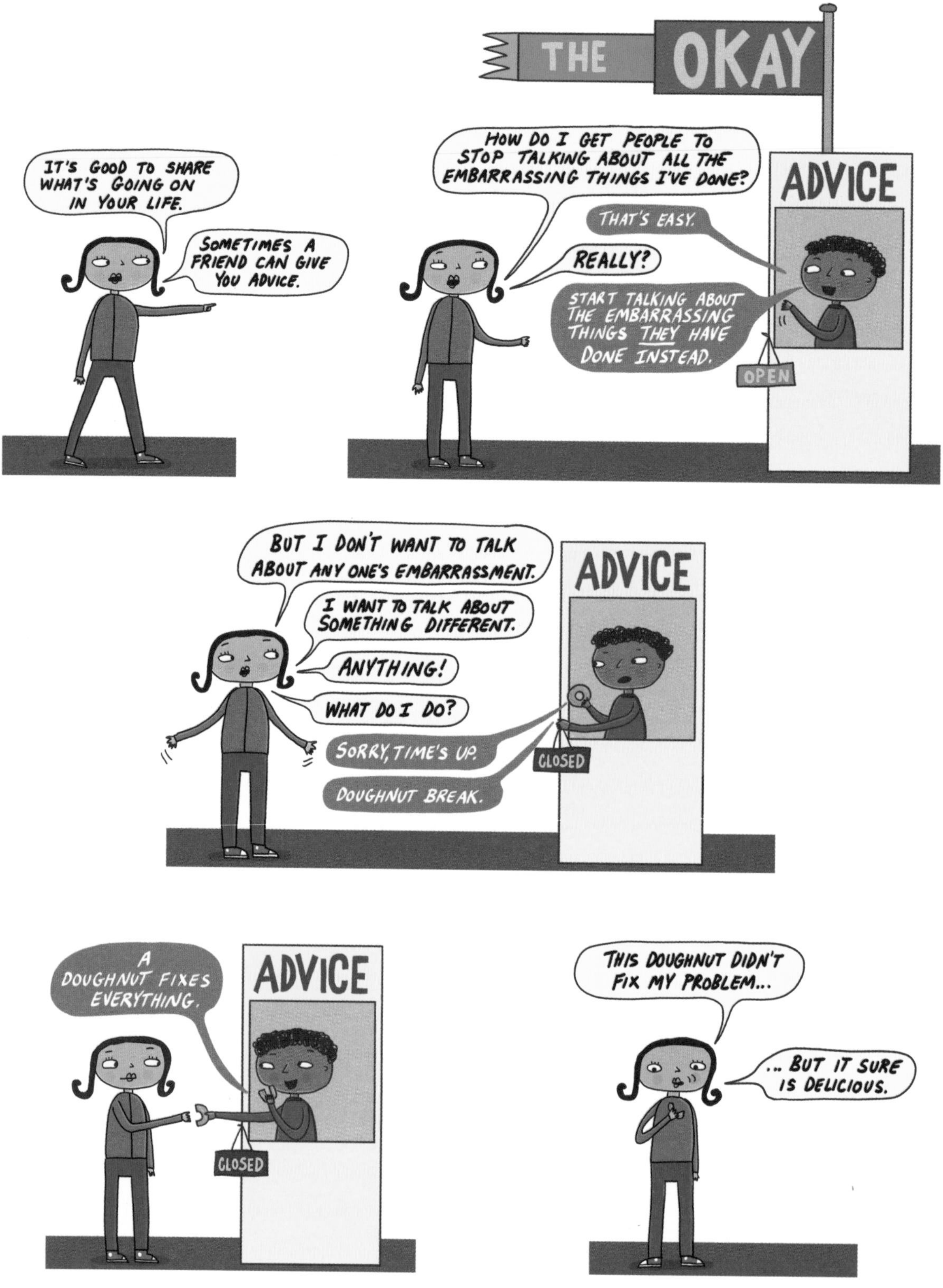
THE OKAY
ADVICE
IT'S GOOD TO SHARE WHAT'S GOING ON IN YOUR LIFE.
SOMETIMES A FRIEND CAN GIVE YOU ADVICE.
HOW DO I GET PEOPLE TO STOP TALKING ABOUT ALL THE EMBARRASSING THINGS I'VE DONE?
THAT'S EASY.
REALLY?
START TALKING ABOUT THE EMBARRASSING THINGS THEY HAVE DONE INSTEAD.
OPEN
BUT I DON'T WANT TO TALK ABOUT ANY ONE'S EMBARRASSMENT.
I WANT TO TALK ABOUT SOMETHING DIFFERENT.
ANYTHING!
WHAT DO I DO?
SORRY, TIME'S UP.
DOUGHNUT BREAK.
CLOSED
A DOUGHNUT FIXES EVERYTHING.
CLOSED
THIS DOUGHNUT DIDN'T FIX MY PROBLEM...
... BUT IT SURE IS DELICIOUS.

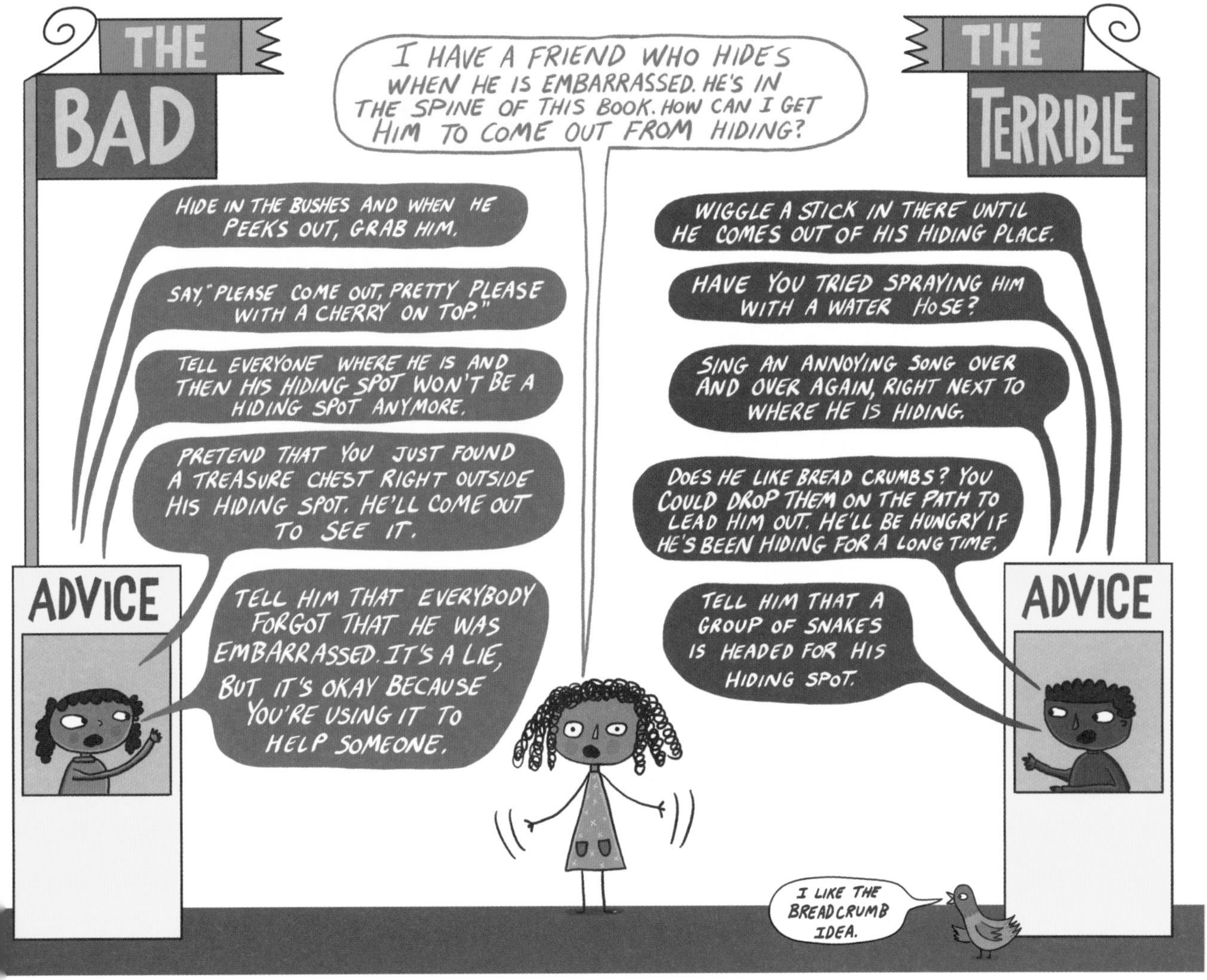
THE BAD
THE TERRIBLE
I HAVE A FRIEND WHO HIDES WHEN HE IS EMBARRASSED. HE'S IN THE SPINE OF THIS BOOK. HOW CAN I GET HIM TO COME OUT FROM HIDING?
HIDE IN THE BUSHES AND WHEN HE PEEKS OUT, GRAB HIM.
SAY, "PLEASE COME OUT, PRETTY PLEASE WITH A CHERRY ON TOP."
TELL EVERYONE WHERE HE IS AND THEN HIS HIDING SPOT WON'T BE A HIDING SPOT ANYMORE.
PRETEND THAT YOU JUST FOUND A TREASURE CHEST RIGHT OUTSIDE HIS HIDING SPOT. HE'LL COME OUT TO SEE IT.
ADVICE
TELL HIM THAT EVERYBODY FORGOT THAT HE WAS EMBARRASSED. IT'S A LIE, BUT IT'S OKAY BECAUSE YOU'RE USING IT TO HELP SOMEONE.
WIGGLE A STICK IN THERE UNTIL HE COMES OUT OF HIS HIDING PLACE.
HAVE YOU TRIED SPRAYING HIM WITH A WATER HOSE?
SING AN ANNOYING SONG OVER AND OVER AGAIN, RIGHT NEXT TO WHERE HE IS HIDING.
DOES HE LIKE BREAD CRUMBS? YOU COULD DROP THEM ON THE PATH TO LEAD HIM OUT. HE'LL BE HUNGRY IF HE'S BEEN HIDING FOR A LONG TIME.
ADVICE
TELL HIM THAT A GROUP OF SNAKES IS HEADED FOR HIS HIDING SPOT.
I LIKE THE BREADCRUMB IDEA.

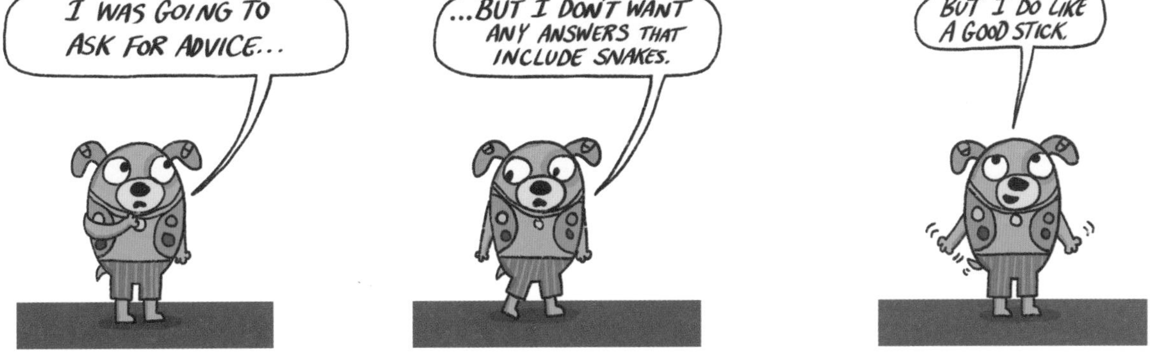
I WAS GOING TO ASK FOR ADVICE...
...BUT I DON'T WANT ANY ANSWERS THAT INCLUDE SNAKES.
BUT I DO LIKE A GOOD STICK.

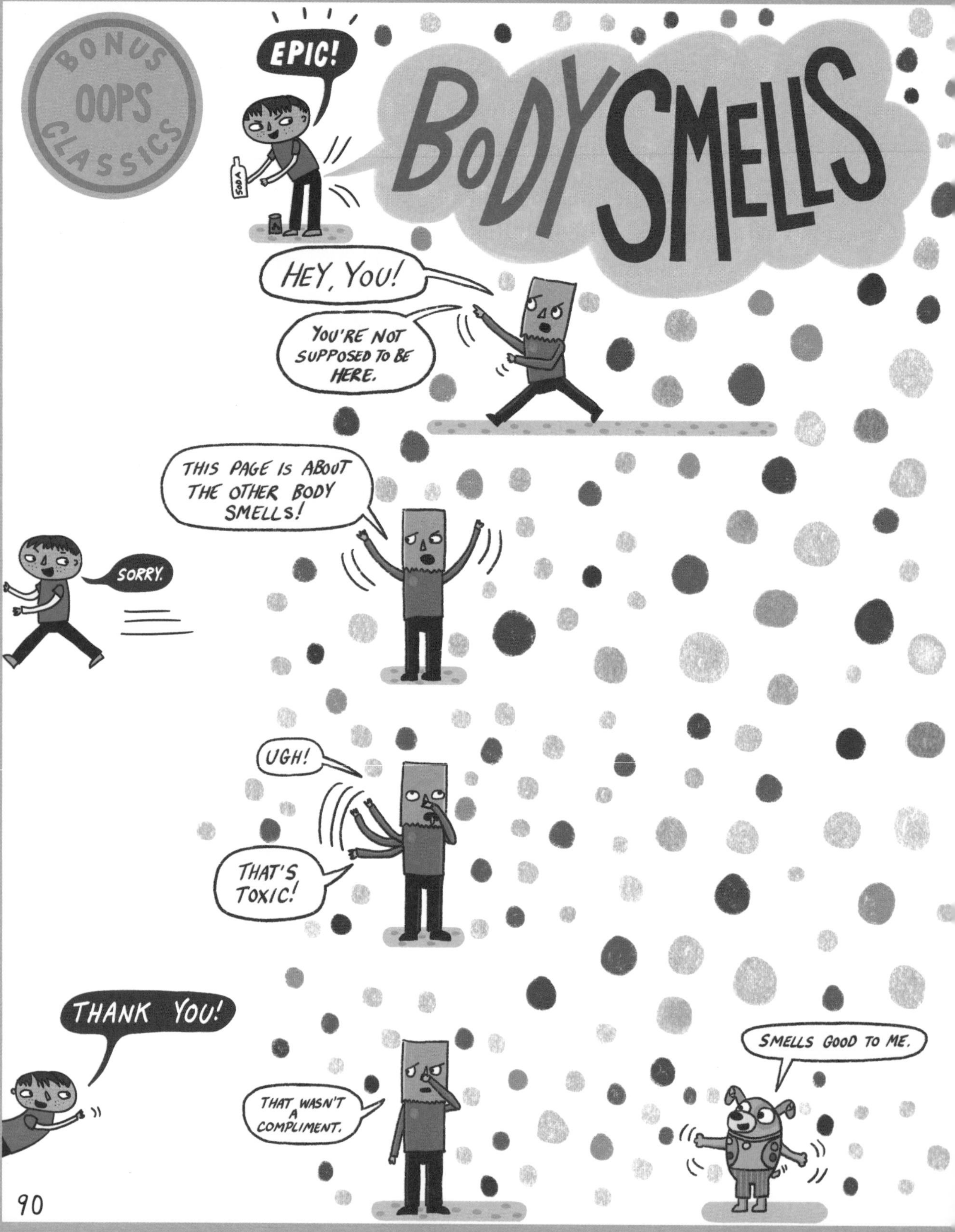

BONUS
OOPS
CLASSICS
EPIC!
SODA
BODY SMELLS
HEY, YOU!
YOU'RE NOT SUPPOSED TO BE HERE.
THIS PAGE IS ABOUT THE OTHER BODY SMELLS!
SORRY.
UGH!
THAT'S TOXIC!
THANK YOU!
THAT WASN'T A COMPLIMENT.
SMELLS GOOD TO ME.

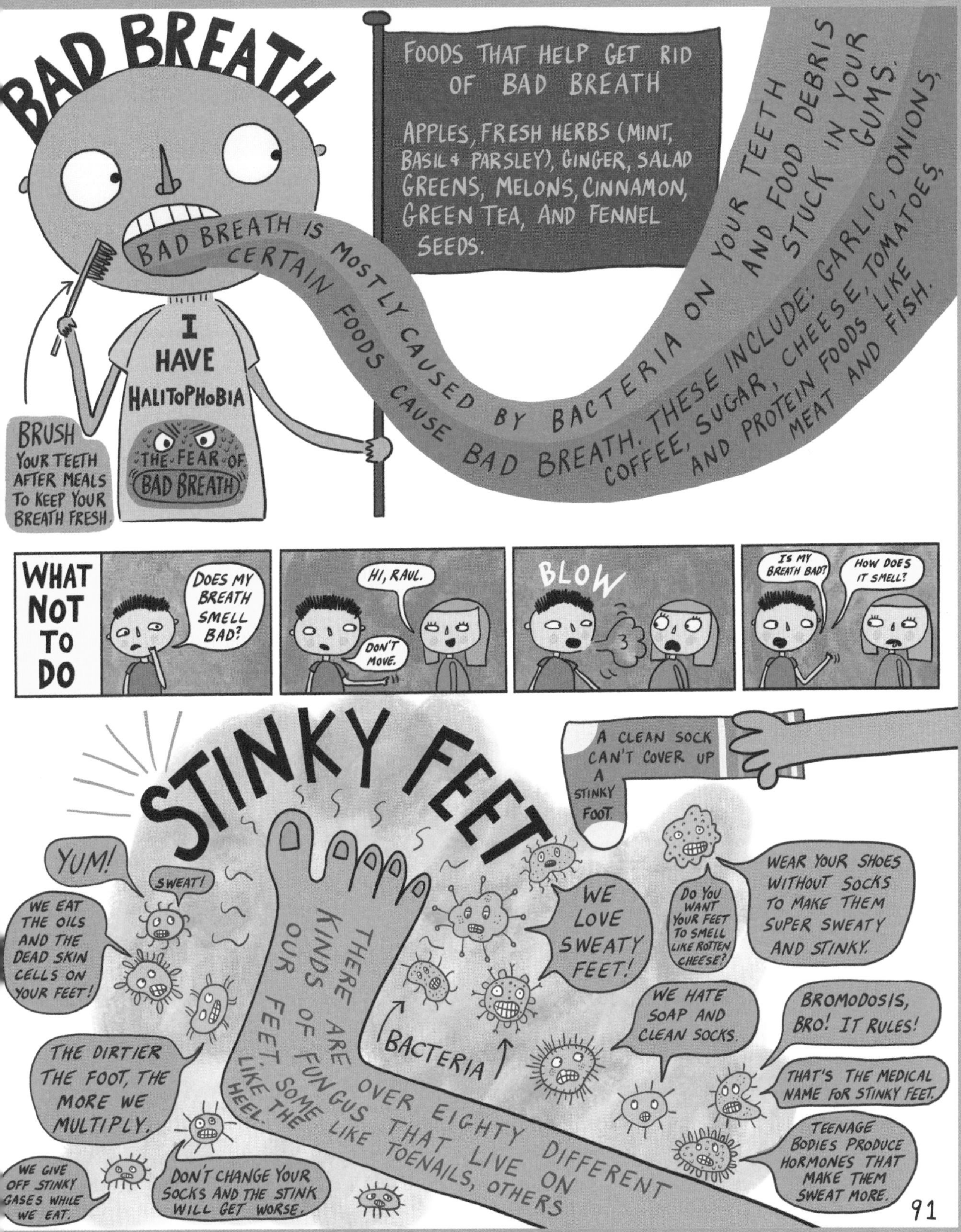
BAD BREATH
FOODS THAT HELP GET RID OF BAD BREATH
APPLES, FRESH HERBS (MINT, BASIL & PARSLEY), GINGER, SALAD GREENS, MELONS, CINNAMON, GREEN TEA, AND FENNEL SEEDS.
BAD BREATH IS MOSTLY CAUSED BY BACTERIA ON YOUR TEETH AND FOOD DEBRIS STUCK IN YOUR GUMS.
CERTAIN FOODS CAUSE BAD BREATH. THESE INCLUDE: GARLIC, ONIONS, COFFEE, SUGAR, CHEESE, TOMATOES, AND PROTEIN FOODS LIKE MEAT AND FISH.
I HAVE HALITOPHOBIA
THE FEAR OF BAD BREATH
BRUSH YOUR TEETH AFTER MEALS TO KEEP YOUR BREATH FRESH.
WHAT NOT TO DO
DOES MY BREATH SMELL BAD?
HI, RAUL.
DON'T MOVE.
BLOW
IS MY BREATH BAD?
HOW DOES IT SMELL?
STINKY FEET
A CLEAN SOCK CAN'T COVER UP A STINKY FOOT.
YUM!
SWEAT!
WE EAT THE OILS AND THE DEAD SKIN CELLS ON YOUR FEET!
THERE ARE OVER EIGHTY DIFFERENT KINDS OF FUNGUS THAT LIVE ON OUR FEET. SOME LIKE TOENAILS, OTHERS LIKE THE HEEL.
WE LOVE SWEATY FEET!
DO YOU WANT YOUR FEET TO SMELL LIKE ROTTEN CHEESE?
WEAR YOUR SHOES WITHOUT SOCKS TO MAKE THEM SUPER SWEATY AND STINKY.
BACTERIA
WE HATE SOAP AND CLEAN SOCKS.
BROMODOSIS, BRO! IT RULES!
THAT'S THE MEDICAL NAME FOR STINKY FEET.
THE DIRTIER THE FOOT, THE MORE WE MULTIPLY.
TEENAGE BODIES PRODUCE HORMONES THAT MAKE THEM SWEAT MORE.
WE GIVE OFF STINKY GASES WHILE WE EAT.
DON'T CHANGE YOUR SOCKS AND THE STINK WILL GET WORSE.

THE ARMPIT

OH NO!

EMMA HAS JUST BEEN RUNNING TO GET TO SCHOOL ON TIME, AND NOW SHE IS SWEATING.

I FORGOT TO WEAR DEODORANT.

SNIFF SNIFF SNIFF

I SMELL TERRIBLE!

WHAT DO I DO?

WASH MY UNDERARMS WITH SOAP AND PAPER TOWELS?

WEAR A SWEATSHIRT ON TOP, EVEN THOUGH IT'S SUPER HOT OUTSIDE?

BUT THEN I'LL SWEAT EVEN MORE.

ARMPIT SWEAT STAIN

THERE'S NOTHING GOOD ABOUT ME!

EMMA'S SWEAT GLANDS ARE DOING THEIR JOB. THEY ARE TRYING TO COOL HER BODY DOWN.

THE HUMAN BODY HAS **2 KINDS** OF SWEAT GLANDS.

YOU'RE SHOWING EVERYONE MY UNDERARM HAIR.

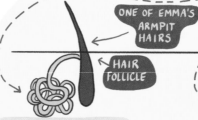

ONE OF EMMA'S ARMPIT HAIRS

SURFACE OF EMMA'S SKIN

HAIR FOLLICLE

APOCRINE GLANDS
THE SWEAT FROM THIS GLAND IS THICK. IT ATTACHES ITSELF TO HAIR FOLLICLES.

ECCRINE GLANDS
THE SWEAT FROM THIS GLAND IS THIN AND WATERY.

I'LL NEVER LIFT MY ARMS UP AGAIN.

HERE'S A FUN QUESTION: WHICH GLAND PRODUCES THE SMELLIEST SWEAT?

THAT IS _NOT A_ FUN QUESTION!

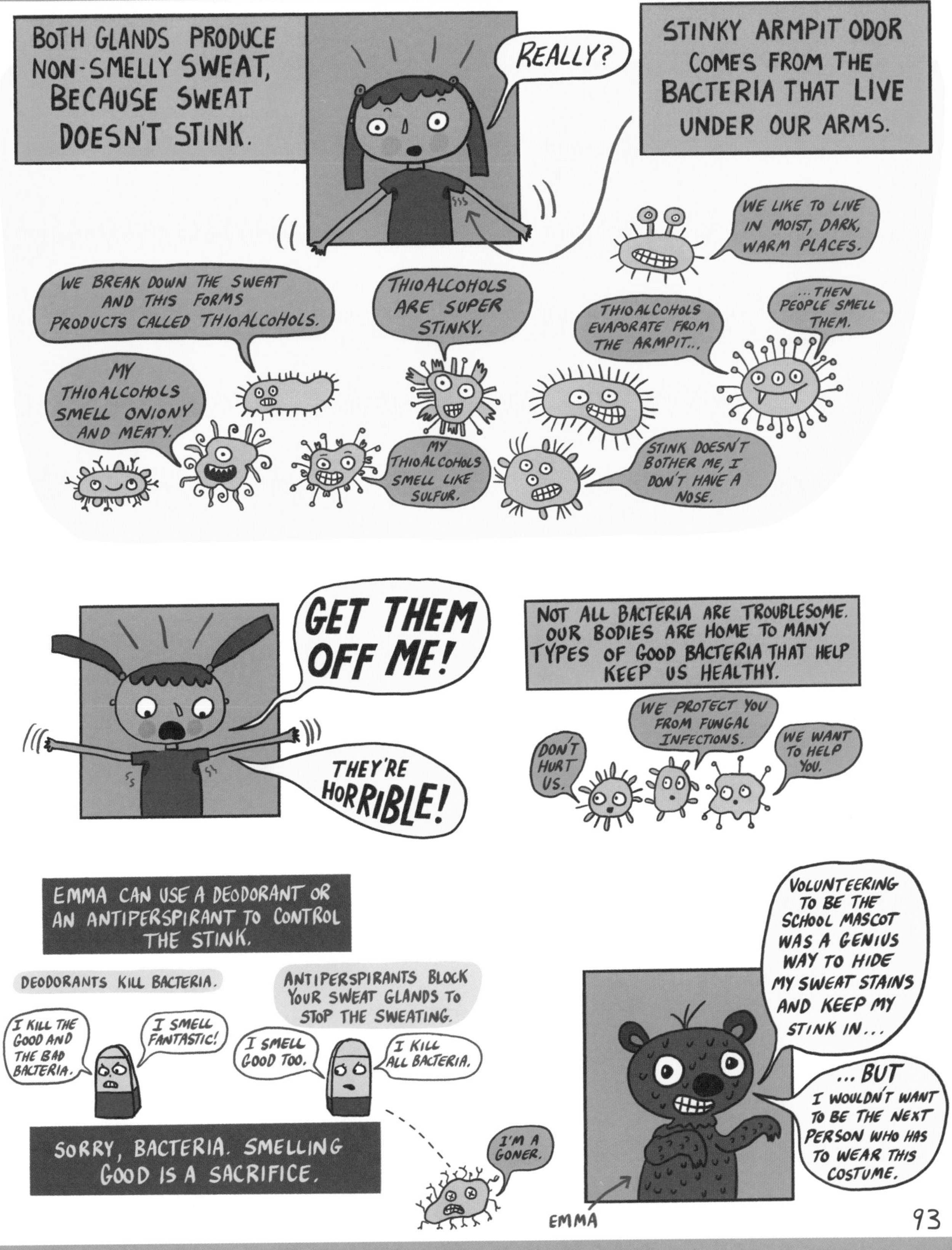

BOTH GLANDS PRODUCE NON-SMELLY SWEAT, BECAUSE SWEAT DOESN'T STINK.
REALLY?
STINKY ARMPIT ODOR COMES FROM THE BACTERIA THAT LIVE UNDER OUR ARMS.
WE LIKE TO LIVE IN MOIST, DARK, WARM PLACES.
WE BREAK DOWN THE SWEAT AND THIS FORMS PRODUCTS CALLED THIOALCOHOLS.
THIOALCOHOLS ARE SUPER STINKY.
THIOALCOHOLS EVAPORATE FROM THE ARMPIT...
...THEN PEOPLE SMELL THEM.
MY THIOALCOHOLS SMELL ONIONY AND MEATY.
MY THIOALCOHOLS SMELL LIKE SULFUR.
STINK DOESN'T BOTHER ME, I DON'T HAVE A NOSE.
GET THEM OFF ME!
THEY'RE HORRIBLE!
NOT ALL BACTERIA ARE TROUBLESOME. OUR BODIES ARE HOME TO MANY TYPES OF GOOD BACTERIA THAT HELP KEEP US HEALTHY.
DON'T HURT US.
WE PROTECT YOU FROM FUNGAL INFECTIONS.
WE WANT TO HELP YOU.
EMMA CAN USE A DEODORANT OR AN ANTIPERSPIRANT TO CONTROL THE STINK.
DEODORANTS KILL BACTERIA.
I KILL THE GOOD AND THE BAD BACTERIA.
I SMELL FANTASTIC!
ANTIPERSPIRANTS BLOCK YOUR SWEAT GLANDS TO STOP THE SWEATING.
I SMELL GOOD TOO.
I KILL ALL BACTERIA.
SORRY, BACTERIA. SMELLING GOOD IS A SACRIFICE.
I'M A GONER.
VOLUNTEERING TO BE THE SCHOOL MASCOT WAS A GENIUS WAY TO HIDE MY SWEAT STAINS AND KEEP MY STINK IN...
...BUT I WOULDN'T WANT TO BE THE NEXT PERSON WHO HAS TO WEAR THIS COSTUME.
EMMA

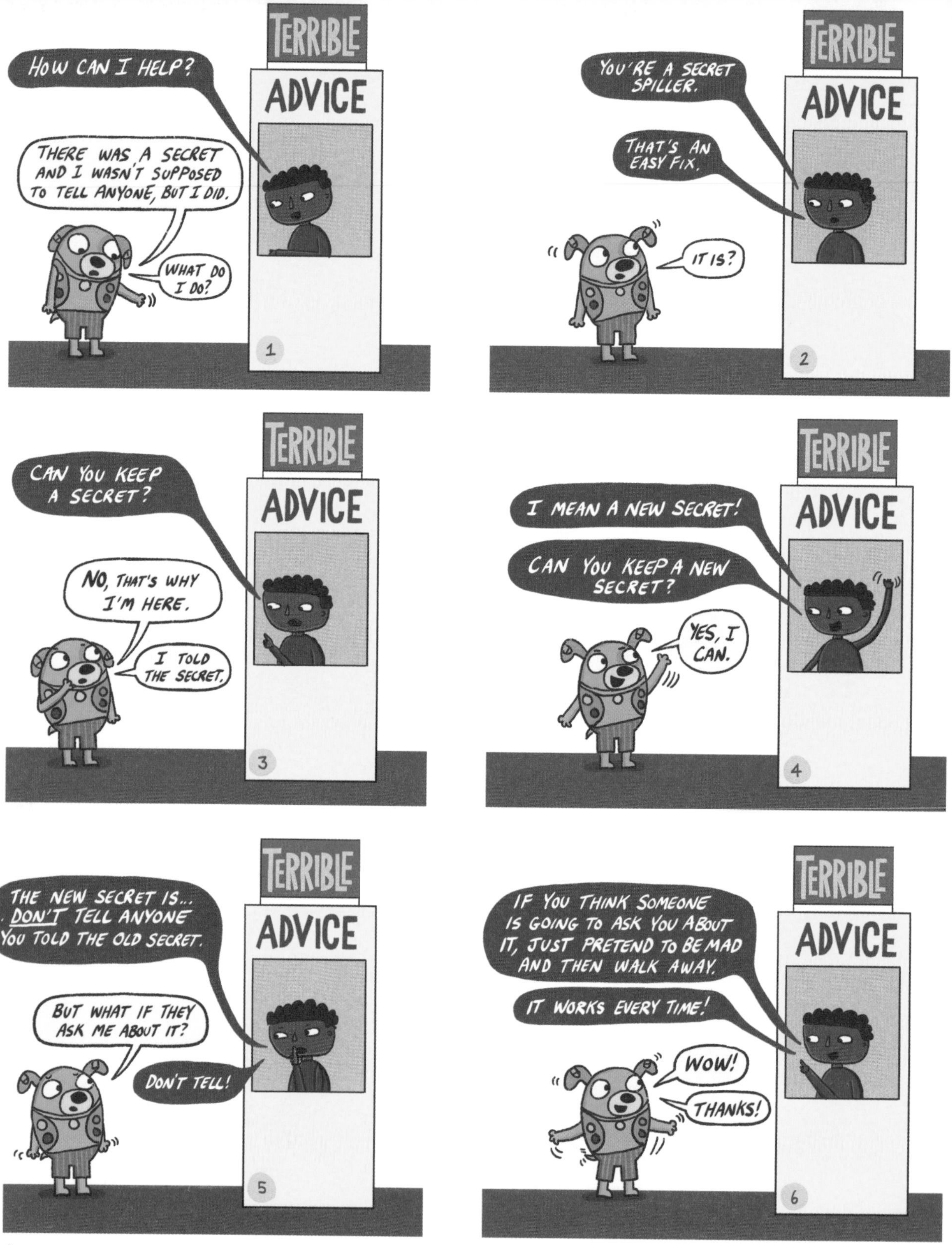
TERRIBLE ADVICE
HOW CAN I HELP?
THERE WAS A SECRET AND I WASN'T SUPPOSED TO TELL ANYONE, BUT I DID.
WHAT DO I DO?
1
YOU'RE A SECRET SPILLER.
THAT'S AN EASY FIX.
IT IS?
2
CAN YOU KEEP A SECRET?
NO, THAT'S WHY I'M HERE.
I TOLD THE SECRET.
3
I MEAN A NEW SECRET!
CAN YOU KEEP A NEW SECRET?
YES, I CAN.
4
THE NEW SECRET IS... ...DON'T TELL ANYONE YOU TOLD THE OLD SECRET.
BUT WHAT IF THEY ASK ME ABOUT IT?
DON'T TELL!
5
IF YOU THINK SOMEONE IS GOING TO ASK YOU ABOUT IT, JUST PRETEND TO BE MAD AND THEN WALK AWAY.
IT WORKS EVERY TIME!
WOW!
THANKS!
6

9

TRANSFORMATIONS

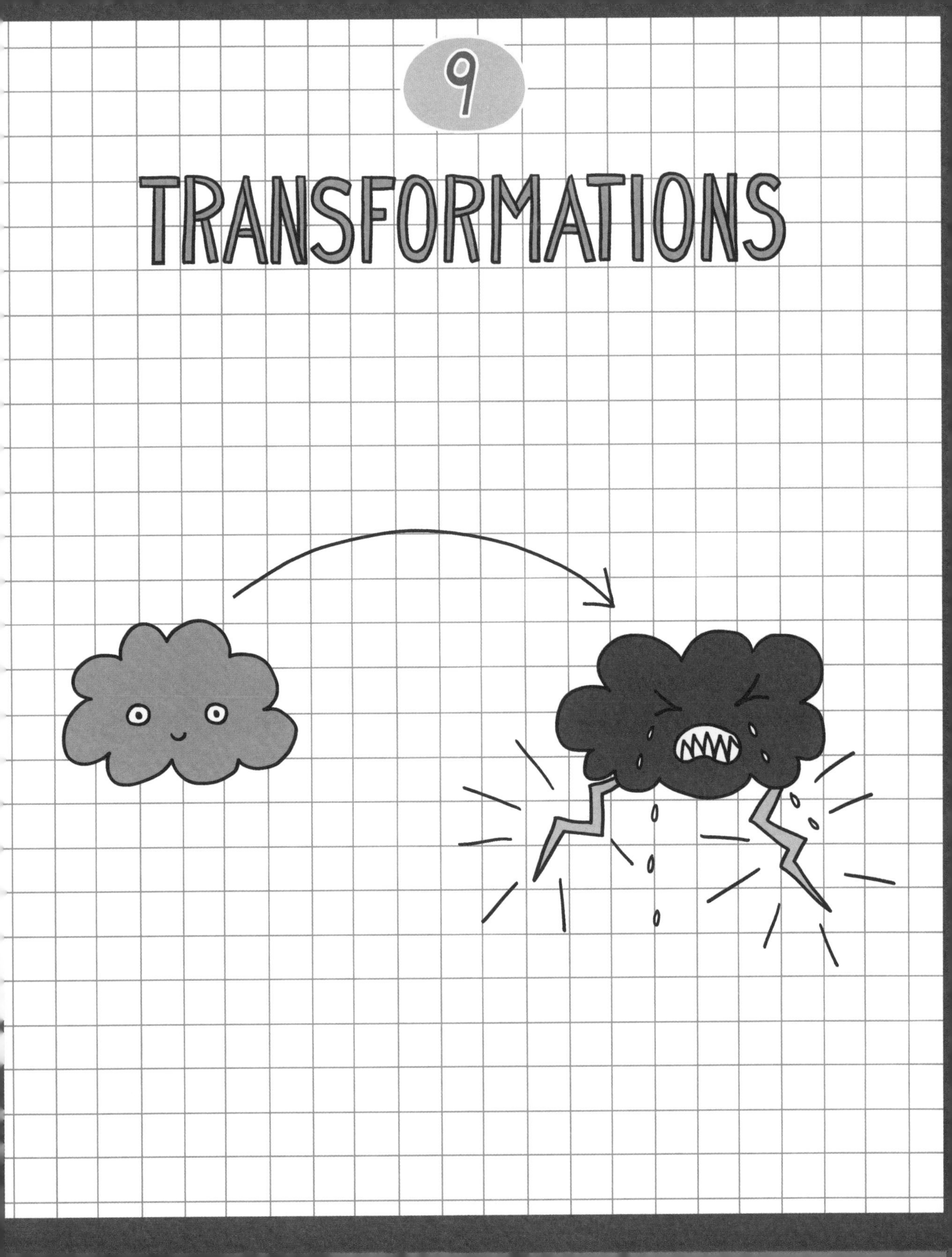

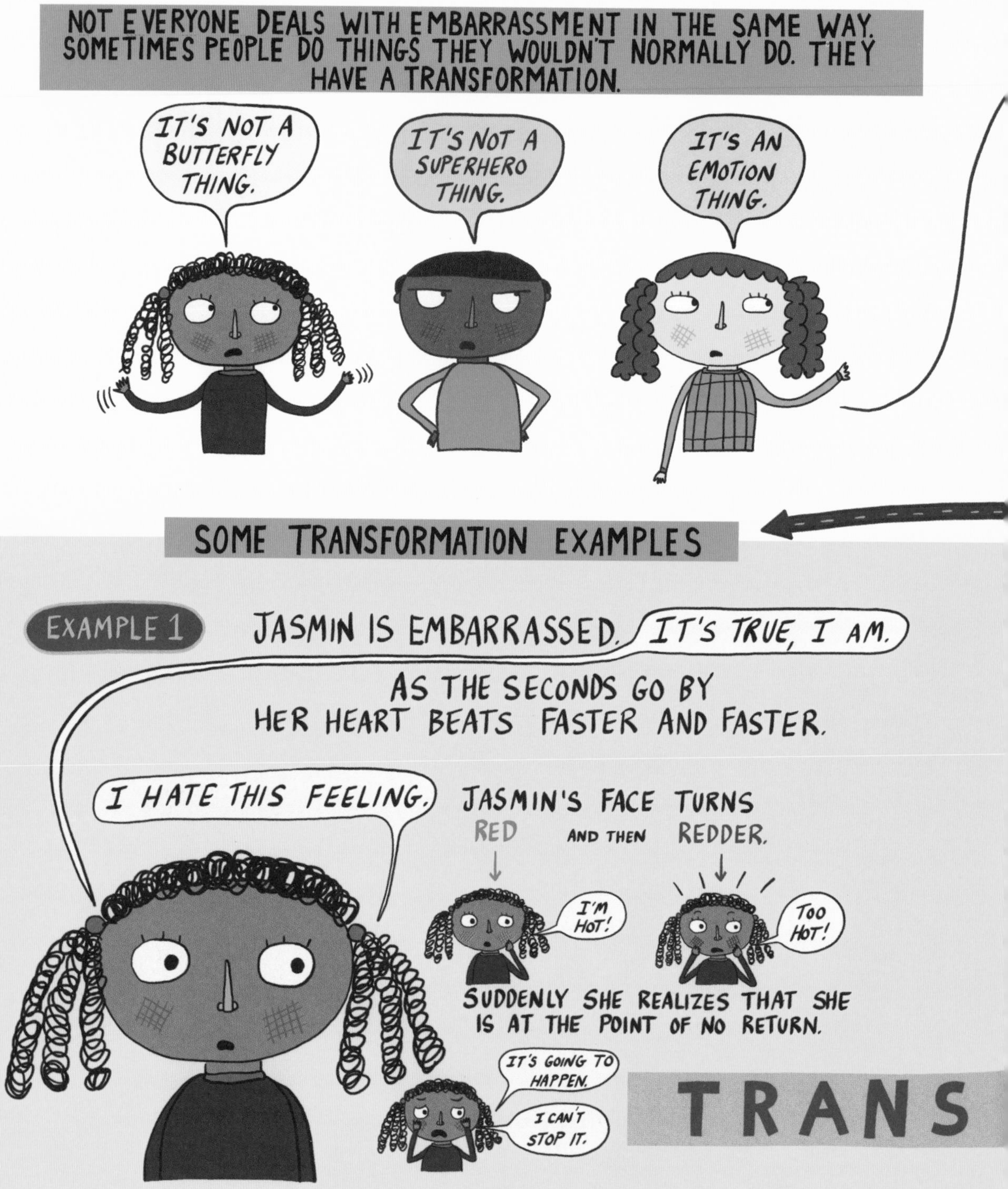
NOT EVERYONE DEALS WITH EMBARRASSMENT IN THE SAME WAY. SOMETIMES PEOPLE DO THINGS THEY WOULDN'T NORMALLY DO. THEY HAVE A TRANSFORMATION.
IT'S NOT A BUTTERFLY THING.
IT'S NOT A SUPERHERO THING.
IT'S AN EMOTION THING.
SOME TRANSFORMATION EXAMPLES
EXAMPLE 1
JASMIN IS EMBARRASSED.
IT'S TRUE, I AM.
AS THE SECONDS GO BY HER HEART BEATS FASTER AND FASTER.
I HATE THIS FEELING.
JASMIN'S FACE TURNS RED AND THEN REDDER.
I'M HOT!
TOO HOT!
SUDDENLY SHE REALIZES THAT SHE IS AT THE POINT OF NO RETURN.
IT'S GOING TO HAPPEN.
I CAN'T STOP IT.
TRANS

IT'S NOT EASY TO BE AROUND AN EMOTIONAL TRANSFORMATION.

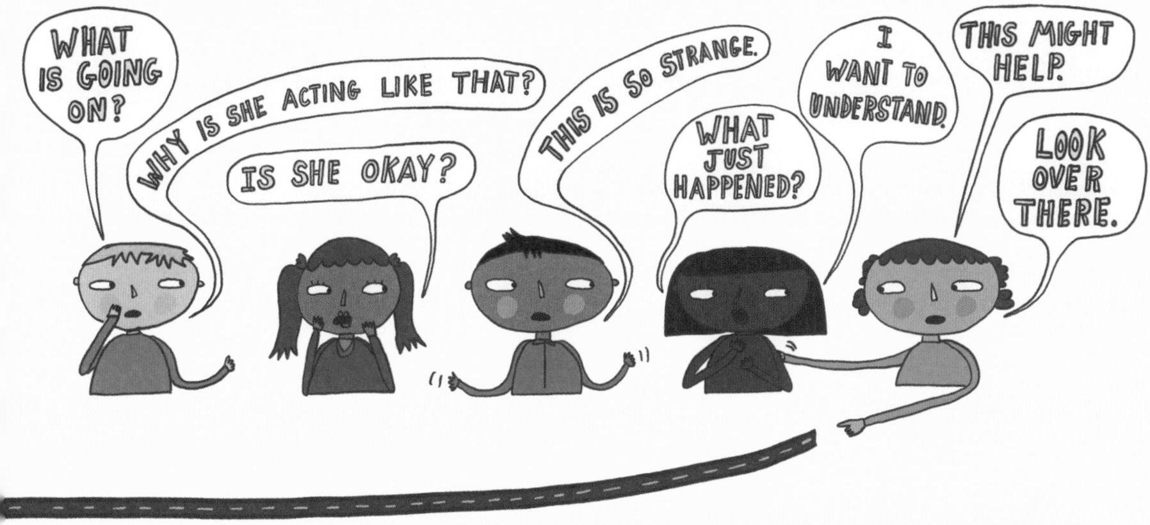

WHAT IS GOING ON?
WHY IS SHE ACTING LIKE THAT?
IS SHE OKAY?
THIS IS SO STRANGE.
WHAT JUST HAPPENED?
I WANT TO UNDERSTAND.
THIS MIGHT HELP.
LOOK OVER THERE.

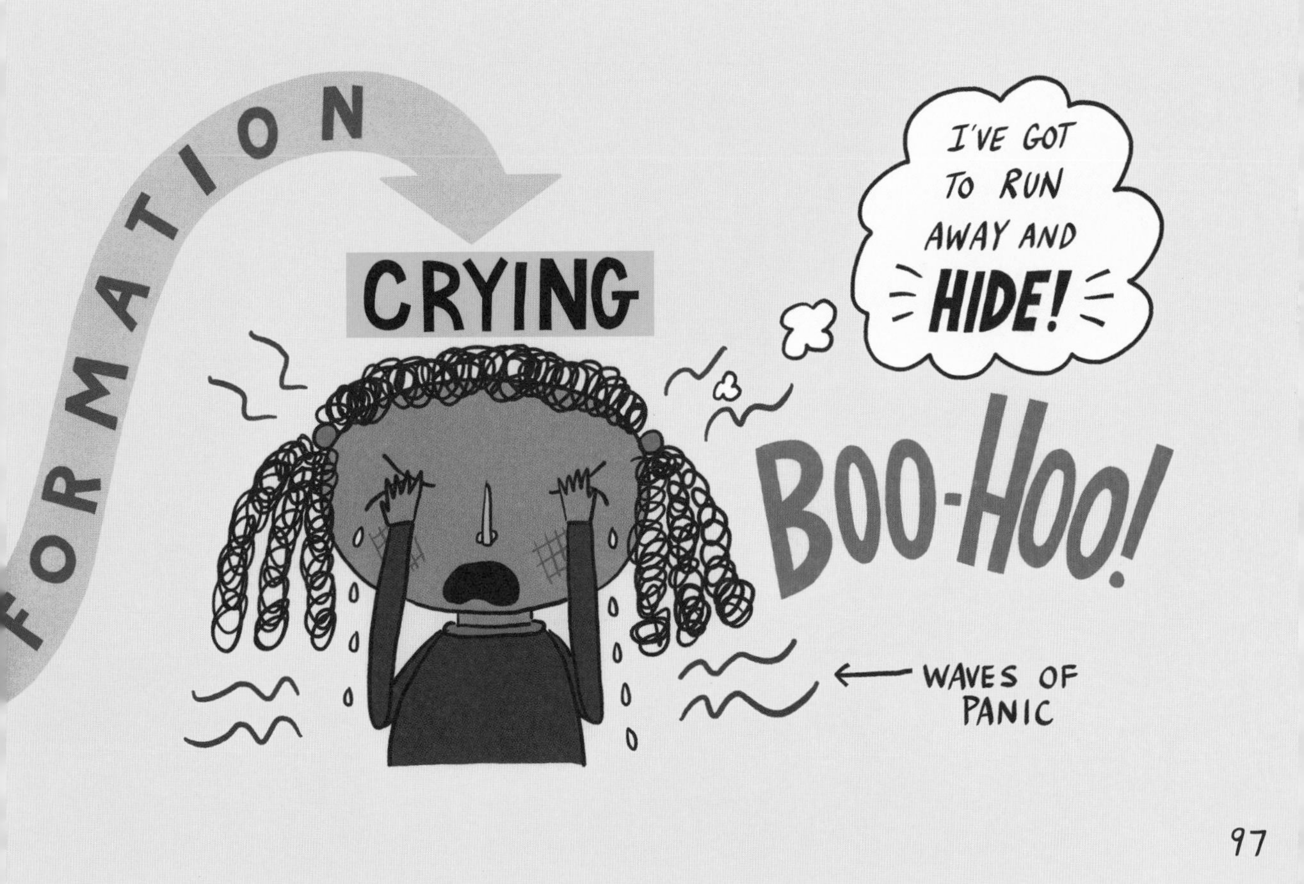

FORMATION
CRYING
I'VE GOT TO RUN AWAY AND HIDE!
BOO-HOO!
WAVES OF PANIC

EXAMPLE 2 BEN IS EMBARRASSED. HE IS GOING TO TRY TO HIDE IT. AS THE SECONDS GO BY HE FEELS MORE AND MORE UNCOMFORTABLE.

BEN CAN'T STOP THINKING ABOUT BEING EMBARRASSED. HE GETS AGITATED.

WHATEVER!

I DON'T CARE.

NOTHING CAN HURT ME!

SUDDENLY HE REALIZES THAT HE IS AT THE POINT OF NO RETURN.

THIS ISN'T MY FAULT.

TRANS

EXAMPLE 3 SUSAN IS EMBARRASSED. SHE DOESN'T WANT ANYONE TO KNOW HOW BADLY SHE FEELS. AS THE SECONDS GO BY SHE FEELS MORE AND MORE DESPERATE.

SHE IS WORRIED ABOUT WHAT PEOPLE ARE THINKING. SHE TRIES TO SAVE HERSELF.

UH-OH.

IT WASN'T ME.

IT WAS ANOTHER KID.

SUDDENLY SHE REALIZES THAT SHE IS AT THE POINT OF NO RETURN.

HE DID IT!

HE WENT THAT WAY.

TRANS

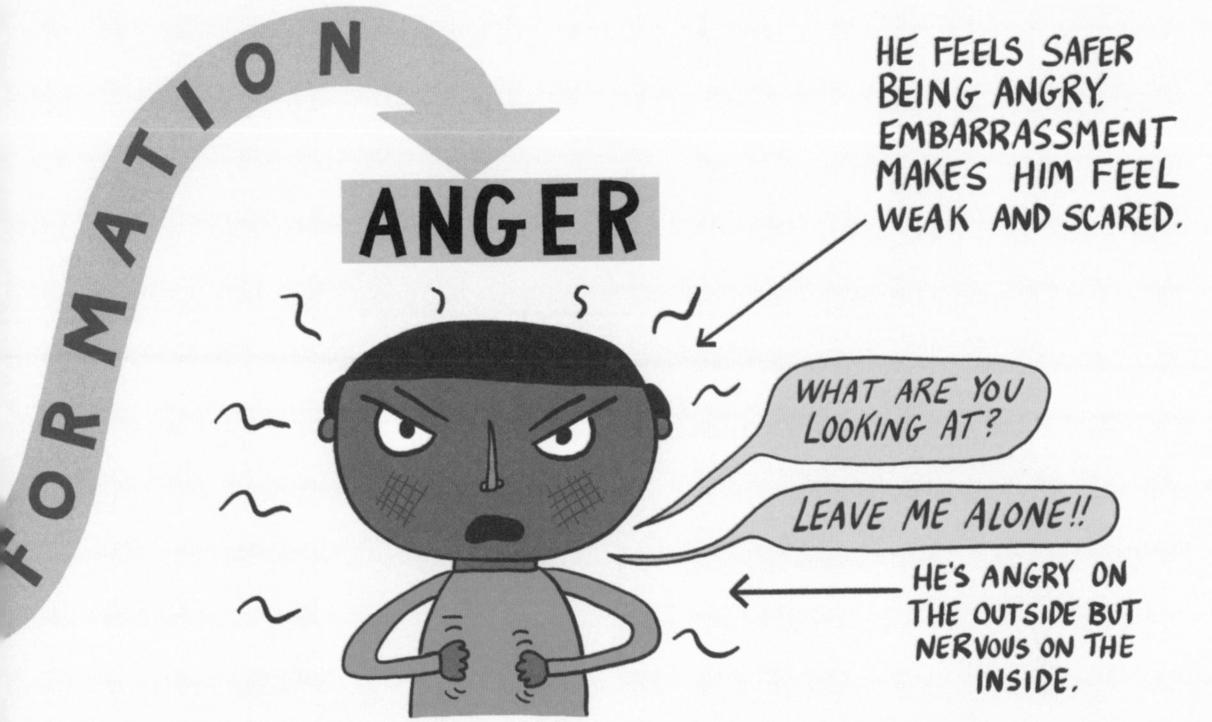
FORMATION
ANGER
HE FEELS SAFER BEING ANGRY. EMBARRASSMENT MAKES HIM FEEL WEAK AND SCARED.
WHAT ARE YOU LOOKING AT?
LEAVE ME ALONE!!
HE'S ANGRY ON THE OUTSIDE BUT NERVOUS ON THE INSIDE.

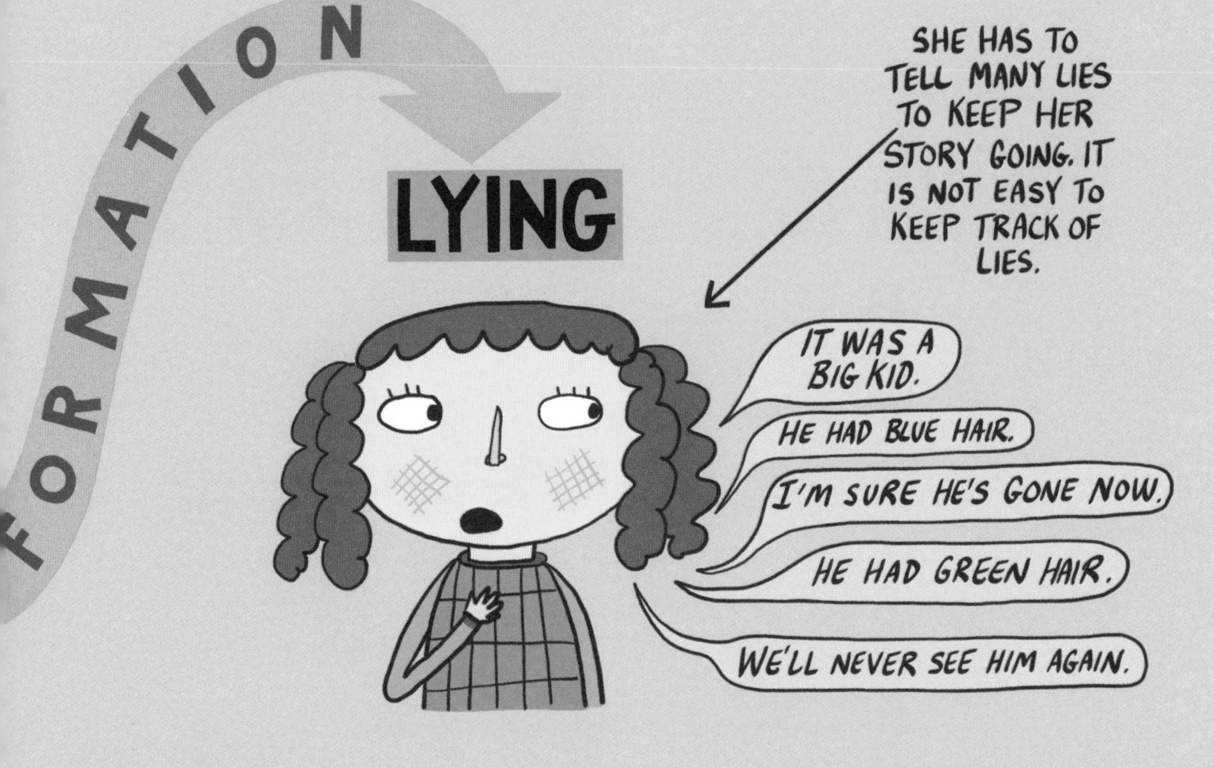
FORMATION
LYING
SHE HAS TO TELL MANY LIES TO KEEP HER STORY GOING. IT IS NOT EASY TO KEEP TRACK OF LIES.
IT WAS A BIG KID.
HE HAD BLUE HAIR.
I'M SURE HE'S GONE NOW.
HE HAD GREEN HAIR.
WE'LL NEVER SEE HIM AGAIN.

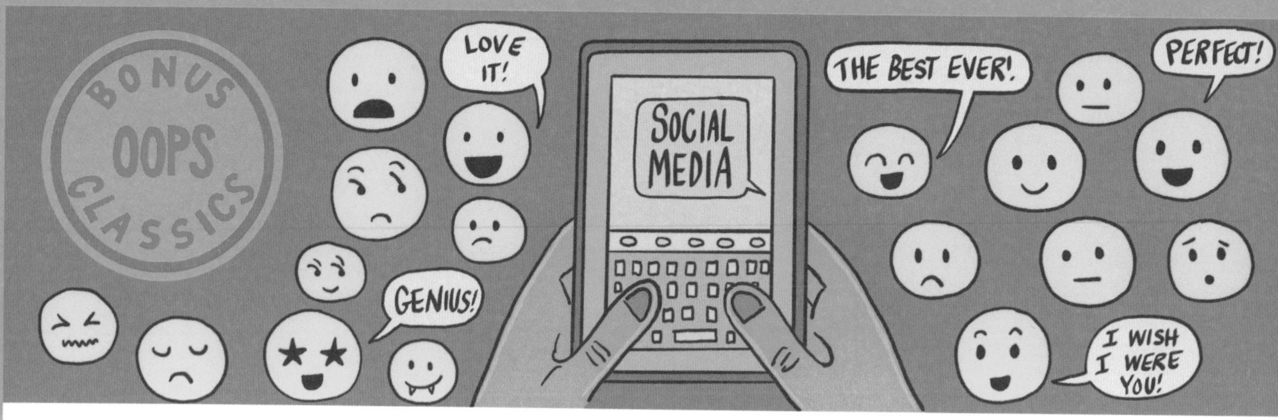
BONUS
OOPS
CLASSICS
LOVE IT!
SOCIAL MEDIA
THE BEST EVER!
PERFECT!
GENIUS!
I WISH I WERE YOU!

LIKE IT!

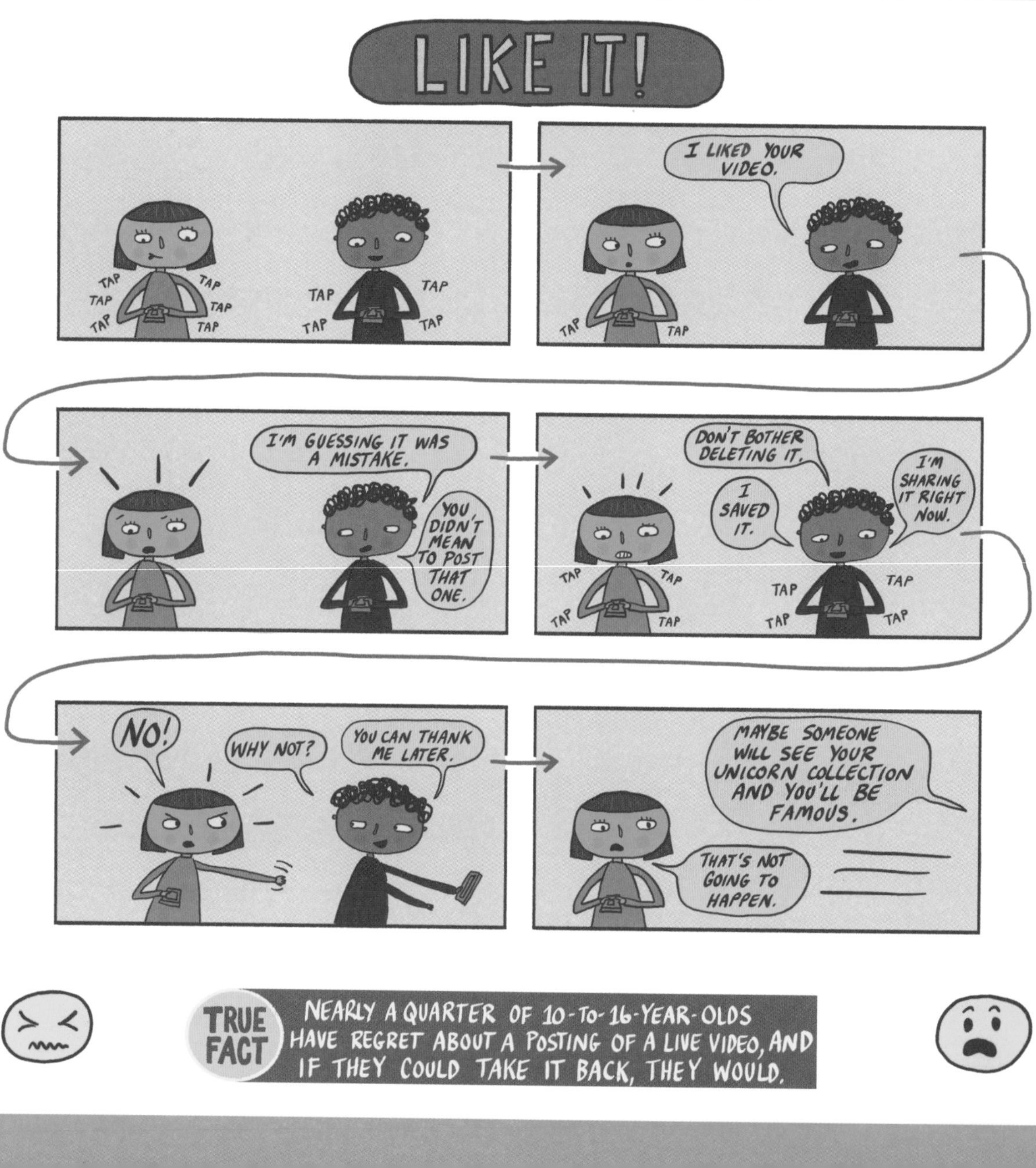
TAP TAP TAP TAP TAP TAP
TAP TAP TAP TAP
I LIKED YOUR VIDEO.
TAP TAP
I'M GUESSING IT WAS A MISTAKE.
YOU DIDN'T MEAN TO POST THAT ONE.
DON'T BOTHER DELETING IT.
I SAVED IT.
I'M SHARING IT RIGHT NOW.
TAP TAP TAP TAP
TAP TAP TAP TAP
NO!
WHY NOT?
YOU CAN THANK ME LATER.
MAYBE SOMEONE WILL SEE YOUR UNICORN COLLECTION AND YOU'LL BE FAMOUS.
THAT'S NOT GOING TO HAPPEN.

TRUE FACT NEARLY A QUARTER OF 10-TO-16-YEAR-OLDS HAVE REGRET ABOUT A POSTING OF A LIVE VIDEO, AND IF THEY COULD TAKE IT BACK, THEY WOULD.

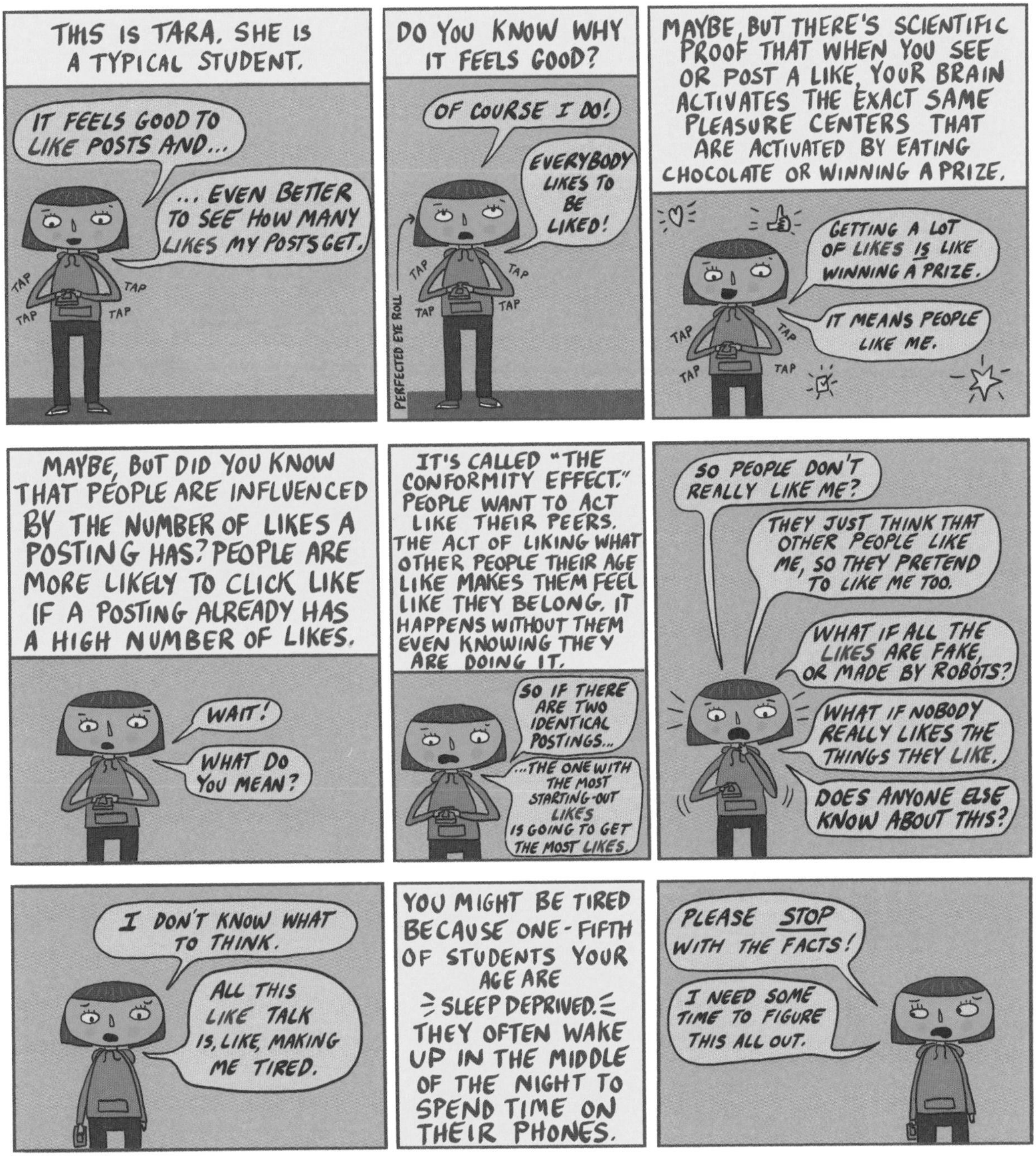
THIS IS TARA. SHE IS A TYPICAL STUDENT.
IT FEELS GOOD TO LIKE POSTS AND...
... EVEN BETTER TO SEE HOW MANY LIKES MY POSTS GET.
TAP TAP TAP TAP
DO YOU KNOW WHY IT FEELS GOOD?
OF COURSE I DO!
EVERYBODY LIKES TO BE LIKED!
PERFECTED EYE ROLL
TAP TAP TAP TAP
MAYBE, BUT THERE'S SCIENTIFIC PROOF THAT WHEN YOU SEE OR POST A LIKE, YOUR BRAIN ACTIVATES THE EXACT SAME PLEASURE CENTERS THAT ARE ACTIVATED BY EATING CHOCOLATE OR WINNING A PRIZE.
GETTING A LOT OF LIKES IS LIKE WINNING A PRIZE.
IT MEANS PEOPLE LIKE ME.
TAP TAP TAP TAP
MAYBE, BUT DID YOU KNOW THAT PEOPLE ARE INFLUENCED BY THE NUMBER OF LIKES A POSTING HAS? PEOPLE ARE MORE LIKELY TO CLICK LIKE IF A POSTING ALREADY HAS A HIGH NUMBER OF LIKES.
WAIT!
WHAT DO YOU MEAN?
IT'S CALLED "THE CONFORMITY EFFECT." PEOPLE WANT TO ACT LIKE THEIR PEERS. THE ACT OF LIKING WHAT OTHER PEOPLE THEIR AGE LIKE MAKES THEM FEEL LIKE THEY BELONG. IT HAPPENS WITHOUT THEM EVEN KNOWING THEY ARE DOING IT.
SO IF THERE ARE TWO IDENTICAL POSTINGS...
...THE ONE WITH THE MOST STARTING-OUT LIKES IS GOING TO GET THE MOST LIKES.
SO PEOPLE DON'T REALLY LIKE ME?
THEY JUST THINK THAT OTHER PEOPLE LIKE ME, SO THEY PRETEND TO LIKE ME TOO.
WHAT IF ALL THE LIKES ARE FAKE, OR MADE BY ROBOTS?
WHAT IF NOBODY REALLY LIKES THE THINGS THEY LIKE.
DOES ANYONE ELSE KNOW ABOUT THIS?
I DON'T KNOW WHAT TO THINK.
ALL THIS LIKE TALK IS, LIKE, MAKING ME TIRED.
YOU MIGHT BE TIRED BECAUSE ONE-FIFTH OF STUDENTS YOUR AGE ARE SLEEP DEPRIVED. THEY OFTEN WAKE UP IN THE MIDDLE OF THE NIGHT TO SPEND TIME ON THEIR PHONES.
PLEASE STOP WITH THE FACTS!
I NEED SOME TIME TO FIGURE THIS ALL OUT.

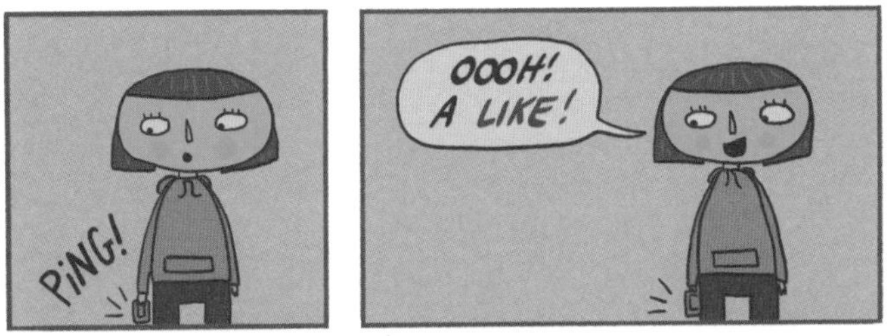
PING!
OOOH! A LIKE!

TRUE FACT ON AVERAGE, 8-TO-12-YEAR-OLDS SPEND AT LEAST SIX HOURS A DAY ON THEIR MOBILE DEVICES. TEENAGERS SPEND NINE HOURS A DAY ON THEIR PHONES.

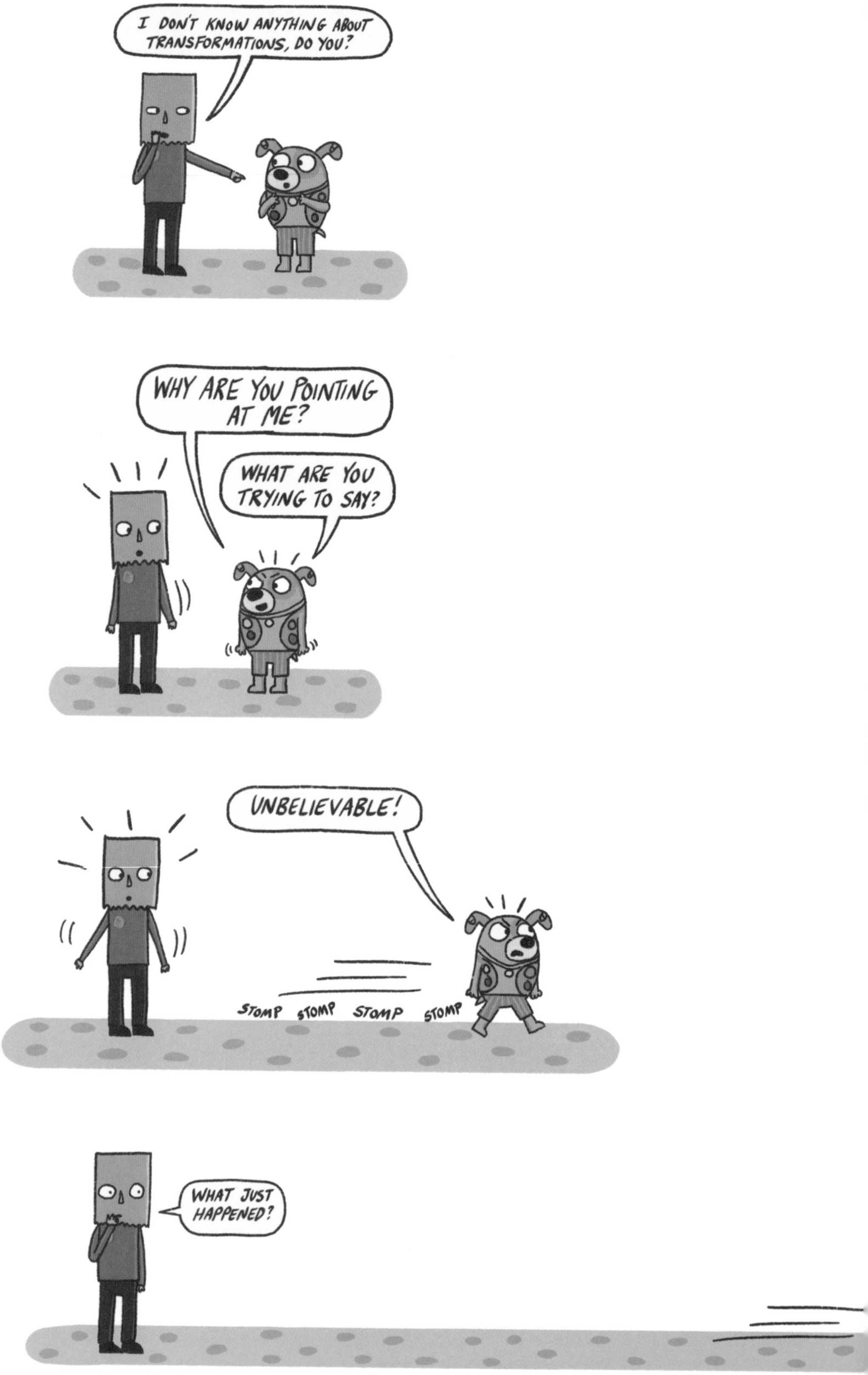
I DON'T KNOW ANYTHING ABOUT TRANSFORMATIONS, DO YOU?
WHY ARE YOU POINTING AT ME?
WHAT ARE YOU TRYING TO SAY?
UNBELIEVABLE!
STOMP STOMP STOMP STOMP
WHAT JUST HAPPENED?

HELP YOU CAN REALLY TRUST

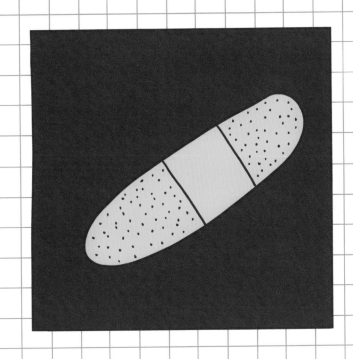

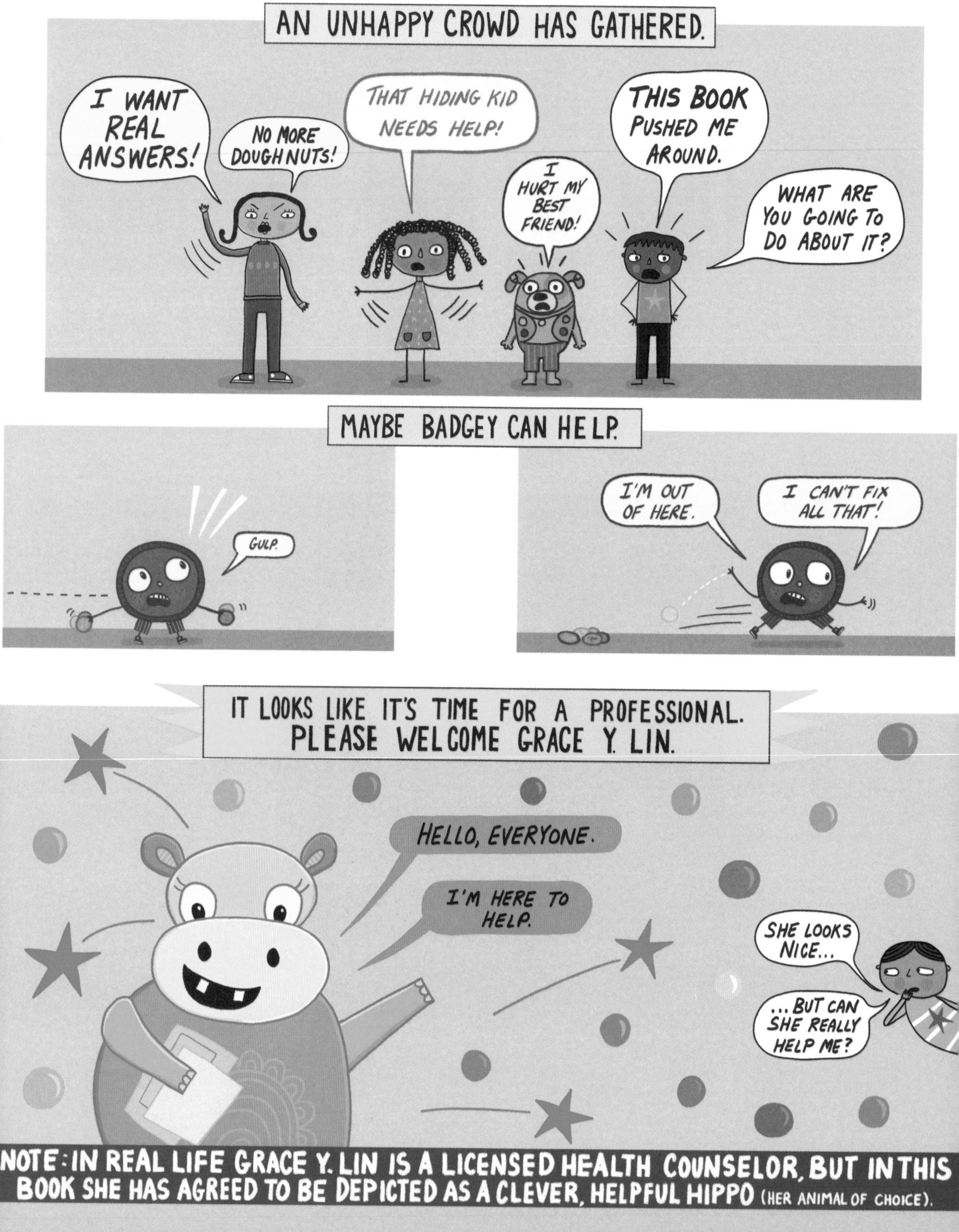
AN UNHAPPY CROWD HAS GATHERED.
I WANT REAL ANSWERS!
NO MORE DOUGHNUTS!
THAT HIDING KID NEEDS HELP!
I HURT MY BEST FRIEND!
THIS BOOK PUSHED ME AROUND.
WHAT ARE YOU GOING TO DO ABOUT IT?
MAYBE BADGEY CAN HELP.
GULP.
I'M OUT OF HERE.
I CAN'T FIX ALL THAT!
IT LOOKS LIKE IT'S TIME FOR A PROFESSIONAL. PLEASE WELCOME GRACE Y. LIN.
HELLO, EVERYONE.
I'M HERE TO HELP.
SHE LOOKS NICE...
...BUT CAN SHE REALLY HELP ME?
NOTE: IN REAL LIFE GRACE Y. LIN IS A LICENSED HEALTH COUNSELOR, BUT IN THIS BOOK SHE HAS AGREED TO BE DEPICTED AS A CLEVER, HELPFUL HIPPO (HER ANIMAL OF CHOICE).

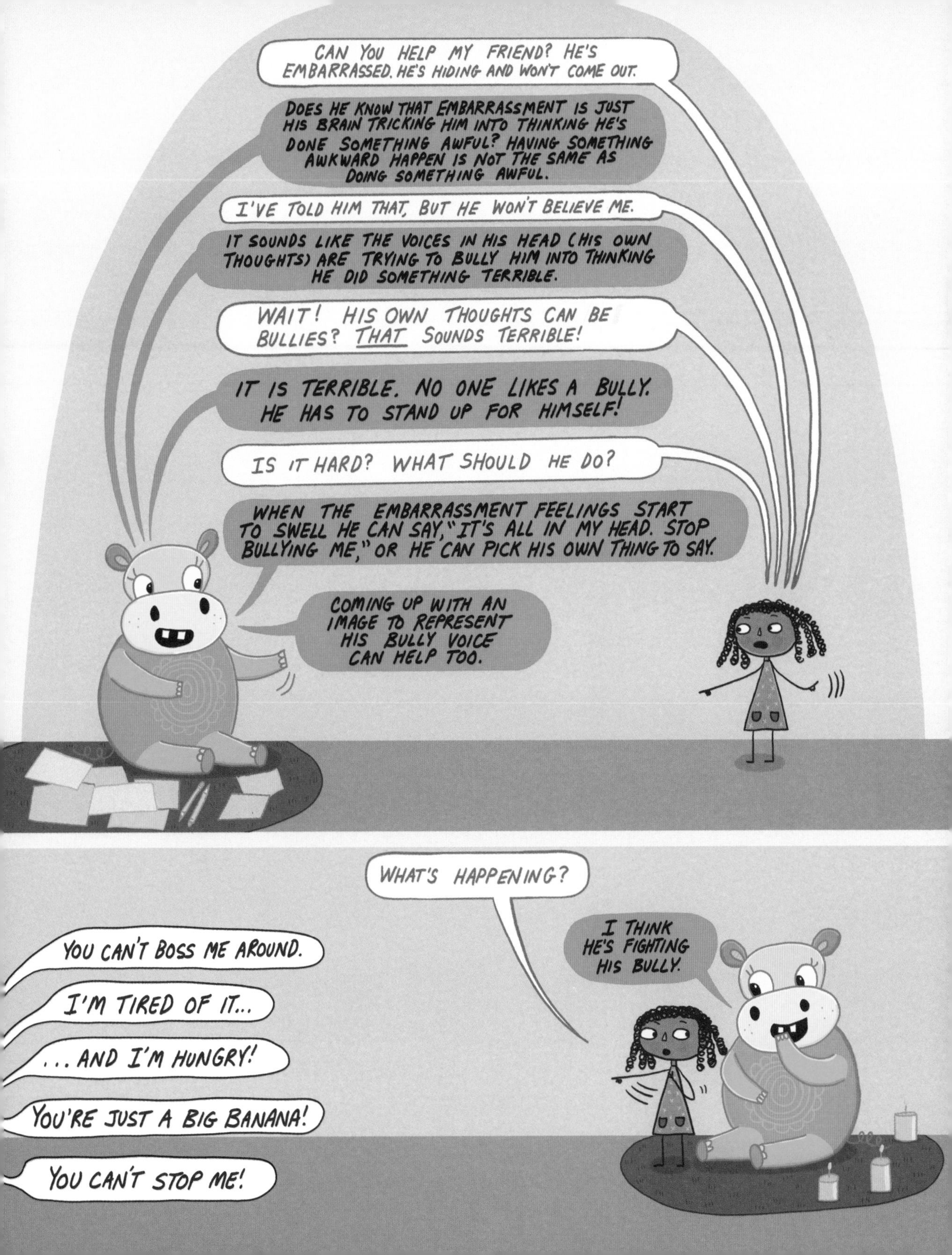

CAN YOU HELP MY FRIEND? HE'S EMBARRASSED. HE'S HIDING AND WON'T COME OUT.
DOES HE KNOW THAT EMBARRASSMENT IS JUST HIS BRAIN TRICKING HIM INTO THINKING HE'S DONE SOMETHING AWFUL? HAVING SOMETHING AWKWARD HAPPEN IS NOT THE SAME AS DOING SOMETHING AWFUL.
I'VE TOLD HIM THAT, BUT HE WON'T BELIEVE ME.
IT SOUNDS LIKE THE VOICES IN HIS HEAD (HIS OWN THOUGHTS) ARE TRYING TO BULLY HIM INTO THINKING HE DID SOMETHING TERRIBLE.
WAIT! HIS OWN THOUGHTS CAN BE BULLIES? THAT SOUNDS TERRIBLE!
IT IS TERRIBLE. NO ONE LIKES A BULLY. HE HAS TO STAND UP FOR HIMSELF!
IS IT HARD? WHAT SHOULD HE DO?
WHEN THE EMBARRASSMENT FEELINGS START TO SWELL HE CAN SAY, "IT'S ALL IN MY HEAD. STOP BULLYING ME," OR HE CAN PICK HIS OWN THING TO SAY.
COMING UP WITH AN IMAGE TO REPRESENT HIS BULLY VOICE CAN HELP TOO.
WHAT'S HAPPENING?
I THINK HE'S FIGHTING HIS BULLY.
YOU CAN'T BOSS ME AROUND.
I'M TIRED OF IT...
...AND I'M HUNGRY!
YOU'RE JUST A BIG BANANA!
YOU CAN'T STOP ME!

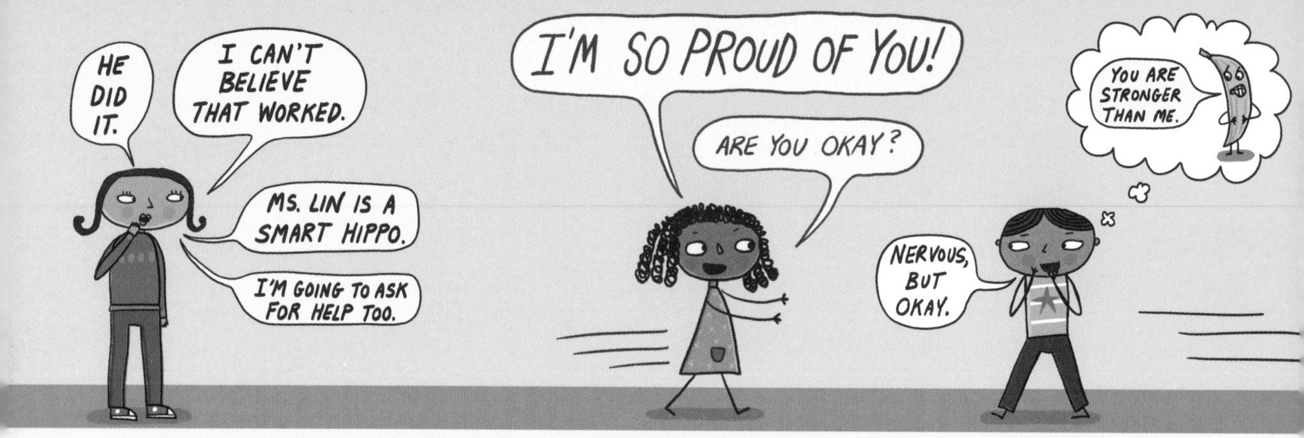
HE DID IT.
I CAN'T BELIEVE THAT WORKED.
MS. LIN IS A SMART HIPPO.
I'M GOING TO ASK FOR HELP TOO.
I'M SO PROUD OF YOU!
ARE YOU OKAY?
NERVOUS, BUT OKAY.
YOU ARE STRONGER THAN ME.

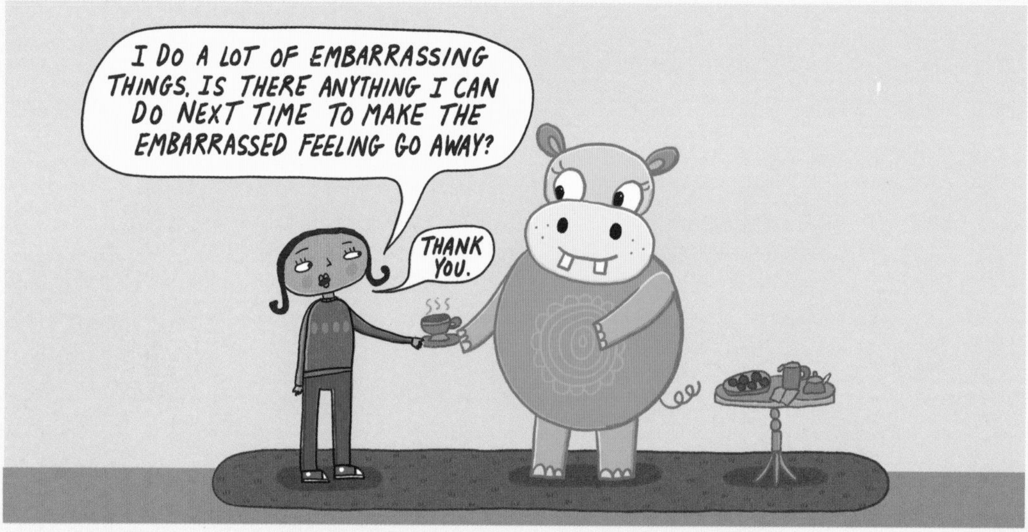
I DO A LOT OF EMBARRASSING THINGS. IS THERE ANYTHING I CAN DO NEXT TIME TO MAKE THE EMBARRASSED FEELING GO AWAY?
THANK YOU.

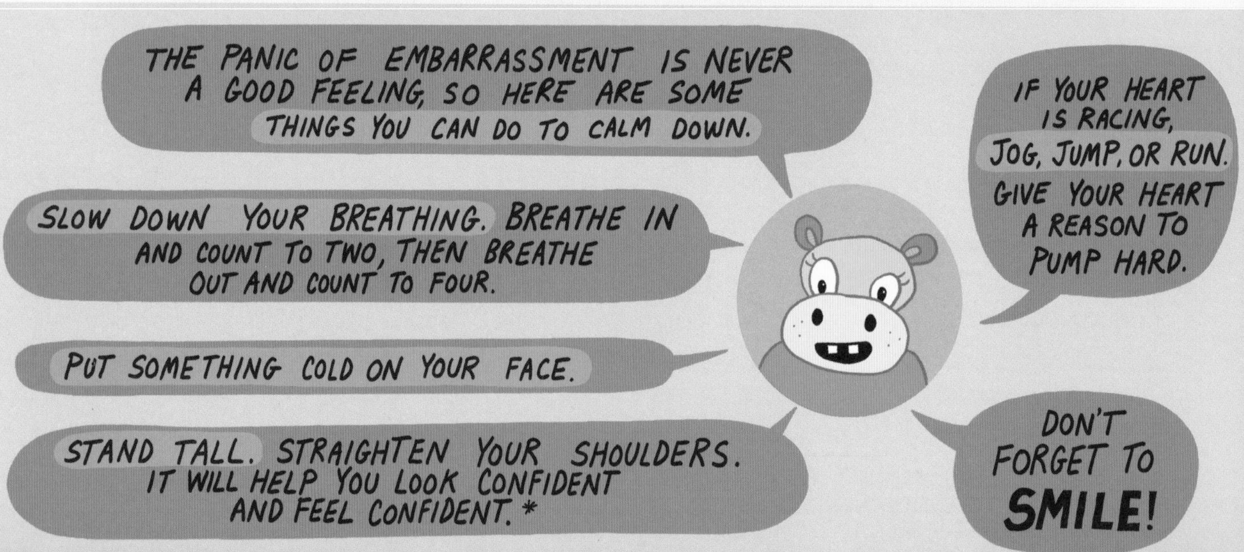
THE PANIC OF EMBARRASSMENT IS NEVER A GOOD FEELING, SO HERE ARE SOME THINGS YOU CAN DO TO CALM DOWN.
SLOW DOWN YOUR BREATHING. BREATHE IN AND COUNT TO TWO, THEN BREATHE OUT AND COUNT TO FOUR.
PUT SOMETHING COLD ON YOUR FACE.
STAND TALL. STRAIGHTEN YOUR SHOULDERS. IT WILL HELP YOU LOOK CONFIDENT AND FEEL CONFIDENT.*
IF YOUR HEART IS RACING, JOG, JUMP, OR RUN. GIVE YOUR HEART A REASON TO PUMP HARD.
DON'T FORGET TO SMILE!

*EVEN IF YOU DON'T FEEL LIKE DOING IT, CHANGING YOUR POSTURE CAN HELP.

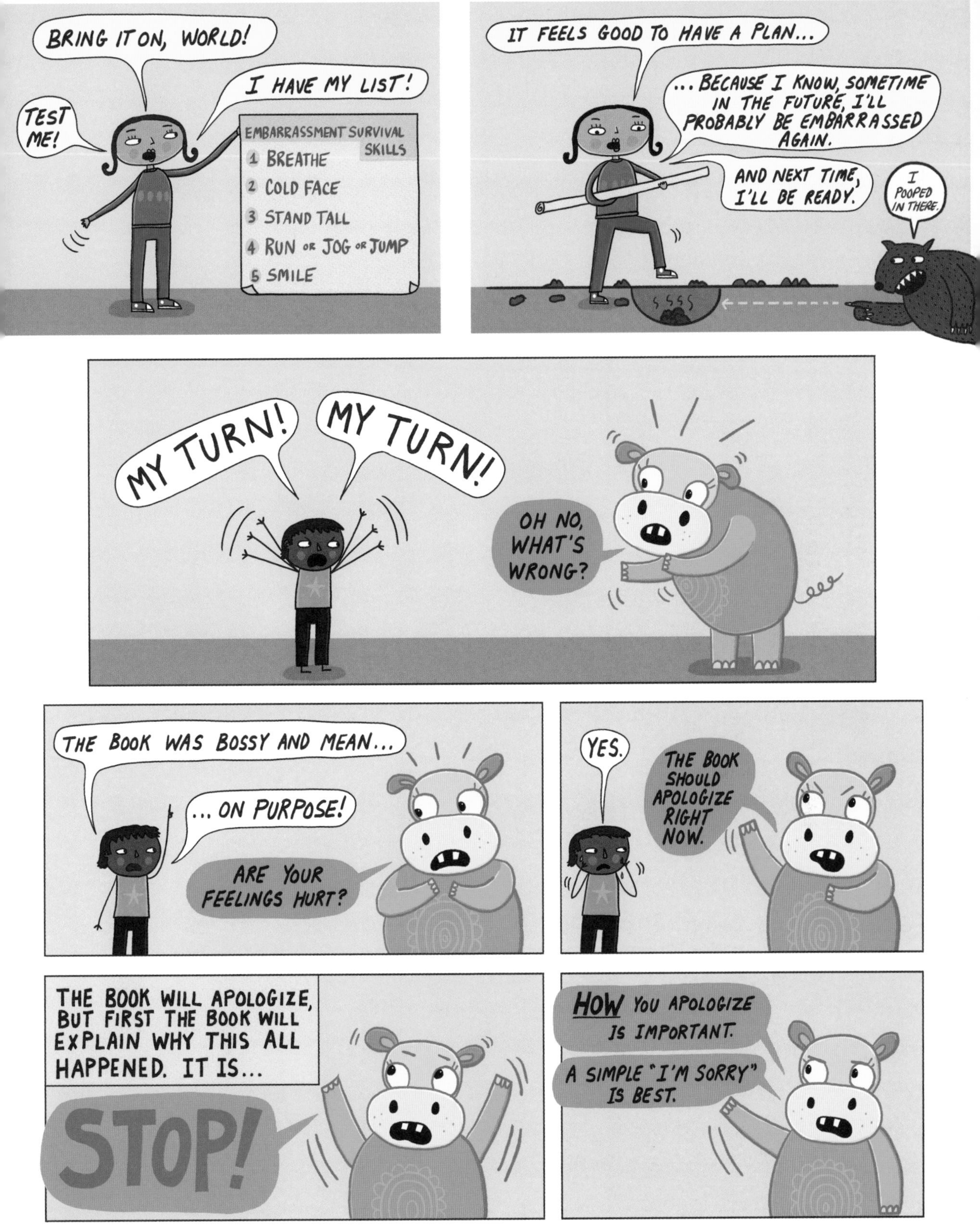

TEST ME!
BRING IT ON, WORLD!
I HAVE MY LIST!
EMBARRASSMENT SURVIVAL SKILLS
1 BREATHE
2 COLD FACE
3 STAND TALL
4 RUN OR JOG OR JUMP
5 SMILE
IT FEELS GOOD TO HAVE A PLAN...
... BECAUSE I KNOW, SOMETIME IN THE FUTURE, I'LL PROBABLY BE EMBARRASSED AGAIN.
AND NEXT TIME, I'LL BE READY.
I POOPED IN THERE.
MY TURN!
MY TURN!
OH NO, WHAT'S WRONG?
THE BOOK WAS BOSSY AND MEAN...
... ON PURPOSE!
ARE YOUR FEELINGS HURT?
YES.
THE BOOK SHOULD APOLOGIZE RIGHT NOW.
THE BOOK WILL APOLOGIZE, BUT FIRST THE BOOK WILL EXPLAIN WHY THIS ALL HAPPENED. IT IS...
STOP!
HOW YOU APOLOGIZE IS IMPORTANT.
A SIMPLE "I'M SORRY" IS BEST.

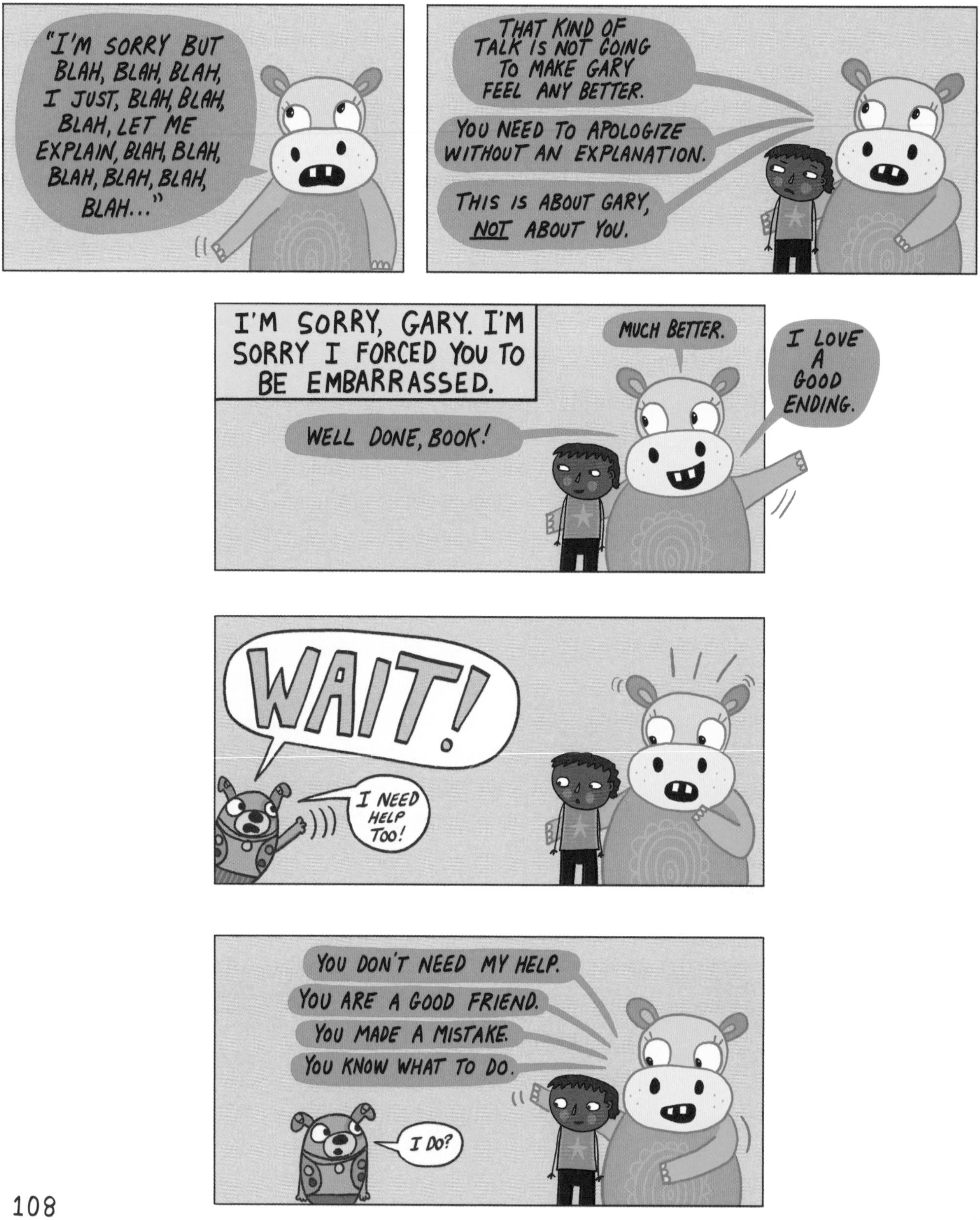
"I'M SORRY BUT BLAH, BLAH, BLAH, I JUST, BLAH, BLAH, BLAH, LET ME EXPLAIN, BLAH, BLAH, BLAH, BLAH, BLAH, BLAH..."
THAT KIND OF TALK IS NOT GOING TO MAKE GARY FEEL ANY BETTER.
YOU NEED TO APOLOGIZE WITHOUT AN EXPLANATION.
THIS IS ABOUT GARY, NOT ABOUT YOU.
I'M SORRY, GARY. I'M SORRY I FORCED YOU TO BE EMBARRASSED.
MUCH BETTER.
I LOVE A GOOD ENDING.
WELL DONE, BOOK!
WAIT!
I NEED HELP TOO!
YOU DON'T NEED MY HELP.
YOU ARE A GOOD FRIEND.
YOU MADE A MISTAKE.
YOU KNOW WHAT TO DO.
I DO?

11

ONE DAY IT WILL BE A GOOD STORY

EMBARRASSMENT

+

TIME

_____

GOOD STORY

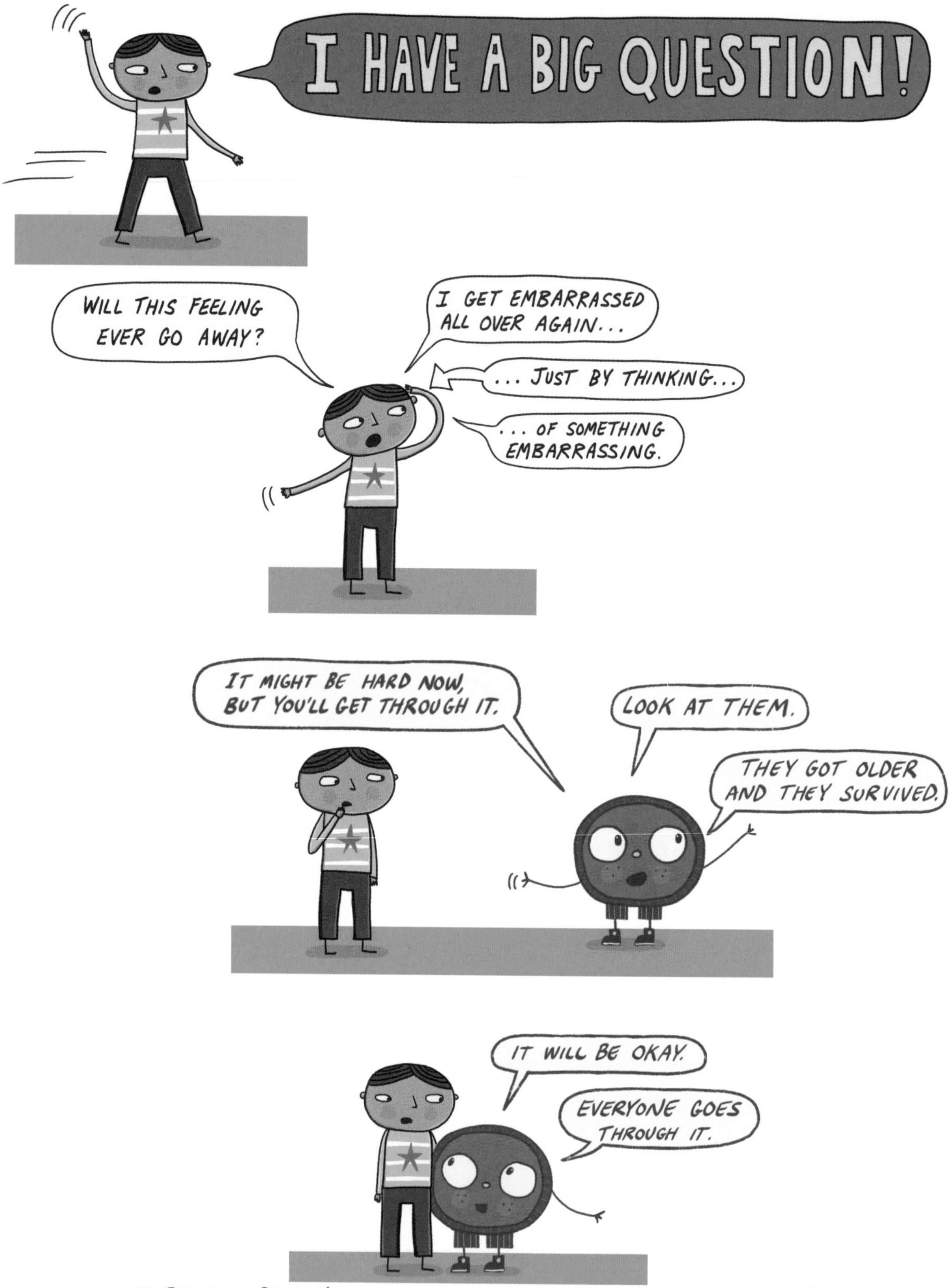
I HAVE A BIG QUESTION!
WILL THIS FEELING EVER GO AWAY?
I GET EMBARRASSED ALL OVER AGAIN...
... JUST BY THINKING...
... OF SOMETHING EMBARRASSING.
IT MIGHT BE HARD NOW, BUT YOU'LL GET THROUGH IT.
LOOK AT THEM.
THEY GOT OLDER AND THEY SURVIVED.
IT WILL BE OKAY.
EVERYONE GOES THROUGH IT.

☐ BELIEVES BADGEY ☐ DOES NOT BELIEVE BADGEY

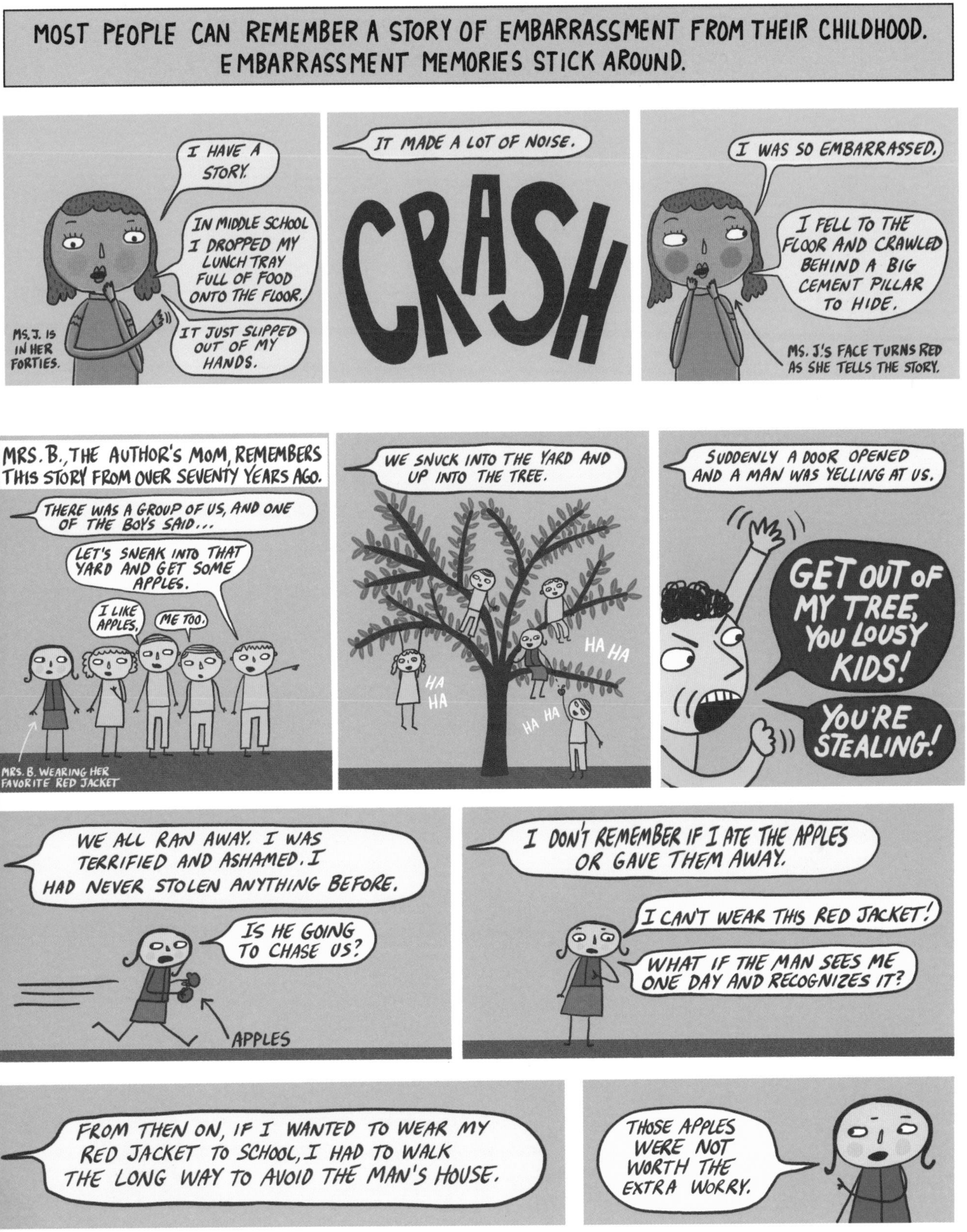
MOST PEOPLE CAN REMEMBER A STORY OF EMBARRASSMENT FROM THEIR CHILDHOOD. EMBARRASSMENT MEMORIES STICK AROUND.
I HAVE A STORY.
IN MIDDLE SCHOOL I DROPPED MY LUNCH TRAY FULL OF FOOD ONTO THE FLOOR.
IT JUST SLIPPED OUT OF MY HANDS.
MS. J. IS IN HER FORTIES.
IT MADE A LOT OF NOISE.
CRASH
I WAS SO EMBARRASSED.
I FELL TO THE FLOOR AND CRAWLED BEHIND A BIG CEMENT PILLAR TO HIDE.
MS. J.'S FACE TURNS RED AS SHE TELLS THE STORY.
MRS. B., THE AUTHOR'S MOM, REMEMBERS THIS STORY FROM OVER SEVENTY YEARS AGO.
THERE WAS A GROUP OF US, AND ONE OF THE BOYS SAID...
LET'S SNEAK INTO THAT YARD AND GET SOME APPLES.
I LIKE APPLES.
ME TOO.
MRS. B. WEARING HER FAVORITE RED JACKET
WE SNUCK INTO THE YARD AND UP INTO THE TREE.
HA HA
HA HA
HA HA
SUDDENLY A DOOR OPENED AND A MAN WAS YELLING AT US.
GET OUT OF MY TREE, YOU LOUSY KIDS!
YOU'RE STEALING!
WE ALL RAN AWAY. I WAS TERRIFIED AND ASHAMED. I HAD NEVER STOLEN ANYTHING BEFORE.
IS HE GOING TO CHASE US?
APPLES
I DON'T REMEMBER IF I ATE THE APPLES OR GAVE THEM AWAY.
I CAN'T WEAR THIS RED JACKET!
WHAT IF THE MAN SEES ME ONE DAY AND RECOGNIZES IT?
FROM THEN ON, IF I WANTED TO WEAR MY RED JACKET TO SCHOOL, I HAD TO WALK THE LONG WAY TO AVOID THE MAN'S HOUSE.
THOSE APPLES WERE NOT WORTH THE EXTRA WORRY.

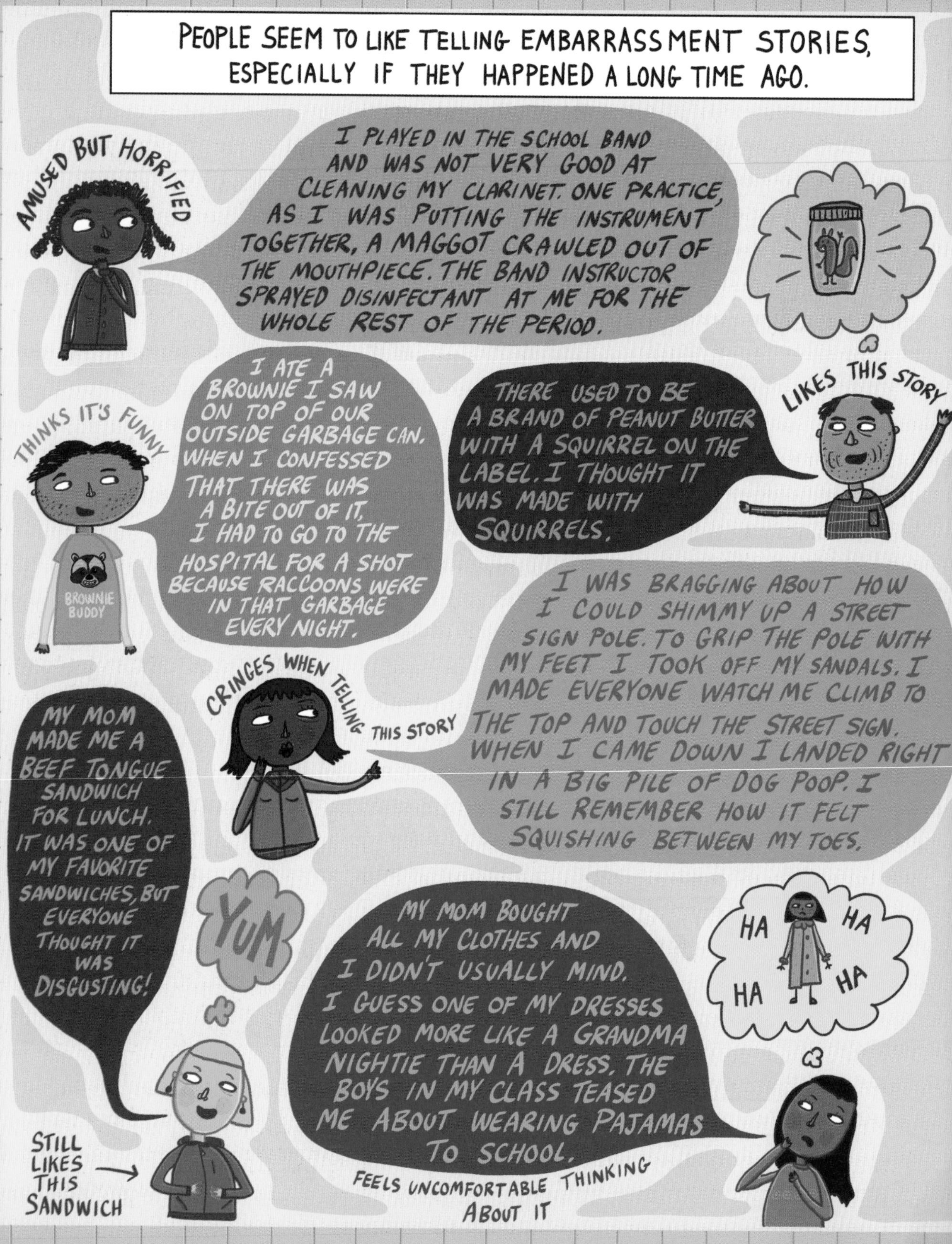
PEOPLE SEEM TO LIKE TELLING EMBARRASSMENT STORIES, ESPECIALLY IF THEY HAPPENED A LONG TIME AGO.
AMUSED BUT HORRIFIED
I PLAYED IN THE SCHOOL BAND AND WAS NOT VERY GOOD AT CLEANING MY CLARINET. ONE PRACTICE, AS I WAS PUTTING THE INSTRUMENT TOGETHER, A MAGGOT CRAWLED OUT OF THE MOUTHPIECE. THE BAND INSTRUCTOR SPRAYED DISINFECTANT AT ME FOR THE WHOLE REST OF THE PERIOD.
THINKS IT'S FUNNY
I ATE A BROWNIE I SAW ON TOP OF OUR OUTSIDE GARBAGE CAN. WHEN I CONFESSED THAT THERE WAS A BITE OUT OF IT, I HAD TO GO TO THE HOSPITAL FOR A SHOT BECAUSE RACCOONS WERE IN THAT GARBAGE EVERY NIGHT.
BROWNIE BUDDY
LIKES THIS STORY
THERE USED TO BE A BRAND OF PEANUT BUTTER WITH A SQUIRREL ON THE LABEL. I THOUGHT IT WAS MADE WITH SQUIRRELS.
CRINGES WHEN TELLING THIS STORY
I WAS BRAGGING ABOUT HOW I COULD SHIMMY UP A STREET SIGN POLE. TO GRIP THE POLE WITH MY FEET I TOOK OFF MY SANDALS. I MADE EVERYONE WATCH ME CLIMB TO THE TOP AND TOUCH THE STREET SIGN. WHEN I CAME DOWN I LANDED RIGHT IN A BIG PILE OF DOG POOP. I STILL REMEMBER HOW IT FELT SQUISHING BETWEEN MY TOES.
MY MOM MADE ME A BEEF TONGUE SANDWICH FOR LUNCH. IT WAS ONE OF MY FAVORITE SANDWICHES, BUT EVERYONE THOUGHT IT WAS DISGUSTING!
YUM
STILL LIKES THIS SANDWICH
MY MOM BOUGHT ALL MY CLOTHES AND I DIDN'T USUALLY MIND. I GUESS ONE OF MY DRESSES LOOKED MORE LIKE A GRANDMA NIGHTIE THAN A DRESS. THE BOYS IN MY CLASS TEASED ME ABOUT WEARING PAJAMAS TO SCHOOL.
HA HA HA HA
FEELS UNCOMFORTABLE THINKING ABOUT IT

A SELECTION OF TRUE STORIES FROM THE OLDER SET

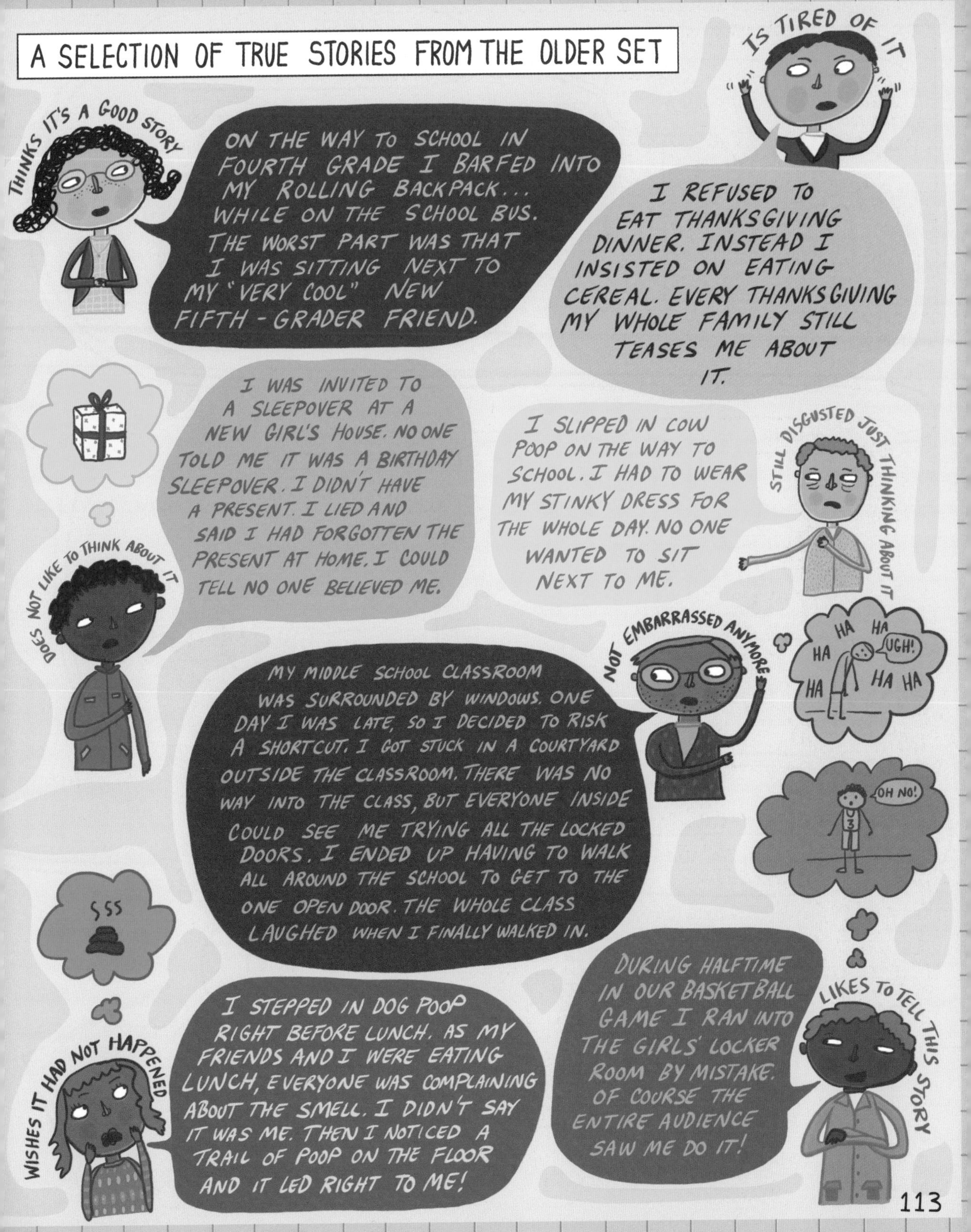
THINKS IT'S A GOOD STORY
ON THE WAY TO SCHOOL IN FOURTH GRADE I BARFED INTO MY ROLLING BACKPACK... WHILE ON THE SCHOOL BUS. THE WORST PART WAS THAT I WAS SITTING NEXT TO MY "VERY COOL" NEW FIFTH-GRADER FRIEND.
IS TIRED OF IT
I REFUSED TO EAT THANKSGIVING DINNER. INSTEAD I INSISTED ON EATING CEREAL. EVERY THANKSGIVING MY WHOLE FAMILY STILL TEASES ME ABOUT IT.
DOES NOT LIKE TO THINK ABOUT IT
I WAS INVITED TO A SLEEPOVER AT A NEW GIRL'S HOUSE. NO ONE TOLD ME IT WAS A BIRTHDAY SLEEPOVER. I DIDN'T HAVE A PRESENT. I LIED AND SAID I HAD FORGOTTEN THE PRESENT AT HOME. I COULD TELL NO ONE BELIEVED ME.
STILL DISGUSTED JUST THINKING ABOUT IT
I SLIPPED IN COW POOP ON THE WAY TO SCHOOL. I HAD TO WEAR MY STINKY DRESS FOR THE WHOLE DAY. NO ONE WANTED TO SIT NEXT TO ME.
NOT EMBARRASSED ANYMORE
HA HA HA HA HA HA
UGH!
MY MIDDLE SCHOOL CLASSROOM WAS SURROUNDED BY WINDOWS. ONE DAY I WAS LATE, SO I DECIDED TO RISK A SHORTCUT. I GOT STUCK IN A COURTYARD OUTSIDE THE CLASSROOM. THERE WAS NO WAY INTO THE CLASS, BUT EVERYONE INSIDE COULD SEE ME TRYING ALL THE LOCKED DOORS. I ENDED UP HAVING TO WALK ALL AROUND THE SCHOOL TO GET TO THE ONE OPEN DOOR. THE WHOLE CLASS LAUGHED WHEN I FINALLY WALKED IN.
OH NO!
WISHES IT HAD NOT HAPPENED
I STEPPED IN DOG POOP RIGHT BEFORE LUNCH. AS MY FRIENDS AND I WERE EATING LUNCH, EVERYONE WAS COMPLAINING ABOUT THE SMELL. I DIDN'T SAY IT WAS ME. THEN I NOTICED A TRAIL OF POOP ON THE FLOOR AND IT LED RIGHT TO ME!
LIKES TO TELL THIS STORY
DURING HALFTIME IN OUR BASKETBALL GAME I RAN INTO THE GIRLS' LOCKER ROOM BY MISTAKE. OF COURSE THE ENTIRE AUDIENCE SAW ME DO IT!

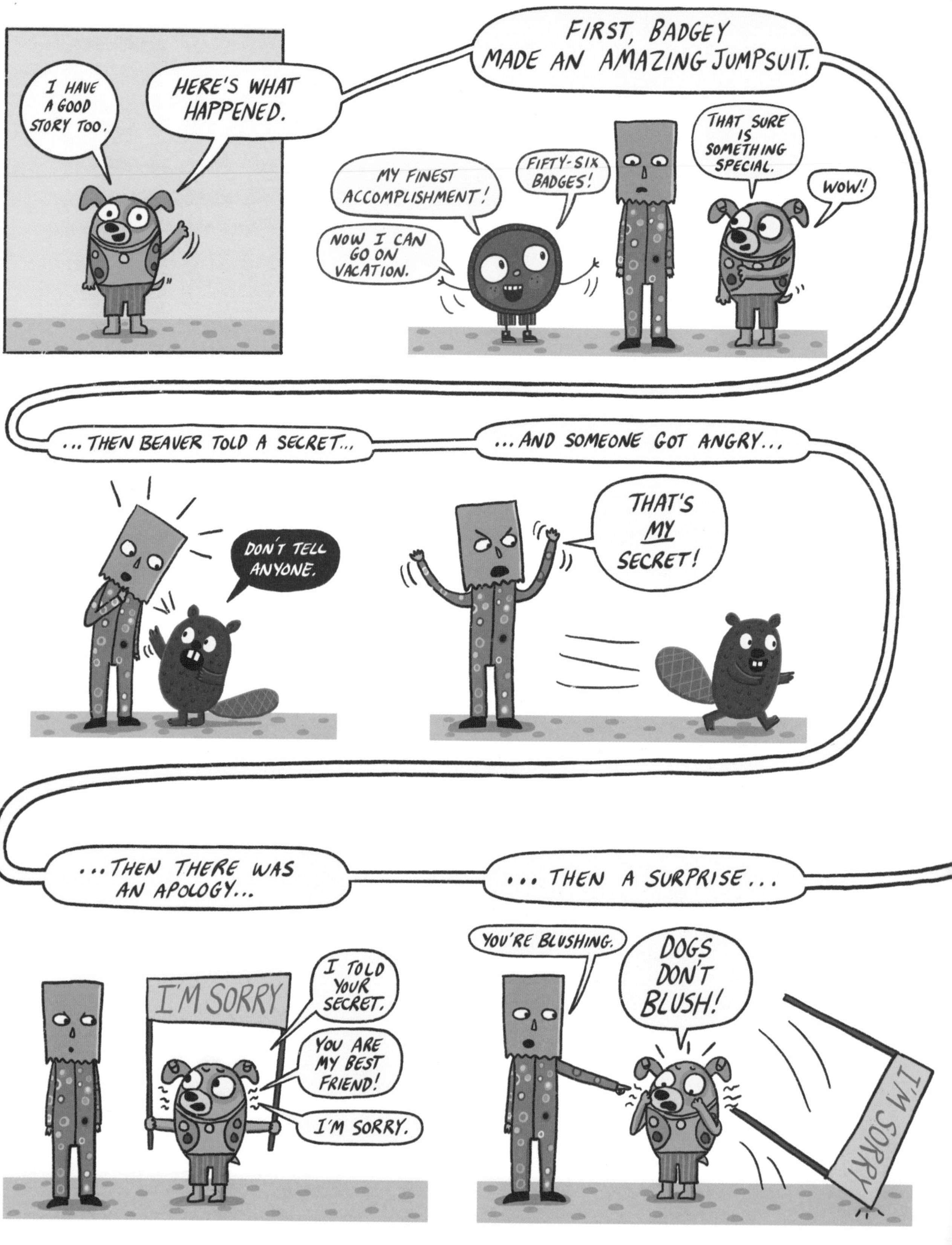

I HAVE A GOOD STORY TOO.
HERE'S WHAT HAPPENED.
FIRST, BADGEY MADE AN AMAZING JUMPSUIT.
MY FINEST ACCOMPLISHMENT!
NOW I CAN GO ON VACATION.
FIFTY-SIX BADGES!
THAT SURE IS SOMETHING SPECIAL.
WOW!
...THEN BEAVER TOLD A SECRET...
DON'T TELL ANYONE.
...AND SOMEONE GOT ANGRY...
THAT'S MY SECRET!
...THEN THERE WAS AN APOLOGY...
I'M SORRY
I TOLD YOUR SECRET.
YOU ARE MY BEST FRIEND!
I'M SORRY.
...THEN A SURPRISE...
YOU'RE BLUSHING.
DOGS DON'T BLUSH!
I'M SORRY

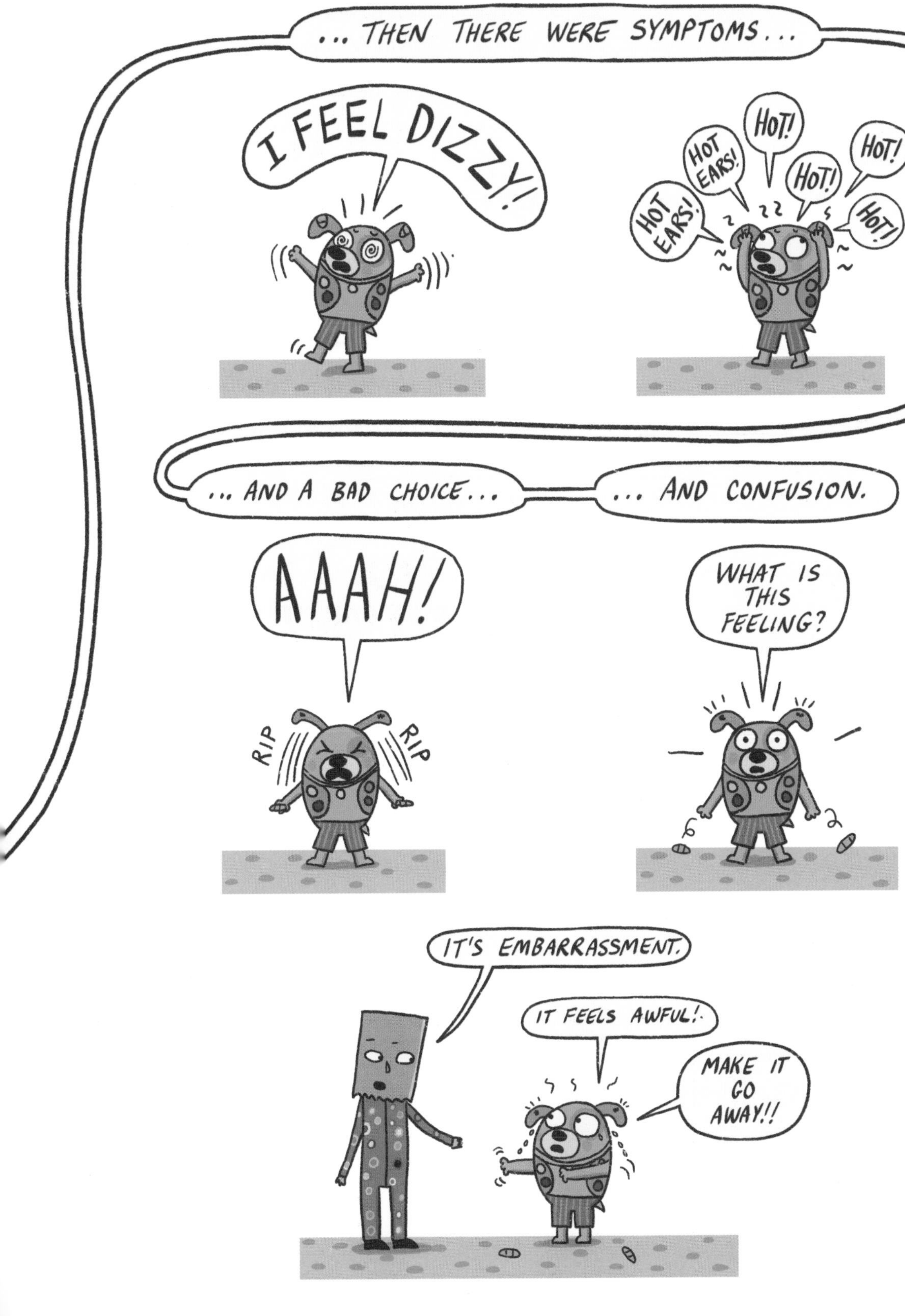
... THEN THERE WERE SYMPTOMS...
I FEEL DIZZY!
HOT EARS!
HOT EARS!
HOT!
HOT!
HOT!
HOT!
... AND A BAD CHOICE...
... AND CONFUSION.
AAAH!
RIP
RIP
WHAT IS THIS FEELING?
IT'S EMBARRASSMENT.
IT FEELS AWFUL!
MAKE IT GO AWAY!!

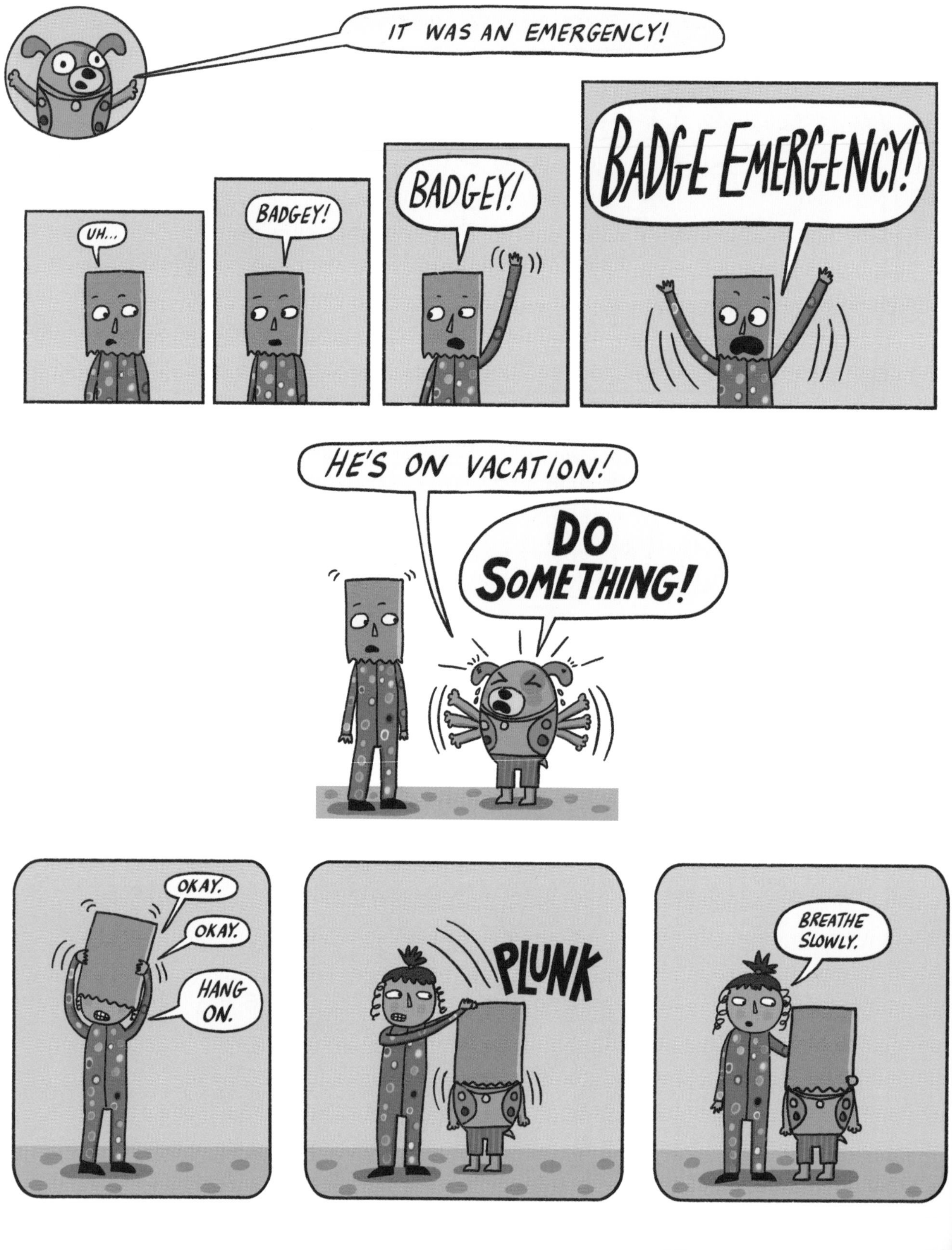
IT WAS AN EMERGENCY!
UH...
BADGEY!
BADGEY!
BADGE EMERGENCY!
HE'S ON VACATION!
DO SOMETHING!
OKAY.
OKAY.
HANG ON.
PLUNK
BREATHE SLOWLY.

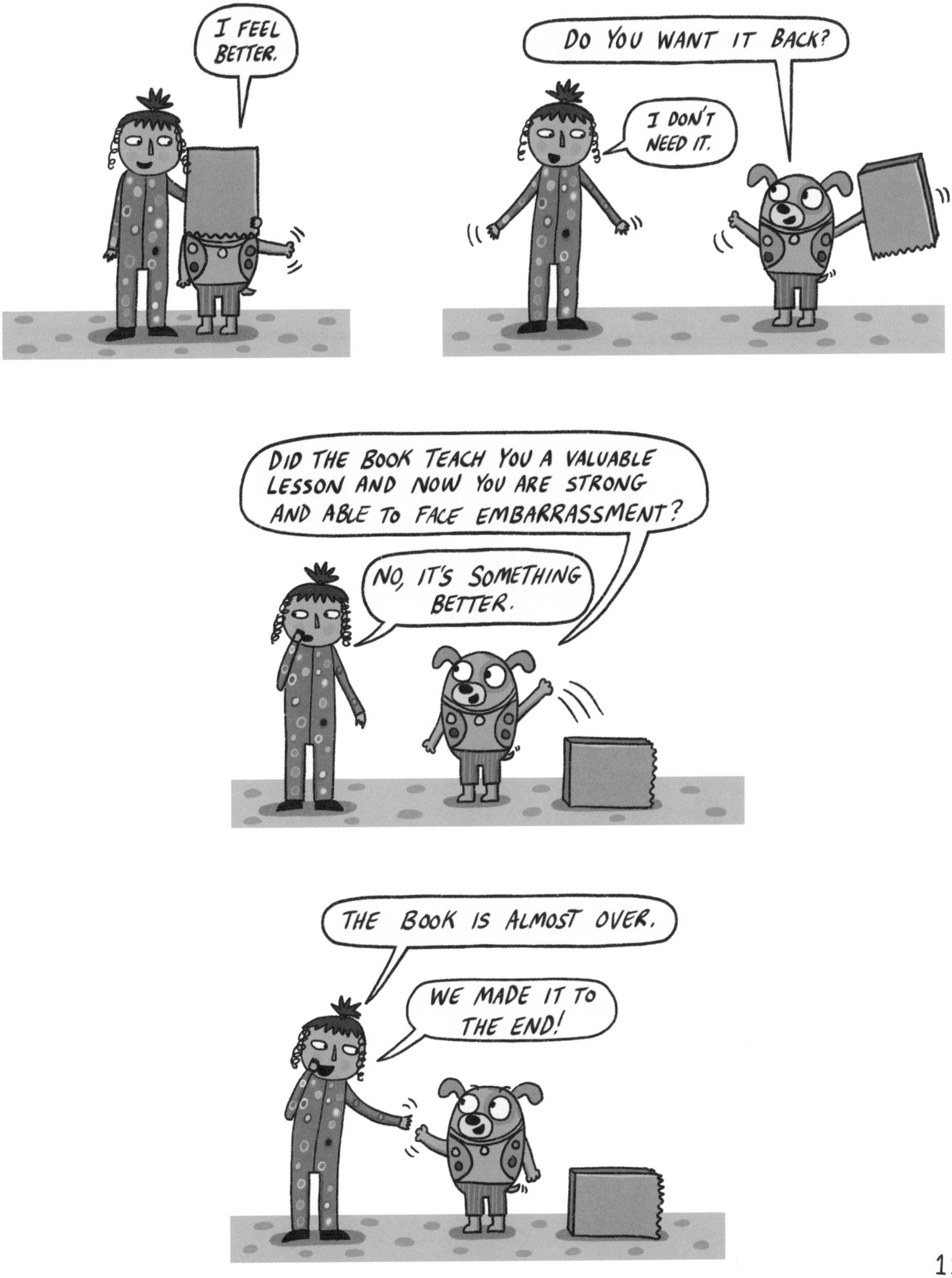
I FEEL BETTER.
DO YOU WANT IT BACK?
I DON'T NEED IT.
DID THE BOOK TEACH YOU A VALUABLE LESSON AND NOW YOU ARE STRONG AND ABLE TO FACE EMBARRASSMENT?
NO, IT'S SOMETHING BETTER.
THE BOOK IS ALMOST OVER.
WE MADE IT TO THE END!

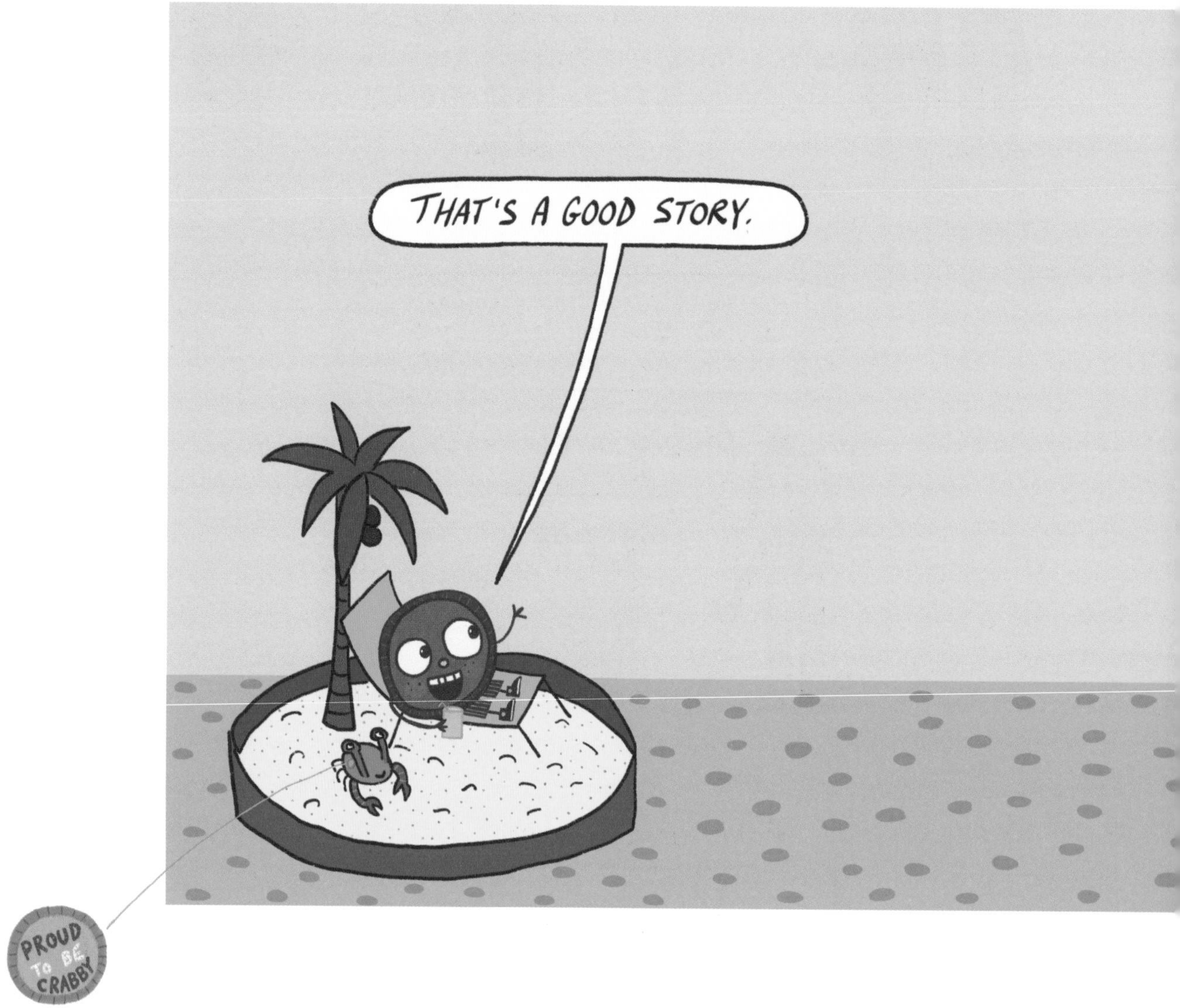
THAT'S A GOOD STORY.
PROUD TO BE CRABBY

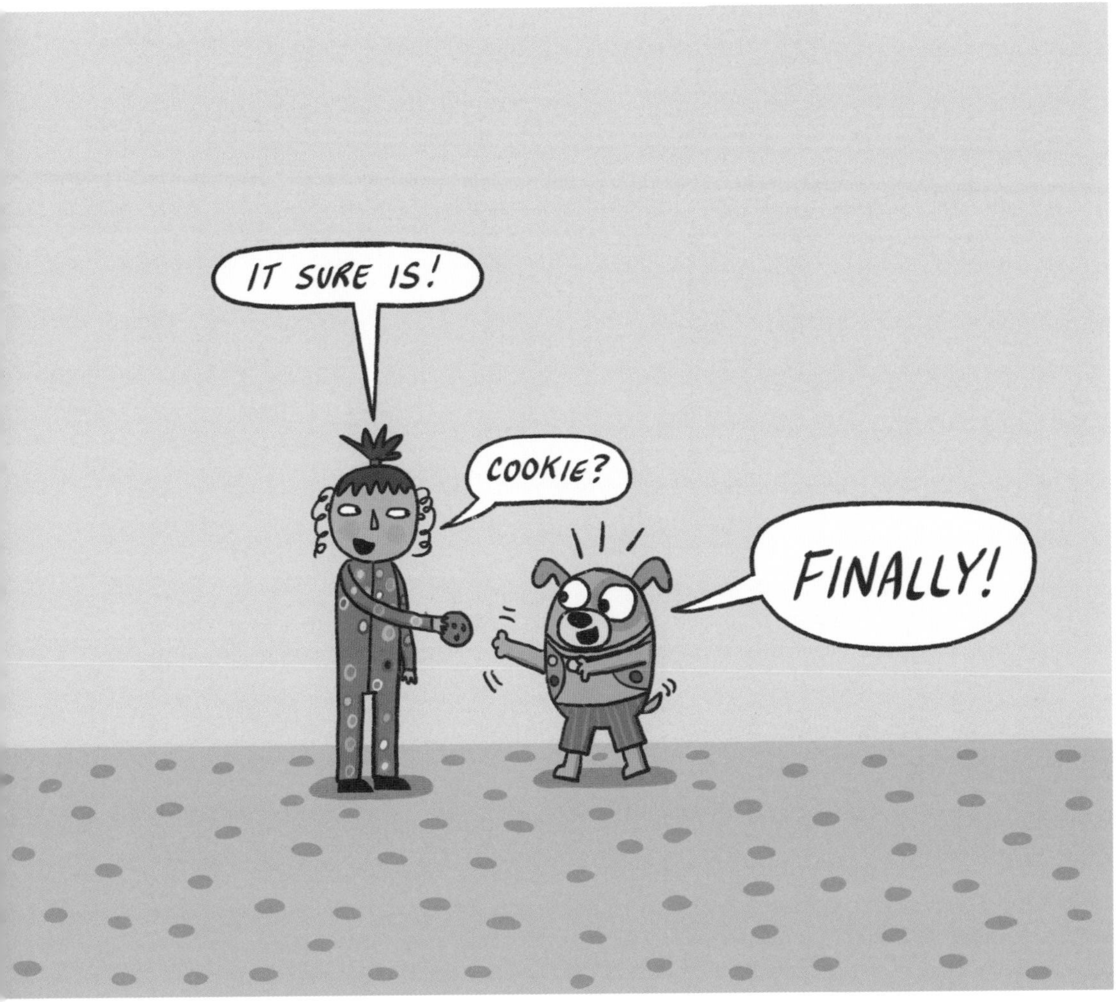
IT SURE IS!
COOKIE?
FINALLY!

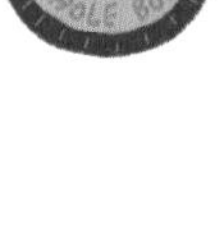
YOU READ A WHOLE BOOK
THE END

THANK YOU, CHRIS DUFFY (MY EDITOR AND FRIEND), FOR ALL YOUR HELP.
—CHARISE MERICLE HARPER

Library of Congress Cataloging-in-Publication Data is available.

ISBN 978-1-5235-1017-7

Design by Jooahn Kwon
Cover illustration by Charise Mericle Harper

Workman books are available at special discounts when purchased in bulk for premiums and sales promotions as well as for fund-raising or educational use. Special editions or book excerpts can also be created to specification. For details, contact the Special Sales Director at the address below or send an email to specialmarkets@workman.com.

Workman Publishing Co., Inc.
225 Varick Street
New York, NY 10014-4381

workman.com

WORKMAN is a registered trademark of Workman Publishing Co., Inc.

Printed in China
First printing October 2020

10 9 8 7 6 5 4 3 2 1